AN ILLUSTRATED HISTORY OF

Tottenham Hotspur

AN ILLUSTRATED HISTORY OF

Tottenham Hotspur

Bob Goodwin

Breedon Books
Publishing Company
Derby

First published in Great Britain by
The Breedon Books Publishing Company Limited
44 Friar Gate, Derby, DE1 1DA.
1995

ISBN 1 85983 012 9

Printed and bound by Butler & Tanner, Frome, Somerset.
Cover printed by Premier Print, Nottingham.

Contents

Dedication
To Karen and Tracey

Introduction

WHEN Anton Rippon of Breedon Books asked me if I would be interested in writing An Illustrated History of Tottenham Hotspur, he could probably not have chosen a worse time, the FA Appeals Committee having just determined Spurs' appeal against the penalties imposed for financial irregularities under the Scholar regime. Although the deduction of 12 points that would almost certainly have meant relegation had been reduced to six, and at least gave Spurs a chance of remaining in the Premiership, the FA Cup ban remained.

Ever since Tottenham first won the trophy in 1901, the competition has held a special place in the hearts of Spurs fans. Spurs had won the Cup a record eight times, it had been good to them, and they had been good for it. There may have been some embarrassing defeats along the way, but to realise that Spurs would not be allowed to compete in the world's most famous knock-out competition was even more painful than losing to Arsenal in the 1993 semi-final.

As a Spurs supporter, though, I was grateful to be given the opportunity to add to the list of books that have chronicled the history of one of Britain's most famous clubs, particularly one that was to be so profusely illustrated with photographs going back to the club's earliest days, many of which have not been seen before.

Thanks to Alan Sugar's determination, arbitrators subsequently not only re-instated Spurs in the FA Cup but cancelled the six-point deduction due to take effect at the end of the season. This did not go down well with football's hierarchy and for a while salt was well and truly rubbed in the wounds as Spurs looked like marching all the way to a tenth FA Cup Final, only to lose in the semi-final to Everton.

It was a season of ups and downs, just like Spurs' entire history has been. In the 113 years since Spurs were formed there have been some great successes, and naturally this book concentrates on them, but there have also been those less than happy times. They have not been overlooked – although not given as much emphasis – for the good times can only be fully appreciated if the bad have also been experienced.

Bob Goodwin
June 1995

Acknowledgements

I could not have written this book without the help of others to whom I offer my sincere thanks: Carolyn, 'Ossie', Barry, Brian, Dave, Dyl, Fred, Graham, John, Julie, Keith, Mark and Martin, the staff of Breedon Books, the staff of the British Newspaper Library, the authors of numerous other books not only about Spurs but many other clubs. There are far too many to mention individually and to do so would run the risk of forgetting somebody. They know who they are and I hope they will understand.

Photographs
Photographs for this book have been supplied by EMPICS/Hulton Deutsch/Howard Talbot.

From Schoolboys to Professionals

IN THE early nineteenth century Tottenham, now an integral part of London, was a 'semi-rural area on the borders of London and Essex providing a pleasant country retreat for substantial citizens'. On the Roman road to Lincoln, there was nothing particularly attractive about the area, the River Lea, the marshes, a few farms, the houses of reasonably well-off families and plenty of open spaces. But that was all to change with the spread of the railways. In the 1840s, the opening of Northumberland Park station on the Northern and Eastern Railway's line from Stratford to Cambridge saw the first residential developments. Large, typically Victorian houses, the type now converted into three or four flats, were built for those fortunate families who could afford to escape from central London.

But the real expansion came in the latter half of the century. Tottenham's population increased from 9,120 in 1851 to 46,456 in 1881 principally due to the advent of 'workmen's trains'. As part of the compensation to be paid for acquiring the land that allowed the Great Eastern Railway to expand into Liverpool Street, the railway company was obliged to provide a cheap travel service. Thousands of London's workers moved out to Tottenham, safe in the knowledge that a 2d (1p) return ticket would quickly get them to work and home again. The working classes flowed out over the Stoke Newington border into Tottenham and the large, comfortable houses that used to line the High Road were soon submerged.

With the influx of the workers and their families came an increase in the demand for schools. Tottenham Grammar was already well established and there were several boarding schools around catering for those Londoners who wanted their children off their hands but still within easy reach. One of the new schools, based in the High Road, was Mr William Cameron's St John's Middle Class School, which was exactly that, a school for the children of middle class families.

Despite the population growth there were still plenty of open spaces and in 1880 some of the pupils of St John's, together with a few friends from the Grammar School, decided to form the Hotspur Cricket Club. Exactly why the name was chosen has never been established for sure. Legend has it that two of the members, brothers Hamilton and Lindsay Casey, were studying the reign of Henry IV and had been enthralled by the battlefield exploits of 'Harry Hotspur', the name given to Sir Henry Percy, teenage son of the Earl of Northumberland and a fierce opponent of the king. True or not it was an apt name. The Tottenham area had been part of the Percy family estates, many of the boys lived in or around Northumberland Park and Percy House was near the headquarters of the local Young Men's Church Association.

The cricket club played for two years but at the end of the 1882 season the members, looking for a winter sport, decided to turn their attention to football. Well-established in the south through the Public Schools and the network of Old Boys Clubs the balance of power in the game was beginning to shift to the north. The first serious challenge to the southern amateurs had just come with Blackburn Rovers reaching the FA Cup Final. Blackburn Olympic were to win the trophy the following season and it was then to be another 18 years before the Cup returned south.

The earliest known records of the Hotspur Football Club are six torn and faded pages that appear to come from the original club book. Written in the hand of Lindsay Casey, honorary treasurer, they record that the club's initial funds, five shillings (25p), came from the cricket club, augmented by sixpenny (2.5p) subscriptions from former cricket club members Hamilton and Lindsay Casey, Edward Beaven, Fred Dexter, John Thompson, Bobby Buckle, Tom and John Anderson, Stuart Leaman, P.Thompson and E.Wall, and a one shilling (5p) subscription from D.Davis, who was called upon to pay twice as much as the others because he had not been a member of the cricket club.

These funds were used to purchase goal posts for 2s 6d (12.5p), flag posts for 1s (5p), flags for sixpence (2.5p) and other essential equipment such as tape for the 'crossbars' and white paint. Later in the year further members joined: C.Iverson, Lovell and John Fisher paid one shilling subscriptions, R.Howlett 1s 6d (7.5p), Tom Bumberry 1s 3d (7p) and Billy Tyrell 9d (4p). These documents also show that Spurs' first-ever match took place on 30 September 1882, a 2-0 defeat by another local team, the Radicals. Sadly no further match details were recorded and the only other result known that season was another defeat, by 8-1 against Latymer, an Edmonton school club whose rivalry with the fledgling Spurs was to prove every bit as keen as the modern day rivalry with Arsenal.

The first meetings of the club took place in some houses being built in Willoughby Lane or under a street lamp in Northumberland Park, but where to play was not a problem. Between the railway line and the River Lea were Tottenham Marshes where other clubs such as Park, Star and Radicals played.

They provided plenty of open space for any bunch of lads willing enough to put in a little hard work and prepare a football pitch. The Spurs lads were so willing, but the same could not be said of other local teams. There were several occasions when Spurs had to defend their pitch by force against gangs of local youngsters who preferred to find their Saturday afternoon entertainment in baiting those who wanted to play. Spurs decided that if they were going to enjoy their sport, then adult help was needed. They approached John Ripsher, a clerk in an iron works who lived with his brother's family in Northumberland Park and had been involved in the running of the cricket club. He was warden of the Tottenham YMCA and took Bible classes at the Parish Church of All Hallows.

A bachelor and 'favourite uncle' type figure, he was very popular with the boys, especially when he readily agreed to lend his support. At his instigation Jim Randall, a clerk in Edmonton County Court and former Radicals player who had switched allegiance to the Hotspur, summoned a meeting for a Friday night in August 1883 held in a basement kitchen at the YMCA. Twenty-one boys attended and by the end of the evening their football club had been properly organised.

Ripsher was appointed president and treasurer, Randall captain, Billy Harston vice-captain and the first committee was made up of Tom Bumberry, W.G.Herbert, Fred Dexter and Billy Tyrell. Matches were to be played at the Park Lane end of Tottenham Marshes, where the only competition would come from Park and the rugby playing University College Hospital. Navy blue was adopted as the club colours and all members were required to wear a scarlet shield on the left side of their jersey with the letter 'H' on it.

The club's second season began on 6 October 1883 with a 9-0 thrashing of Brownlow Rovers. Although Billy Harston was later to recall the team line-up as: S.Leaman; W.Tyrell and F.Dexter; H.D.Casey and F.Lovis; W.Lomas, F.Cottrell, Dr Alec Watson, J.T.Fisher, W.Harston and R.Buckle. he made no reference to Jack Jull who was said by the *Tottenham and Edmonton Weekly Herald* in their first report of a Spurs game to have 'done good service for the Hotspur'. And perhaps we must ask what Dr Watson was doing playing for a schoolboys' football team!

Billy Harstons' line-up may look a little strange to modern football fans with its two full-backs, two half-backs and six forwards. But that was football in those days – two wingers, two inside-forwards and two centre-forwards. What a difference to today's 4-5-1s, 3-2-4-1s or even 1-4-3-1-1s!

For novices Spurs did remarkably well in their second season – 15 victories against five defeats – and much of the time they were up against older and more experienced opponents. Many of the games did not last a full 90 minutes, often coming to an early conclusion because of bad light or, as against Brownlow Rovers on 10 November, because the ball burst. Sometimes Spurs or their opponents did not field a full complement of players for the entire game and it was not unusual for goals to be disputed.

Certainly Spurs were proving popular for there were even enough members for a second XI to be fielded, but if Spurs were having few problems on the pitch, the same could not be said for their off-field activities. During a meeting of the YMCA Council there was such a noise coming from the

Spurs in 1884-85, the first season that the word Tottenham was added to the Hotspur title. Back row (left to right): R.Amos, L.Brown, T.Wood, T.W.Bumberry, J.Anderson, John Ripsher (president), H.D.Casey. Middle row: J.H.Thompson, W.C.Tyrell, F.Lovis, J.C.Jull (captain), H.Goshawk, W.Hillyer, S.Leaman (second team captain), F.Bayne, J.Randall. Front row: J.G.Randall, R.Buckle, G.F.Burt, G.Bush, P.Moss, W.Mason, W.Harston, F.Cottrell, H.Bull.

basement where Spurs used to practise that a member of the Council was sent to investigate. A ball disappeared up the chimney. Just as it emerged to be on the receiving end of a full-blooded kick, the light was turned off and the council member choose that precise moment to open the door. He returned to the council covered in soot. Playing cards and sampling mulberries from the YMCA's garden did not endear Spurs to their elders and betters and by the end of the season they had been told to find somewhere else to practise.

With the help of the Vicar of Tottenham, Revd Wilson, Ripsher found them a new home at Dorset Villas, Northumberland Park, and on the field Spurs continued to impress. Of 28 matches played in 1884-85, 18 were won and five drawn. A reputation for entertaining football was already being established and not only were players from disbanding clubs keen to join their ranks but people were even making their way to the Marshes just to watch Spurs play.

At the end of the season Spurs cancelled their last game so that they could go to Kennington Oval and watch Blackburn Rovers beat Queen's Park for the second successive season to retain the FA Cup. Rovers' success left it's mark on Spurs who immediately changed their colours to Blackburn's blue and white halves.

At this time the important decision was also taken to rename the club Tottenham Hotspur. There was already a club known as London Hotspur and correspondence for the two was

continually being confused. The change of name was for no reason other than to stop this happening.

Perhaps it was the excitement of watching a Cup Final that led to Spurs entering a cup competition for the first time the following season. In the London Association Cup they were drawn to play St Alban's, not a team from the Hertfordshire town but a London house team, and in front of a crowd of about 400 pulled off a 5-2 victory. Any taste for cup glory this provided did not last long, though. In the next round they were hammered 8-0 by the Casuals, but even to play such a famous club showed how a team of schoolboys had progressed in only three years. All other matches played this season were friendlies and whilst the details of every game are not known, Spurs were reported to have won 24 and drawn two of the 37 games played with 111 goals scored and 51 conceded.

The only condition attached to Spurs' tenancy of Dorset Villas had been that they should attend church every Wednesday. This they did for two years without problems until they were expelled after some members were caught playing cards during a service. Again Ripsher came to their rescue, securing accommodation at the Red House in the High Road. Visitors to White Hart Lane today will be familiar with this building. On the opposite corner to the White Hart public house and adorned with a beautiful cockerel mounted clock, it was later purchased by Spurs and formed part of the club's offices

Spurs, pictured before the club's first-ever competitive match, a 5-2 win over St Alban's in a London Association Cup-tie before 400 spectators. Back row (left to right): W.C.Tyrell, F.Lovis, J.Jull, John Ripsher (president), H.Bull, H.D.Casey. Front row: T.W.Bumberry, R.Amos, R.Buckle, W.Mason, W.Harston, F.Cottrell. The team are wearing blue and white quartered jerseys after Blackburn Rovers, one of the great clubs of the era.

until the current West Stand was built in the 1980s.

What a marvellous friend John Ripsher was to those early Spurs. Despite the number of members, finance was always a problem and more than once the boys went to him concerned they had no ball for the next day's match. "The Lord will provide" would be his reply and, sure enough, Ripsher would turn up the next day with a ball, sometimes two. A pillar of the community, he must have been greatly embarrassed by the antics of his charges but he stuck by them and there can be no doubt that without his support Spurs would have gone the way of many other clubs and simply disappeared.

Far from disappear Spurs went from strength to strength. In 1886-87 they did not get past the first round of the London Association Cup but they did reach the semi-final of the East End Cup, although that turned into something of a farce. The match against London Caledonians was fixed to take place at Millwall's North Greenwich ground on 19 March but the pitch was in such a state both clubs agreed to play a friendly. The tie was rearranged for the following week at Spurs

but the Calies failed to appear. Spurs kicked-off, duly scored and promptly claimed the tie, only to be ordered to play again. Three weeks later Spurs lost 1-0 with the exiled Scots going on to draw twice with the infant Millwall Rovers in the Final before they were declared joint winners.

Spurs' progress continued unabated in 1887-88, although a 6-0 defeat by Hendon in the London Senior Cup may not look that way. Hendon, though, were a strong adult team and losing to them was no disgrace. With the benefit of hindsight the most important event of the season was the first meeting with Royal Arsenal. A friendly played on 19 November, it was abandoned after 75 minutes due to bad light with Spurs leading 2-1 but they did not do so well in the return on 4 February, going down 6-2 at Plumstead.

Continued success brought it's own problems with up to 4,000 fans flocking to the Marshes for an afternoon's free entertainment. Spurs had been forced to rope off the pitch but they could do nothing about the coarse remarks, mud and even rotten vegetables, hurled by the crowd at their opponents. They received many complaints but what could they do? They were, after all, playing on public land and it was not as if they had a private ground where they could have any control over spectators or even charge for admission. But all that was soon to change.

Despite the pessimists who insisted that people would not pay to watch something they had grown used to seeing for free, Bobby Buckle, Jack Jull, Ham Casey and secretary Frank Hatton, who had joined Spurs only a year earlier when the Park club folded, convinced the doubters that if the fare was good enough then the public would pay to watch it. A suitable site was found in Trulock Road, just off Northumberland Park. Part of it was already occupied by Foxes FC, with whom Spurs had a good relationship, but there was more than enough room for both clubs and for a rent of £10 per season Spurs were allocated a pitch tenanted by a tennis club during the summer. A brave decision, and one not without risk, the confidence of Buckle and Co was not misplaced. Although the numbers prepared to dip into their pocket hardly compared with those who watched Spurs on the Marshes, there were enough for Spurs to finish the season showing a healthy profit of £6. One guinea (£1.05) of that came from a donation by the Football Association when Spurs agreed to join football's governing body and £1 12s 6d (£1.63) from the match against Royal Arsenal on 9 March.

The highlight of the season came in October when the Old Etonians visited Northumberland Park in the London Senior Cup. FA Cup Finalists only five years before, they ran out 8-2 winners but that was only after an inspired second half saw them score five goals without reply. Continuing to enhance their reputation for playing an attractive game, Spurs' steady, if not spectacular, advance continued over the next couple of seasons despite the relative lack of competitive football.

The Football League, dominated by the professional clubs of the Midlands and north, was formed in 1888 but there was no equivalent for London and the south where the game was controlled by the amateurs of the Old Boys' clubs. Since the FA's decision to accept professionalism in 1885 the FA Cup, originally the exclusive property of the southern clubs, had found a permanent home in the north, but the southerners were totally opposed to the idea of footballers being paid to play sport and when Woolwich Arsenal decided in 1891 to pay their players they were immediately expelled from the London FA and banned from all local cup competitions. At Woolwich Arsenal's instigation a meeting of southern clubs was called for February 1892 at Anderton's Hotel in Fleet Street, the same hotel that had hosted the meeting four years earlier at which the first steps in the formation of the Football League had been taken.

Seconded by Millwall, Woolwich Arsenal's resolution, "That a league be formed for London and the south," was overwhelmingly passed by the 26 clubs present. Twelve clubs were elected to membership but they did not include Spurs who were bottom of the poll with only a single vote. However, that was as far as plans went. The amateur clubs were concerned that to play against professionals might incur the wrath of their governing bodies and they did not want to suffer the same penalty as Woolwich Arsenal. Within two weeks five clubs pulled out and the idea was dropped.

In 1892-93, Spurs did get to compete in a league competition for the first time though, even if not on the scale of the proposed 'Southern League'. John Oliver, president of Westminster Criterion, sponsored the formation of the Southern Alliance. Spurs were one of ten founder members and played Old St Stephen's, Slough, Polytechnic, Windsor & Eton, Erith and Upton Park. They finished third but the competition was not a success. Some clubs failed to complete their fixtures and the standard of play was simply not good enough.

Spurs were attracting good players to their ranks, evidenced by the fact they lost only 1-0 to the famous Casuals in the fourth round of the London Senior Cup at Northumberland Park before a crowd of 3,000, and they deserved good quality opponents if they were to be retained.

The increasing domination of the FA Cup by the professional clubs led to the introduction of the FA Amateur Cup in 1893-94. Spurs were invited to compete and in the first round they knocked out Vampires. They were drawn to meet Clapham Rovers in the next round but the match never took place. On 21 October 1893, Spurs were due to meet Old St Mark's in the first round of the London Senior Cup. They invited Ernie Payne, who had spent the previous season playing for Fulham but was now out of favour there, to appear at outside-left. He readily accepted and on his way to Northumberland Park called in at Fulham's Half Moon, Putney, ground to collect his kit. It had disappeared. There was no problem providing him with shirt, shorts and stockings but no suitable boots could be found so Spurs gave him ten shillings (50p) to buy a pair. When

Fulham got to hear of this they complained to the London FA accusing Spurs of poaching and professionalism. On 1 November 1893 Spurs were hauled before the Council of the London FA.

The charge of poaching was dismissed but to the astonishment of the football world Spurs were found guilty of misconduct. Even though it was always understood that the boots Payne bought were the property of the club, the council decided he had been offered 'an unfair inducement' to play for Spurs. Payne was suspended for a week, Spurs for two and Northumberland Park was closed for a fortnight. An appeal was unsuccessful and so the match against Clapham Rovers never went ahead. With the decision being ridiculed by the sporting press, Spurs received a tremendous amount of publicity. Public support was overwhelming and when the ground reopened for a London Charity Cup-tie against Crusaders on 9 December, some 2,000 spectators attended.

Other clubs were keen to meet Spurs and when they played at Southampton St Mary's on Boxing Day, a crowd of 6,000 was reported, many of them curious to see the team that had caused such a stir. A decision taken by the short-sighted members of the London FA that should have discredited Spurs had exactly the opposite effect and it was the governing body that felt the public and sporting wrath.

All this did not impress Spurs senior London rivals much, though. Newly-professionalised Millwall Athletic, having just seen Woolwich Arsenal elected to the Football League, moved to the forefront of attempts to form a Southern League. As a result of meetings early in 1894 an initial League of nine clubs was set up, with a Second Division of seven quickly being added. Spurs were not even invited to apply for membership.

Watching all this was John Oliver. He realised that Spurs were a club who, with the right guidance, could really go places. At the 1894 annual meeting John Ripsher stood down as president to be replaced by Oliver. His first act was to arrange and pay for the erection of a stand at Northumberland Park. Although Spurs were now the sole occupants of the ground, and hired a field in Edmonton for the reserves, the only previous 'stand' had been one or two wagons. The new stand, with dressing-rooms underneath, and providing seating for 100 people, was partially blown down during a gale a few weeks after it went up but was soon repaired. Oliver also secured the service of Spurs' first trainer, Arthur

Norris, at a salary of ten shillings (50p) per week.

Whether it was the influence of Norris or the increasingly high standard of players attracted to Spurs by the prospect of jobs in Oliver's carpet making business is not clear, but whatever the reason Spurs continued to attract publicity, but now for their performances on the pitch. Early in the season they recorded their first victory over the Casuals, 3-1. In the FA Amateur Cup they easily saw off Old Harrovians 7-0, City Ramblers 6-1, Romford 8-0, London Welsh 4-2 (in a second replay) and Beeston 2-0 before being brought back down to earth by the holders and eventual runners-up, Old Carthusians, who beat Spurs 5-0. In their first venture into the FA Cup, Spurs reached the fourth qualifying round before going out in a replay to Luton Town 4-0.

They were now not only able to compete with the best of the amateurs but had the beating of them. Yet if Spurs were to go any further, they had to take the plunge into professionalism. Woolwich Arsenal, the first London club to turn professional, had become the south's standard bearer in the Football League in 1893 and were holding their own in the Second Division. Millwall Athletic had adopted the paid game in 1893 and two years later were the first champions of the Southern League. Swindon Town, Southampton St Mary's, New Brompton (later Gillingham), Luton Town and Reading had all taken the momentous decision. It was a risk, but so too was the decision to find a private ground and that had paid off. Plans to raise the subject were clearly formulated early on. Clubs who had taken the step were approached for advice and supporters quietly sounded out.

Obviously much-behind-the scenes lobbying went on before a meeting was called for 16 December 1895 at The Eagle pub in Chesnut Road. Bobby Buckle, player, committee member, secretary, treasurer or auditor since the club's formation, put forward the proposal that the meeting should accept the committee's recommendation to adopt professionalism. In support it was pointed out that other clubs were taking the step and if Spurs wanted to compete they had to go with the flow. Rejection would leave them unable to secure the best players, unable to match their rivals and ultimately see them left behind.

Certainly the playing strength of Spurs had been recognised by the FA with the club being granted automatic progress to the first round of the Amateur Cup where they were due to meet Chesham. Spurs had to grasp the nettle, and grasp it now. The proposal was not without its opponents, though, particularly those concerned about the financial implications. Could the club afford to pay players? What guarantee was there crowds would increase to meet the extra expenditure? Indignant denials were made to suggestions that the committee had something to hide. Yes, the club was £65 in debt, but £60 of that was owed to Mr Oliver and there were many attractive home games to come.

At times the discussion was heated and the meeting certainly lasted longer than had been expected. Eventually the proposal was voted upon and although several members abstained, only one hand was raised in opposition. Tottenham Hotspur FC was now a professional club.

Trainer Norris was sent to Scotland to secure new recruits and returned after Christmas with Spurs' first professionals, full-back John Montgomery and centre-forward J.Logan. Montgomery was one of only two paid players in the professional Spurs' only competitive match that season. Charlie Lanham was the other who returned home from a first round FA Cup-tie at Stoke on the wrong end of a 5-0 scoreline.

Spurs fared a lot better in friendlies attracting Reading, Millwall Athletic, Burslem Port Vale, Woolwich Arsenal, Middlesbrough, Swindon Town and even Aston Villa to Northumberland Park, although Villa apparently found the dressing-room facilities so primitive they refused to use them and hired the Northumberland Arms instead. Enticing well-known clubs to North London was all well and good, but it did not provide competitive football and Spurs were never sure attendances would be big enough to cover the substantial guarantees some clubs demanded. League football was essential and Spurs therefore put their name forward as one of the three clubs to be elected to the Second Division of the Football League at its meeting on 19 May 1896.

Spurs fared marginally better than they had in their first attempt to join the Southern League, two votes now but joint bottom with Macclesfield of the ten applicants. This decision was not really that surprising. Woolwich Arsenal, still London's only Football League representatives, were struggling financially and northern and Midlands clubs were not keen on making the time consuming and expensive trip to London once a season, let alone twice. Spurs did not despair though. Several new players, including experienced Scots Richard McElhaney, Jimmy Milliken and Willie Newbigging, were signed and in June they applied to join the Southern League. Such was their obvious strength that this time they were voted straight into the First Division.

FA Cup Winners

AS IF to mark another step forward following election to the Southern League, Spurs' club colours were changed from the red and blue that had been worn since 1892-93 to chocolate and gold. Spurs also joined the United League and with the FA Cup, Wellingborough Charity Cup and a full programme of friendlies, 70 matches were played in 1896-97. Fourth place in the Southern League was satisfactory, bottom of the United League was not, but the real worries were financial. Guarantees to visiting clubs continued to be a burden, the paying support was not as great as hoped for, losses were being sustained and if Spurs wanted to make their mark better, more expensive players were needed.

Casting aside the financial worries, the close season saw wholesale changes to the playing staff. Almost an entire new team was signed: Scots Joe Cullen, Jimmy Hartley, Sandy Hall, Joe Knowles, Bob Tannahill, David Black, Jimmy Davidson, Bob Stormont and Bill Joyce; Englishman Tom Meade; and Spurs' first international, the Welshman John L. Jones. To help with the finances Spurs enlisted the help of Charles Roberts, at that time a trooper in the Herts Yeomanry and well-known fund-raiser. He organised a military tournament for June 1897 but a profit of over £100, although helpful, was not enough to wipe out the losses.

And, of course, Spurs were a football club which should not have needed to rely on non-football activities. Roberts advised that capital was required and suggested the club should become a limited company so that the committee members could avoid personal liability and shares could be offered to the public.

He argued that Spurs were an asset to the area and surely their supporters, local residents and in particular tradesmen, would support a share issue. A meeting was called for 2 March 1898. Again Bobby Buckle was called upon to propose the resolution but this time it was passed without dissent. John Oliver, Charles Roberts, Bobby

Buckle, Ralph Bullock and John Thompson were elected directors.

At the same meeting it was agreed to appoint Frank Brettell as Spurs' first secretary-manager. A Liverpudlian who had played for Everton and served on their committee, he was tempted away from Bolton Wanderers and well received in North London.

Some 8,000 shares were offered to the public but the issue was to be a disappointing failure with only 1,558 being taken up in the first year. The season did, however, see an improvement on the pitch with Spurs finishing third in the Southern League and second in the United League. Even better results might have been secured if the ground had not been closed for two weeks after Spurs fans, so incensed by Luton Town's tactics, assaulted three visiting players.

More fans were also coming through the turnstiles with over 14,000 squeezing into Northumberland Park for the Good Friday United League fixture against Woolwich Arsenal. Although the ground was said to have a capacity of 30,000, it was clearly not suitable to hold even half that number and a disaster was only narrowly averted. To get a better view about 80 people climbed on to the roof of a refreshment bar. It collapsed but fortunately only five people needed medical treatment. The writing was on the wall, though, a successful team with attendant big crowds would need a bigger ground. Joining Spurs over halfway through the season, Brettell had no say in the players under his control until it ended but he then set about using his contacts in the north to secure the services of several top players, Bob Cain, Harry Erentz, James McNaught, Jimmy Melia, Tom Smith and John Cameron included.

In the 1898-99 season third place in both the United League and the Thames & Medway League was not matched by a disappointing seventh position in the Southern League. Some consolation came in the FA Cup with Spurs

In January 1899 Spurs played one of their last games at the old Northumberland Park ground when Newton Heath (forerunners of Manchester United) visited North London for an FA Cup-tie. The sides draw 1-1 before Spurs won the replay at Clayton 5-3. This picture, showing Spurs (wearing striped shirts) on the defensive, gives some idea of the appearance of this former ground.

overcoming Wolverton, Clapton and Luton Town in the qualifying rounds and Newton Heath (later Manchester United) and Sunderland in the competition proper before going out to Stoke.

At the end of the season Brettell left to take up a more lucrative post as manager of the reconstituted Portsmouth club and despite many applicants John Cameron was appointed his replacement, but with the added burden of playing. He immediately set about signing new talent, George Clawley, Ted Hughes, Sandy Tait, David Copeland, John Kirwan, Tom Morris and Tom Pratt.

At about the same time John Oliver resigned as chairman with Charles Roberts taking his place. Oliver had guided Spurs through difficult times, the adoption of professionalism, the formation of a limited company and entry into regular league competition. It later transpired that his business was in serious financial difficulties and Oliver fell upon hard times, partly alleviated by Spurs

staging a benefit match for him in January 1901. At the same time Spurs changed their colours for the last time, adopting blue and white as a tribute to Preston North End, one of the great clubs of the era.

But the major event of the summer was the discovery of the new ground that had been in the mind of the club ever since the refreshment stand collapse against Woolwich Arsenal some two years earlier. At the rear of the White Hart public house in the High Road was some former nursery land acquired by the brewers Charringtons with the intention of building a housing estate to provide custom for their establishment. A new landlord, who had previously run a hostelry near Millwall's ground, took over and allowed the rumour to spread that a football club was going to start up on the vacant land. When Charles Roberts learned of this he approached the landlord, who claimed never to have heard of Spurs, and

Tottenham defending again as goalkeeper Cullen saves from a Newton Heath forward. Spurs had already defeated Wolverton, Clapton (after two games) and Luton Town (after three) and went on to beat Sunderland before losing to Stoke in the later stages of the 1899 FA Cup.

In September 1899, White Hart Lane was officially opened with a friendly game against First Division Notts County, who were then one of the leading clubs in the country. A crowd of around 5,000 saw Spurs win 4-1, helped by a hat-trick from David Copeland. These pictures from the game show that White Hart Lane was quite a well-appointed ground for the era.

Buckle immediately visited Charringtons and after some persuasion a lease was agreed. The only stipulation was that Spurs had to guarantee crowds of 1,000 for first-team games and 500 for reserve-team games. That was no problem but Spurs now had two grounds and that could have proved a thorny situation. Luck was on their side, though, for when the landlord of Northumberland Park, not knowing about the new ground, approached Spurs offering them 'a

suggested that the Tottenham club should take on the ground.

If the brewers were agreeable the landlord would raise no objection, so Roberts and Bobby

Spurs were one of the pioneers of matches against foreign opposition and in January 1901 they beat a German Association XI 9-6 on a snow-covered White Hart Lane pitch. Although the game produced 15 goals, the crowd for the fixture was sparse, the bitterly cold weather and the Tuesday afternoon kick-off no doubt the reasons.

handsome sum' for the surrender of the lease they quickly accepted.

Suggestions were invited for a suitable name for the new ground, to where the old Northumberland Park stands were moved. Gilpin Park was favourite but no official name was ever adopted and it simply became known as White Hart Lane. Ready for the start of the 1899-1900 season, the first match played on the new enclosure was a friendly against Notts County before a crowd of 5,000, who paid a total of £115.

In the Southern League, Southampton were hot favourites for a fourth successive title but Spurs started the season in great form. Eleven of the first 13 Southern League games were won (two of them were later expunged due to Cowes and Brighton United resigning from the League) and by Christmas it was a three-cornered fight for the title between Spurs, Southampton and Frank Brettell's Portsmouth. On Christmas Day, Spurs beat Portsmouth 3-0 at White Hart Lane but the following day lost 3-1 at Southampton. By February, Southampton were top but they then embarked on their run to the FA Cup Final and dropped out of the running for the title.

Spurs travelled back from the return fixture at Portsmouth in March having lost 1-0 but that was one of only four Southern League games in which they tasted defeat and while Portsmouth pushed them right to the end, a 2-1 win at New Brompton in the last match ensured Spurs their first-ever championship. In the Southern District Combination, where Spurs finished second, they met Woolwich Arsenal for the first time in competitive matches. On 17 April, Spurs won 4-2 but seven days later lost 2-1 at the Manor Ground

in a game that was abandoned after 75 minutes 'due to the use of bad language'.

John Cameron made only one significant change in the playing staff for 1900-01 and to some extent that was forced upon him. Tom Pratt, top scorer with 54 goals in 60 appearances in all matches, complained he was unable to settle in London and was allowed to return to his previous club, Preston North End. Cameron secured Sandy Brown, another Scot, another former Preston man and top scorer for Portsmouth, as his replacement. And what a replacement he proved to be.

Not helped by injuries that deprived the side of John Jones, Tom Morris, Ted Hughes and David Copeland, and forced continual positional changes, Spurs began their defence of the Southern League title poorly and although they recovered to finish fifth, the title always seemed destined for Southampton. It was only with the return of Copeland in the new year – just in time for the FA Cup – that Spurs began to look like the team of a season earlier.

Delayed by the death of Queen Victoria, the first round of the Cup did not take place until February when Spurs were drawn against Preston North End for the second year running, only this time at White Hart Lane. Playing for Preston was Tom Pratt and he gave a masterful display, whereas at the other end Sandy Brown was having an awful match. Preston took the lead after 28 minutes when a poorly taken corner was cleared to the edge of the box. Johnny McMahon, the Preston full-back, hit the ball back in and, more by luck than judgment, it found a way past the unsighted Clawley. Spurs piled on the pressure for the rest of the game and Preston had little option but to defend, but when Spurs did get past the massed ranks of the visitors' defence the nervous Brown would either let them down or the visiting 'keeper, Peter McBride, would pull of a heroic save. There were only nine minutes left when Jack Kirwan put another cross into the Preston box. The ball was not really Brown's but by a 'superhuman effort' he managed to get to it and grab the equaliser.

For the replay four days later, Spurs travelled up to Southport on the Monday to prepare. With Ted Hughes replacing the injured James McNaught and John Jones returning after injury for Bob Stormont, the team was to remain the same for the rest of the Cup campaign.

A crowd of only 6,000 turned up, perhaps a sign of Lancashire confidence. If that was the case then they got a nasty shock. Spurs took the lead through Cameron after only six minutes and although it was then Spurs' turn to defend, they did not simply fall back in numbers as Preston had done in the first match but continually looked for the opportunity to break out and add to the score. This they did twice before the interval with Brown getting both goals. In the second half Tom Becton scored from a free-kick for Preston but Brown completed his hat-trick from a Kirwan centre before a late goal from Pratt left the final score-line looking a little flattering to the home team.

In the second round the Cup holders Bury, who had outplayed Southampton 4-0 at the Crystal Palace to maintain the Football League's grip on the trophy, were called upon to visit White Hart Lane. They had been forced to win all their matches away from home to take the trophy and in the first round had overcome the Wednesday at Owlerton. The omens did not look good for Spurs when Bury took the lead after only two minutes and for the next 20 minutes the visitors were on top. Gradually Spurs managed to get back in the game and on 30 minutes Smith broke down the right and his lovely cross gave Brown the chance to equalise. The second half was tense and started in Bury's favour but after ten minutes Brown was again on the end of a Smith centre to put Spurs ahead. Bury were not going to give up the Cup easily and put Spurs under a lot of pressure but the defence held firm and were it not for an injury to Smith that left him almost a passenger, Spurs could have added to their score from several good counter attacks.

Having put out two top Football League sides 3,000 Spurs fans travelled to Reading for the third round in confident mood. It was their turn for a shock. Reading could not compete with Spurs in terms of skill but they had the hunger and determination to upset their opponents. Hard and physical – over-physical according to some reports – their strong, ruthless tackles threw Spurs out of their stride and for long periods it looked as if the spoilers would overcome the artists. Reading took the lead after 15 minutes, a break down the right, a cross into the centre and from 20 yards Clawley was well beaten by Dick Evans' shot. Spurs had chances to equalise but their finishing was poor and it was only for a short spell after half-time that they looked like finding the net.

It was during this spell that Kirwan got the equaliser. Picking up the ball on the edge of the box he tried a quick shot. Accurate and with some pace, Charles Cotton, the Reading 'keeper, should have saved it but he was clearly taken by surprise and could do nothing more than help the ball into his net. The match was more even now but shortly before the end Spurs had that stroke of luck that leads every Cup-winning team to claim their name is on the trophy. Clawley failed to hold a shot from the left and the ball was spinning towards the net behind him when Sandy Tait rushed back and punched it clear. A certain penalty, or so Reading thought. But Clawley was between the referee and the ball and the referee had not seen the incident. The linesman should have but when consulted was certain Tait had not used his hand. A goal-kick was given and amidst furious protests from the Reading players and allegations of 'cheat' from the Reading supporters Spurs lived to fight another day.

Not that Spurs needed to fight. In the Thursday replay Reading were just as committed but Spurs were a different team, in control from first minute to last. They took the lead after only seven minutes. Cameron and Brown worked the ball towards goal before finding Copeland. He nodded the ball down, and took deliberate aim before blasting it past Cotton. Before half-time Smith found Brown and Spurs were two up. Seven minutes after the restart the whole forward line combined in a move that left the Reading defence chasing shadows. The ball ended up at Brown's feet and he promptly finished the scoring.

The semi-final draw had already been made and after the game officials of West Bromwich Albion, somewhat surprisingly, persuaded the Spurs directors to agree to the match taking place at Villa Park on Easter Monday. If Albion hoped the venue would give them an advantage they

In February 1901, Spurs beat Bury 2-1 in an FA Cup-tie at White Hart Lane. Here goalkeeper George Clawley, who had recovered well from a fractured leg, punches the ball clear. In those days, of course, goalkeepers wore the same jersey as the rest of the team.

could not have been more wrong. Half north London made the journey to Birmingham. Playing the close-passing, flowing football that had become Spurs' trademark they totally outclassed an Albion side that relied far too much on 'kick and rush'. It took Spurs 15 minutes to come to terms with West Brom's vigorous style but it was a surprise that half-time arrived without Spurs scoring.

That was put right within five minutes of the restart when Ted Hughes found an unmarked Kirwan, Brown got his head to Kirwan's centre and Spurs were on their way. Ten minutes later Cameron's corner was converted by an unmarked Brown who then embarked on a solo run from the centre circle before scoring from 30 yards. Albion's pride stirred, they at last had the upper hand for a short time but ten minutes from the end the ball was fed out of defence to Cameron, who found Smith and from his centre Brown scored his fourth.

Such was the measure of Spurs' superiority that even though no Southern League team had managed to win the Cup there were many, admittedly mostly from London, who made Spurs favourites to beat either Aston Villa or Sheffield United in the Final. They had drawn 2-2 at Nottingham in the semi-final two days earlier and were due to replay three days later at Derby's Baseball Ground. It was Sheffield United who won through to the Final and travelled down to Crystal Palace for a match in which interest was truly tremendous.

Fully 114,815, at that time a world record for a football match, witnessed one of the best Finals in

years. The early play favoured United but Spurs gradually overcame their nerves and it was not long before a fine move between Copeland and Kirwan saw Brown put Cameron through, only for the Spurs' player-manager to be pulled up for offside. United then got the upper hand with Clawley making one smart save from George Hedley and Erentz two desperate clearances before, with only 12 minutes gone, an unsighted Clawley was beaten by Fred Priest's 20-yard effort.

With the wind and sun behind them Spurs were up against it as United looked for a second goal but after 25 minutes a free-kick 40 yards out was met by Sandy Brown's forehead and Spurs were level. Both sides had good chances to take the lead before the interval. Clawley making several good saves and big Bill Foulke an excellent one-handed save from an unchallenged Tom Smith, but the scores remained level at half-time.

Five minutes after the restart a picture goal gave the vast majority of the crowd belief that the Cup would return to London. Jones started the move with a pass to Kirwan, who in turn found Cameron free to run at goal. Brown's marker was forced to move across to cover Cameron, leaving Brown free to take Cameron's pass and blast it past Foulke.

Spurs' lead lasted for only a minute and when United got their second, their supporters must have believed it was their name on the Cup. Lipsham shot from the left, Clawley failed to hold his shot cleanly but as Walter Bennett rushed in, recovered to put the ball behind. The linesman signalled a corner, but the referee did not agree. It

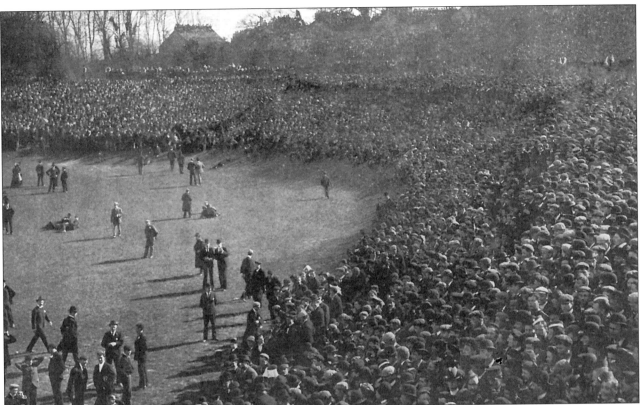

In April 1901, the biggest crowd ever to watch a football match converged on the Crystal Palace to watch Spurs meet Sheffield United in the FA Cup Final. Here, part of the 114,815 attendance spills on to the pitch. It is probable that the majority of the spectators saw little or nothing of the action.

A general view of play in the 1901 FA Cup Final, when Spurs and Sheffield United draw 2-2, both Tottenham's goal coming from Sandy Brown, on his way to a record number in the FA Cup for one season. In that campaign Brown scored in every round.

was only as Clawley placed the ball for a goal-kick that referee Kingscott amazed everybody by indicating a goal. The reaction of the crowd told its own story as they booed, hooted and jeered the official. Impartial observers confirmed that when Clawley fumbled the ball it got no closer than a foot to the line before being scrambled to safety and this was later confirmed by film of the incident.

The most annoying thing was Kingscott's refusal to consult his linesman even though he had been well behind the play but the linesman equally well up with it. The decision gave United fresh impetus but drained the heart from Spurs and with United having the better of the exchanges, Spurs had their defence to thank for taking the match to a replay. That replay was set to take place at Everton's Goodison Park the

In contrast to the huge crowd at the Crystal Palace there were barely 20,000 present when Spurs and Sheffield United replayed the 1901 FA Cup Final at Burnden Park, Bolton. Here, Tottenham are on the attack.

following Saturday, but with Liverpool due to play a home League game that day they protested and the replay was switched to Bolton's Burnden Park.

The first match had drawn a record crowd for a Cup Final but the replay was watched by the lowest crowd since the early days of the competition. Spurs fans were aggrieved at the idea of having to travel all the way to Lancashire and United's fans no doubt thought their team had done the hard bit by drawing in London, but the major reason for an attendance of only 20,470 was the refusal of the Lancashire & Yorkshire Railway Company to offer cheap fares.

Unlike the first game, Spurs started much the better but luck was not with them and they were unable to carve out any clear cut chances. There was only five minutes to the half-time whistle when Ernest Needham charged through the middle before releasing Bert Lipsham on the left. He took the ball down the wing and passed inside to his partner Fred Priest, who had moved into space and had little difficulty in scoring. This stirred Spurs and before the break Foulke was twice called upon to make excellent saves to keep United ahead.

In the second half it was a different game. Spurs took control and within ten minutes Cameron had got the equaliser. The move started in defence with Sandy Tait finding David Copeland. He rounded Harry Thickett, exchanged passes with Brown and then passed to Cameron whose long-range shot beat Foulke all ends up. With Spurs' half-back line in control and the rain coming down, United's goal was under constant threat and it was no surprise when Needham only half-cleared to Smith who guided the ball into the net. Spurs now dominated and could have scored more goals than the one

Brown headed home from the last of three quick corners.

A goal in every round and 15 in all, it was appropriate that Sandy Brown should get the goal that finally saw off United's challenge. John Jones collected the Cup from Lord Kinnaird and when the team returned to South Tottenham station hours later they were greeted by fireworks and an enormous crowd of delirious supporters. After 18 years the Cup was back in the south. It was to be another 20 before it returned.

The Cup-winning team was perfectly balanced for a knockout competition – good solid defence, hard-working and talented half-backs, creative inside-forwards, wingers with speed and skill and a centre-forward always likely to score. Goalkeeper George Clawley, 6ft 1in and particularly adept at dealing with crosses and long-range shots, helped Southampton win the Southern League in both 1897 and 1898 before a year back home in the Potteries with Stoke. His first year at Spurs was ruined when he broke a leg in October 1899, and he did not return to the team until April 1900. He stayed with Spurs for two years after the Cup win, returned to Southampton, collected a third Southern League title in 1904 and finished his career with the Saints in 1907.

Harry Erentz and Sandy Tait at full-back complimented each other perfectly. 'Tiger' Erentz, solid, reliable and consistent, joined Spurs in May 1898 from Newton Heath immediately becoming a great favourite. He stayed at White Hart Lane until released in 1904, but broke his leg soon after joining Swindon Town and was forced to retire. 'Terrible' Tait, he of the magnificent moustache, spent six years with Preston before joining Spurs in May 1899 and was regarded as the best left-back in the Football League. Hard but fair and

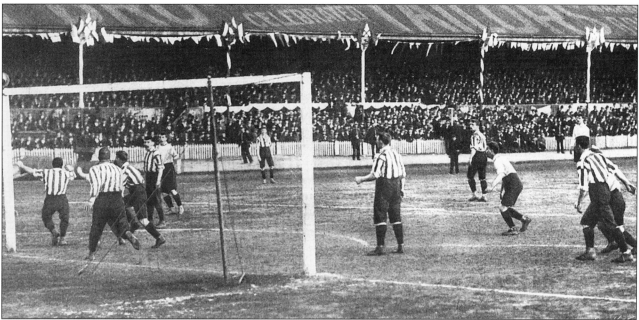

The ball is coming over from a corner-kick and Spurs' Sandy Brown (hidden) is about to head a goal past Sheffield United goalkeeper Billy Foulke. Spurs won the replay 3-1 and thus became the first non-Football League side – since the League was formed, of course – to win the FA Cup.

with a famed sliding tackle, although he looked an intimidating figure he was not not a dirty player, merely strong with great anticipation and positional sense which compensated for a lack of pace. Tait remained with Spurs until 1908 when he went into management with Leyton.

The great strength of the team was in the half-back line. Tom Morris, signed from Gainsborough Trinity in the 1897 close season, was the engine room. With amazing stamina he never tired, helping out the defence one minute then rushing upfield to support the attack, but equally was never flustered. Morris retired from playing in 1912 but remained on the Spurs' groundstaff until his death in 1942.

Spurs secretary-manager John Cameron, also still a player then, is seated (left) with the FA Cup. Tottenham chairman C.D.Roberts is seated right. The other directors are (from left to right) J.Hawley, T.A.Deacock, M.F.Cadman and R.Bullock, who later emigrated to the United States.

Ted Hughes provided the intelligence. A reserve with Everton his chance came when he replaced James NcNaught for the replay against Preston. An untiring worker, great in the air and always keen to support the attack his outstanding form in the Cup run earned him a recall to the Welsh team.

The skill was provided by John L.Jones, a great tactician with almost 20 years experience who had joined Spurs in May 1897 after three years with Sheffield United. His work with David Copeland and John Kirwan was responsible for much of Spurs' most exciting play.

On the right wing was Tom Smith, one of the fastest wingers of his day. Not short on skill, he looked to get past his back before putting in crosses for his inside and centre-forwards to feed off. Another former Preston star, his retirement at the end of the 1901-02 season came far too soon and it was some years before Spurs truly replaced him. If Smith provided the speed, then John Kirwan on the opposite wing provided the trickery. One of the most exciting wingers in the game, his markers never knew what strokes he would pull and there were few full-backs who did not have to call on their half-back to provide cover when Kirwan confronted them. An Irish international who started with Southport, he had a year with Everton who were most upset when he moved to Spurs in July 1899.

At inside-right was John Cameron, another former Everton player and a typically Scottish inside-forward with great dribbling ability and precision passing. Originally a centre-forward, he

Tottenham Hotspur in 1900, pictured with the Southern League Championship Shield.

still had the goalscorer's eye for the half-chance and regularly found the net. At inside-left was former centre-forward and winger David Copeland, signed from Bedminster in May 1899. A foraging type of player he had a remarkable understanding with Kirwan and they formed possibly the most effective left-wing partnership in the country. Spurs were devastated when Copeland and Kirwan took their talents to the newly-formed Chelsea in 1905.

Spearheading all this talent was Alexander 'Sandy' Brown. A true opportunist who looked idle at times, Brown came alive when there was the chance of a goal but he was not unaware of his colleagues and created as many goals as he scored himself. After one more year in north London, Brown returned to Portsmouth and later had two years with Middlesbrough, winning the Scotland cap he was deprived of as a Spurs player due to the April 1902 Ibrox Disaster.

By early 1901, Spurs had only won six Southern League matches and on Boxing Day had lost 3-1 at eventual champions Southampton. Hopes of retaining the title had almost disappeared and not surprisingly the FA Cup took priority. Performances did improve in the second

half of the season, but Spurs had far too much ground to make up and had to be content with fifth place. In the Western League it was exactly the opposite – a good start was not maintained and the club finished third, although Spurs did not put too much store on that competition and frequently fielded reserve sides to keep the Cup team fresh.

The winning of the FA Cup was expected to be the start of a serious challenge by Spurs to become one of the best clubs in the land but that was not to be. Indeed performances in both League and Cup were not to touch the same peaks until after World War One.

The 1901-02 Southern League campaign began with Spurs mounting a serious challenge to Southampton and Portsmouth, but defeat at home to Portsmouth on Christmas Day and at Southampton a day later proved crucial. They went out of the FA Cup to Southampton in a first round second replay at Reading's Elm Park and while they maintained a place near the top of the table, a dismal run-in saw them finish five points behind champions Portsmouth.

The magic of the Cup saw some optimism at White Hart Lane the following two seasons. In

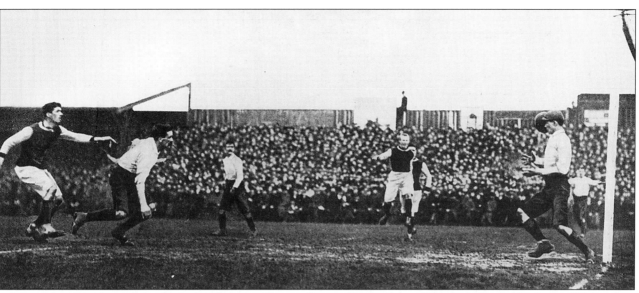

Aston Villa centre-forward Joe Bache has Spurs goalkeeper George Clawley in a real tangle during the third-round FA Cup-tie between the sides at White Hart Lane in March 1903, when Villa emerged 3-2 victors.

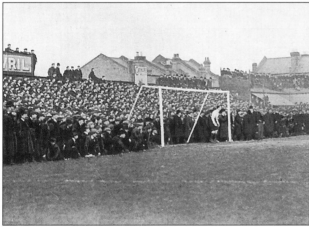

Another Spurs-Villa game, but one which ended in controversial circumstances. The FA Cup-tie at White Hart Lane in February 1904 was abandoned with Villa leading 1-0 when the crowd invaded the pitch. The FA ordered the tie to be replayed at Villa Park, where it was Spurs who came away with a 1-0 victory.

1902-03 West Bromwich Albion were defeated in a first round replay at the Hawthorns and Bristol City at home in the second round. Aston Villa were the visitors in the third round and 24,500 spectators saw a titanic battle before Villa ran out 3-2 winners.

In 1903-04 Spurs again got through to the third round before going down to League champions Sheffield Wednesday in a replay, but not before Spurs had found themselves in trouble with the authorities. After a great win at Everton in the first

Spurs press on the edge of the Millwall penalty area during the Southern League match at White Hart Lane in September 1903. Spurs lost 1-0 in front of a crowd of 16,000.

round, Spurs were paired with Aston Villa at White Hart Lane again. The opportunity for revenge saw 32,000 people cram into the ground and benches were put around the edge of the pitch to help accommodate them. At half-time, with Villa one up, those occupying the benches decided to stretch their legs on the pitch. They were followed by thousands from the terraces and when the teams returned for the second-half, the spectators were either unable or refused to return to their places. The referee was forced to abandon the match and Spurs were called before the FA, fined £350 and ordered to replay the tie at Villa Park.

Much to everyone's surprise, Spurs won 1-0 with a goal from John 'Bristol' Jones. So named to avoid confusion with John L.Jones. the inside-forward had been signed from Bristol City in the summer of 1902 and was regarded as one of the best in his position in the country. Sadly, he died in September 1904 from typhoid having been diagnosed as suffering from influenza when he reported for pre-season training.

Spurs did win the Western League in 1903-04 and finished second in both the Premier Division of the London League and the Southern League, but they had never been a serious threat to champions Southampton, an atrocious start to the season having seen them win only one of their first nine Southern League games. Highly entertaining football was still being provided but it was not winning trophies. Publicly no pressure was being put upon John Cameron but when he suddenly resigned in March 1907 he blamed his decision on 'differences with the directorate'. Former referee Fred Kirkham was appointed to his place.

Into the Football League

WHILST maintaining a position in the upper reaches of the Southern League and twice more reaching the FA Cup quarter-finals, Spurs were not making real progress and in that regard they were not helped by the ultra-conservative approach of the Southern League, in stark contrast to the progressive attitude of the Football League. In 1905, Clapton Orient and the newly-formed Chelsea were refused admission to the Southern League but were welcomed into a Football League anxious to spread its influence from its powerbase in the north and Midlands. In 1907 Fulham, Southern League champions for the previous two seasons, made the move after efforts to combine the two leagues had been thwarted by the southerners. The Football League was proving the more attractive competition and it soon became apparent that unless the Southern League was prepared to adopt a more radical approach, then a rapid decline was inevitable.

In February 1908, Spurs director Morton Cadman returned from a Southern League meeting to report that he had not even been able to find a seconder for an important resolution that might still recover lost ground. Charles Roberts was furious and, with the full backing of his fellow directors, announced that Spurs would

Spurs' staff in 1905. Back row (left to right): J.Over (groundsman), T.Deacock, W.Hickling, J.Whitbourne, J.Eggett, J.Shackleton, W.Bull, T.A.Deacock (director), M.F.Cadman (director). Second row: T.Sinton (steward), J.Cameron (secretary-manager), J.Watson, J.Walton, E.Hughes, T.Morris, O.Burton, J.George, J.Freeborough, C.D.Roberts (chairman), J.Hawley (director). Seated: F.McMullan, H.Chapman, A.Glen, H.Stansfield, A.Tait (captain), C.O'Hagan, W.Murray, P.Kyle, J.McNaught, J.Brearley, G.Cox (director). On ground: S.Mountford (trainer), J.Chaplin, W.Berry, C.Carrick, J.Darnell, J.Nie (assistant trainer).

Spurs fight desperately to clear the ball in the first few minutes of their first-round FA Cup replay against Middlesbrough at White Hart Lane in February 1905. Two minutes before time, O'Hagan headed the only goal of the game following a corner and Spurs were through to the next round.

be seeking election to the Football League. Similar announcements by Queen's Park Rangers and Bradford (who were astonishingly in the Southern League) resulted in the Southern League, largely at Millwall's urging, passing resolutions that the conduct of the three clubs was objectionable and calling upon them to resign. When they refused a rule change was passed giving the League power to expel the rebels.

Both Football League and Southern League meetings were fixed for 27 May 1908, with the Southern League bringing theirs forward half an hour so the two clashed exactly. Bradford had resigned from the Southern League but Spurs and QPR had refused to do so and were both expelled with Coventry City and Southend United taking their places.

At the Football League meeting Spurs were competing with Chesterfield, Grimsby Town, Lincoln City, Bradford and Boston United. The first three, seeking re-election, could rely on the loyalty vote and Bradford City's promotion to Division One had removed the main objection to Bradford's election, so although Spurs had been assured of support they knew there were no guarantees. Yet again, when it came to a vote, they were disappointed. Chesterfield and Grimsby finished top of the poll with 32 and 23 votes. Bradford's 20 was two more than Lincoln and enough to see them elected. Spurs collected only 14 and were left to either crawl back to the Southern League or try to survive without league competition. They had unofficially been told the Southern League would have them back; but only in the Second Division, and had seen QPR readmitted on condition they played all their matches in mid-week.

There was no going back and Spurs only hope seemed to lay in the possibility of the Football

League adopting a Third Division. That hope was soon dashed but fresh hope arose when relegated Stoke decided they could not survive on Second Division attendances and resigned from the Football League pledging their support to Spurs. A special Football League meeting was called for 29 June, Stoke then reversed their decision but were too late to withdraw their resignation and had to go into a ballot with Spurs, Lincoln, Rotherham Town and Southport. In the first vote Spurs and Lincoln both finished with 17, Stoke got six and Rotherham and Southport nil. A second ballot saw Spurs and Lincoln win 20 votes each, leaving the decision to the management committee. They gave it to Spurs by five votes to three. Spurs not only took over Stoke's fixtures but also signed three players from them, Frank Bentley, Joe Brough and James Morton. Before the season began, manager Fred Kirkham left. He had not proved popular with players or fans and had been highly criticised in many quarters. The directors decided not to replace him but to take on his duties themselves.

Spurs' first Football League match could not have been more attractive – FA Cup holders Wolverhampton Wanderers at White Hart Lane. Wolves were favourites but 20,000 spectators saw Spurs make the perfect start; a 3-0 victory with two goals from Vivian J.Woodward and the other from Tom Morris. Woodward – whose mere presence shows the importance Spurs attached to the game as he did not usually play football until the cricket season had finished – had the honour of scoring Spurs' first Football League goal after only six minutes. A Joe Walton free-kick, given after Wolves' goalkeeper Tommy Lunn had carried the ball outside his area, was parried by Lunn and fell nicely for Woodward to knock home.

It was a great start and one that continued to surprise perhaps even Spurs. By the new year the battle for promotion was between Bolton Wanderers, Spurs, West Bromwich Albion, Birmingham and Derby County. Albion were four points ahead of Bolton, who in turn were a point ahead of Spurs, but both Bolton and Albion had played a game more. With three games left Spurs and Bolton were one point behind Albion but all three Spurs games were away (to Burnley, Bradford and Derby). Bolton had two at home (Stockport County and Derby), and a visit to Clapton Orient. Albion had to play Glossop North End at home and Stockport and Derby away. All three clubs had to meet Derby in the last week of the season.

While Bolton were beating Stockport and Albion were beating Glossop, Spurs won at Burnley. While Spurs were winning at Bradford and Bolton at Clapton, Albion could only pick up one point at Stockport. The last week of the season began with Albion losing at Derby. Spurs were next to face the Rams and knew that victory or a draw of no more than 1-1 would secure promotion. A 2-2 draw would be no good as goal-average would leave Albion ahead and a Bolton victory in their last game would give them the title. Bobby Steel got Spurs' goal in the 1-1 draw they needed in a match as tense as any Cup Final. Bolton did beat Derby two days later to take the title, but this hardly mattered to Spurs, they were in Division One and that was all that mattered.

At the end of the season Spurs and Everton sailed to South America for a series of matches in Argentina and Uruguay against local teams and each other. On the way out the two teams played cricket on ship with Walter Bull proving Spurs' star batsman. It was not Spurs' first foreign tour but certainly the most adventurous they had undertaken. On the way home the ship's parrot was given to Spurs, having been used as a prop by one of the party who dressed up as Long John Silver for a fancy dress contest.

Spurs found life much harder in the First Division than they had in the Second but were not helped by Vivian Woodward's shock close season decision to quit Spurs and return to Chelmsford. The outstanding centre-forward of his era, Woodward had spent eight years with Spurs playing for England at both full and amateur level and leading the United Kingdom team to the Olympic title in 1908.

Spurs struggled from the start and did not recover from Woodward's loss until December 1909, when Percy Humphreys was signed from Chelsea. Ironically he had become available only because Chelsea had persuaded Woodward out of retirement to play for them. Humphreys' goals kept Spurs in with a chance of staying up but when Chelsea visited White Hart Lane for the last match of the season, the position was simple: Bolton were relegated and a draw or win for Spurs would see Chelsea accompany them; a Chelsea win would send Spurs down. Spurs got the win they needed, 2-1 with the goals coming from Billy Minter and, perhaps inevitably, Percy Humphreys.

Over the next four years Spurs' results improved little. There was no need for more last-day heroics, but they never finished out of the bottom half of the table and had little success in

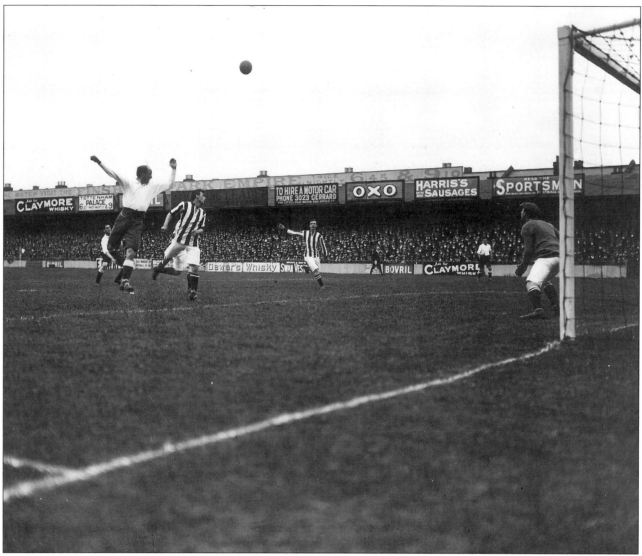

Spurs' Sandy Young heads wide against West Brom at White Hart Lane in September 1911. Spurs won 1-0 but later in the season the Baggies gained revenge by knocking Tottenham out of the FA Cup.

the FA Cup. The directors received a lot of criticism for refusing to enter the transfer market, replying that there were no players available who were better than those already on the staff and those they could secure were not worth the money demanded. Nothing changes in football!

They did at least recognise the need for a professional manager and in January 1913 Peter McWilliam, former Newcastle and Scotland international, was appointed. He slowly prised the purse strings open but, as if Spurs' failure to make an impression in the First Division was not bad enough, 1913 saw a new threat develop. Woolwich Arsenal were relegated that year after nine years of continual struggle. In 1910 Arsenal had been in a financial crisis and sought the assistance of Fulham chairman, Henry Norris, a man with a burning desire to see a London club challenging for the Football League title. His original idea was to merge Arsenal with Second Division Fulham, leaving him with a First

Division club playing at Craven Cottage, but this had been thwarted by the Football League.

Norris retained his interest in Fulham but concentrated his efforts on Arsenal, soon realising that if they were to fulfill his ambitions they would have to move from Plumstead. Finding a suitable site took some time, but early in 1913 news got out that he had found the perfect place at Highbury; right on Spurs' doorstep. Spurs, Clapton Orient and even Chelsea bitterly opposed Norris's plan and complained to the Football League. An acrimonious special meeting of the management committee was held in March 1913 but Arsenal won the day. Not because the committee supported Arsenal's plans but because the regulations gave them no right to interfere. The rules were soon changed but not soon enough from Spurs' point of view.

Clapton Orient had been Spurs' only serious competition for North London football fans and

Battle around the Bradford City goalmouth in a First Division game just before Christmas 1911. The Yorkshire club won 3-2 and on the last day of the season completed a double over Spurs with a 3-0 win at Valley Parade.

Spurs at White Hart Lane before the first game of the 1912-13 season. From left to right: Middlemiss, Darnell, Bliss, Tattersall, Rance, Collins, Lunn, Grimsdell, Lightfoot, Minter, Brittan. Spurs lost the game, against Everton, 2-0 and thus embarked on their worst-ever start to a League season, their first victory not coming until 23 November, after ten defeats and three draws. Despite this dreadful start, Spurs still avoided relegation.

Sheffield Wednesday score their second goal at White Hart Lane in September 1912. They went on to win 4-2 and in the next game Spurs went down 6-1 at Blackburn.

An aerial battle in the game against Manchester City at White Hart Lane in September 1913. Billy Minter scored twice as Spurs won 3-1.

Tottenham's Middlemiss in a race for possession with Chelsea's Taylor during the 2-1 defeat by the Pensioners at White Hart Lane just after Christmas 1913.

in 1909 Spurs had invested some £50,000 in rebuilding the West Stand. Now they had London's oldest professional club only a penny bus ride down the Seven Sisters Road and, being right next to an underground station, Arsenal had the advantage of easy access from Central London. But Arsenal were in the Second Division and Spurs the First, and as long as it stayed that way then Spurs should have the upper hand. It very nearly changed within a year, though, Spurs finishing 17th and Arsenal just missing promotion on goal-average.

To supplement a £5,000 profit on the season Spurs embarked on a European tour including six games in Germany where they experienced at first hand the bitter anti-British feelings that were soon to erupt into World War One and, amongst other things, lead to the internment of several British footballers who had been coaching in that country when war was declared. Well received in Italy and Switzerland, the Spurs party was treated diabolically by the Germans who were not interested in football. All they wanted was to beat the English and they were prepared to go to any lengths to achieve their objective.

Their tactics were violent, the referees openly biased and the spectators not just verbally violent but physically so. Avoiding the crude challenges of opponents was the least of Spurs' worries, for in one match they came under a hail of stones and missiles and in another, goalkeeper Tiny Joyce had his head cut open by an umbrella-welding thug who was loudly applauded by his countrymen. On their return chairman Roberts said that Spurs would never visit Germany again, and it was to be many years after his death before they did.

War with Germany broke out in August 1914 but with the government anxious that life should continue much as normal, football was not suspended. Spurs had an atrocious season, winning only eight games, suffering some heavy defeats and finishing bottom of the First Division. It would be easy to put the blame on the war, and certainly they were weakened by the loss of the many players who were quick to enlist; quicker than those at a lot of clubs, but the fact is that relegation had been a threat for years; it just came, so it turned out, at the worst possible time.

After only one season of wartime football, the

FA decreed that the game should be suspended for the duration, a decision which, had it been taken in the earliest days of the war, might have been influenced by public opinion which then reflected a growing feeling that it was hardly patriotic to see healthy young men playing football while others of their generation were in the trenches of Western Europe.

Of course, there were also practical difficulties. Getting a team together had proved hard enough for many clubs but when travelling problems were considered it was clear that the game could not carry on as it had in peacetime. The authorities now felt that football was good for morale, providing people with a distraction from the war effort, and they wanted it to continue, if only on a regional basis. Henry Norris set about organising the London Football Combination but this led to a dispute with the Football League, who threatened to expel any club competing in it. The dispute was only resolved thanks to the intervention of the FA.

Spurs' opening game in the Combination was on 4 September 1915 when they made their first visit to Highbury, the ground on which they were to play many of their 'home' matches for the last three years of the war. In September 1916, the Ministry of Munitions announced that White Hart Lane was being closed to football and taken over as a factory; more than 11 million gasmasks being made there before the Armistice.

Arsenal and Clapton Orient immediately offered Spurs the use of their grounds and Spurs played roughly half their games at Highbury and the other half at Orient's Homerton ground. Arsenal's willingness to allow Spurs the use of Highbury might be seen as some apology for their intrusion into Spurs' territory. If it was regarded in that way things certainly changed early in 1919. The Football League had decided to increase the First Division by two clubs, as they had in 1898 and 1905. After the 1898 test matches, with Burnley due to replace Blackburn Rovers and Stoke having seen off Newcastle's challenge, both Blackburn and Newcastle had been elected to the First Division. In 1905 Liverpool and Bolton Wanderers received the promotion they had won but Bury and Notts County, due for relegation, had been reprieved. Spurs expected the same would happen this time and were very surprised, not to say annoyed, when Henry Norris began canvassing support for Arsenal to be promoted.

Norris had invested some £125,000 (equivalent to about £3 million today) in Arsenal. The Gunners were £60,000 in debt, and the players who had so nearly taken them up in 1914 and to sixth place (it was in fact fifth but only years later was the error realised) in the last pre-war season were either four years older or had departed. They might well be able to win their way out of the Second Division but there was no guarantee and Norris simply could not afford to take the risk. He based Arsenal's plea on the fact they had been members of the Football League longer than Spurs. That cannot be disputed but ignores the fact that Wolverhampton Wanderers and Birmingham, fourth and fifth in the Second Division table in 1915, had both been in the League longer than Arsenal. Indeed, Wolves were founder members.

If there was any merit in Norris's suggestion that length of membership gave a club a better right to promotion, then both Wolves and Birmingham had a better claim, but neither of them had the gall to put forward such a case. Perhaps even more important, though, Norris's attitude ridiculed the belief promotion should be won on the field, not in the boardroom.

The other club due for relegation was Chelsea but Norris did not challenge their right to remain in the First Division. They had finished a point ahead of Spurs and one behind Manchester United but it had subsequently been established that United's 2-0 defeat of Liverpool on 2 April 1915 had been fixed as part of a betting scandal. If the score had been reversed then Chelsea would have been safe and United in the relegation spot. Even Norris could not suggest relegating Chelsea in such circumstances. Norris began his challenge to Spurs by sending a circular letter to other clubs. Spurs did the same but perhaps they were so convinced in their own mind that right was on their side they did not take the threat from Arsenal seriously enough. Norris, a former Fulham councillor, knighted in 1917 and elected to Parliament in 1918, was a man of influence and wealth with many important friends. He put all those attributes to good use, pressuring and cajoling here, reminding people of good turns done there, calling in favours owed.

The League meeting took place in March 1919 and it was soon apparent that Norris' plans had the backing of his close friend and League president John McKenna, chairman of Liverpool. In the past voting for the four clubs to go up had been dealt with in one ballot but it was obvious Chelsea would top the poll, leaving few votes for Arsenal and Spurs to garner and Spurs likely to win, so McKenna suggested that

Chelsea should be re-elected without a vote. Nobody objected. He then proposed Derby County and Preston North End, first and second in Division Two, should be elected and this was again done without a vote, leaving one place to be decided.

To many people's surprise, not least Charles Roberts', McKenna then made a speech urging the clubs to elect Arsenal. Only then did Roberts realise how utterly he had been outmanœuvred. The ballot gave Arsenal 18 votes, Spurs eight, Barnsley five, Wolves four, Nottingham Forest three, Birmingham two and Hull City one. Following hot on the heels of Arsenal's move to Highbury they had stolen Spurs' First Division place. Was it any wonder Roberts considered emigrating to Germany? Perhaps he felt as 'sick as a parrot', but certainly not as sick as the parrot that had been Spurs' mascot since the 1909 tour. A few days after the League meeting it died! No logical explanation for the League's decision has ever been given. There were rumours, but nothing was proved and with the principal players long since departed, the mystery will remain forever.

Promotion – and Cup Winners Again

SPURS' anger at the Arsenal situation can only be imagined but they showed the injustice of the whole fiasco in the only way that really matters, by strolling away with the Second Division title in 1919-20. The only major additions to the pre-war playing staff were half-back Bert Smith and winger Jimmy Dimmock but from the difference in performances it was as if an entire new team had been signed. The season started with a 5-0 win at Coventry and continued that way with a free-scoring attack netting 102 goals and only 32 conceded. It was not until the thirteenth match that the first defeat was sustained and only three more were to follow as Spurs collected a record 70 points to finish six clear of Huddersfield Town.

They might have made as big an impact in the FA Cup too if tragedy had not befallen captain Tommy Clay. In the first round Spurs won 4-1 at Bristol Rovers and then saw off West Stanley 4-0 and West Ham United 3-0 at White Hart Lane before Aston Villa's fourth round visit. First choice centre-half Charlie Rance was injured so Spurs were forced to call up Jimmy Archibald for only his fourth senior game with Bert Smith moving to Rance's position.

If this weakened Spurs it was not apparent as two teams committed to attack gave the crowd a brilliant display; only to come up against two defences playing equally well. On the play Spurs deserved to win but Villa got the only goal when Clay went to make an easy clearance and somehow only managed to slice the ball past Bill Jacques. It was a mistake that lived with Clay for the rest of his life, while Villa went on to win the Cup. The team that won promotion contained some of the most famous names in Spurs' history. Goalkeeper Bill Jacques, signed from Coventry City in May 1914, was big, brave and quite at home against intimidating centre-forwards licensed to charge the 'keeper, even when in possession. The war took away much of Jacques' career and when it was over he only had a few years at the top before illness caused him to retire in 1923. Captain Tommy Clay was possibly the finest right-back to have donned a Spurs' shirt and won five England caps. Signed from Leicester Fosse in January 1914 after impressing for Leicester against Spurs in the Cup he went on to give Spurs 15 years truly great service. A strong tackler, immaculate passer and very astute tactically if he had a fault it was a lack of pace but he made up for that with his positional sense and there were few wingers who got the better of him. Early on John Pearson, signed from Arbroath in February 1913, occupied the left-back slot but midway through the season lost his place to Bob Brown, a summer signing from Thorneycrofts. The half-back line, Bert Smith, Charlie Rance and Arthur Grimsdell provided the great strength of the team. Smith, formerly with Huddersfield Town and another who went on to win England honours, was the midfield workhorse, a great tackler but also very skilful in his own right. Rance joined Spurs from Clapton having twice helped them to win the Amateur Cup. Regarded as the best amateur in his position in the country he added a stability to the middle line that had been sadly lacking before the war. At left-half was the immaculate Grimsdell, a schoolboy star signed from Watford in March 1912. Aggressive, skilful, a tireless worker, while Clay provided the tactical skill on the right Grimsdell was the counter-balance on the left.

With a great long-range shot he provided the heart of the team until his release in 1929, one of the most complete half-backs in the history of the game. On the wings Fanny Walden and Jimmy

Tommy Clay puts through his own goal to score the only goal of the home FA Cup fourth-round tie against Aston Villa in March 1920. At the end of the season, though, Spurs had ample consolation with promotion to Division One.

Part of the record crowd of 52,179 who saw the Spurs-Villa Cup-tie at White Hart Lane which ended Tottenham's interest in the competition for another season. Twelve months later, however, Spurs were to gain ample revenge over Villa, on their way to winning the trophy for a second time.

Dimmock never gave opposing defences a minute's rest. Walden, 5ft 2in, 8st 9lb, was signed from Northampton Town for a record £1,700 in April 1913. With a never ending repertoire of tricks one of the finest sights at White Hart Lane was to see him take the ball up to some big, burly full-back, push the ball past him, run off the pitch to avoid a crushing tackle and look over his shoulder to see his marker left on his backside. Dimmock on the other hand was a dribbler, relying on balance and close ball control to tie his opponent in knots. A local discovery, he replaced Jimmy Chipperfield in November 1919 and went on to become the hero of Spurs fans, young and

old alike. Between these two was Jimmy Cantrell, 38 years old and with the experience that goes with age. He was unlike so many of his contemporaries, relying on skill and subtlety as opposed to the pure physical strength so prevalent then. At inside-left Bert Bliss, a blistering shot with a shoot on sight policy signed as a junior from Willenhall Swifts, worked perfectly with Grimsdell and Dimmock, devouring the chances they created. Billy Minter started the season at inside-right but gave way to Jimmy Banks in January 1920. Minter was a great servant to Spurs working for the team and scoring regularly after being signed from Reading in June 1906. Banks, more a creator than scorer, provided an effective link between Smith and Walden always looking to get the little winger in or slip the ball through to Cantrell.

If Spurs' League and Cup performances that season did not convince the League of the mistake they had made 12 months earlier they certainly did in 1920-21. Sixth place in the First Division, three above Arsenal, was their best-ever placing but it was in the FA Cup they really shone. In the first round Bristol Rovers were the visitors. Any hopes they had of springing a surprise were dashed within two minutes as their right-half, Dennis Howes, was injured. He returned after treatment but did not last long and Rovers played most of the game with only ten men. Jimmy Seed gave Spurs the lead with a long-range drive after four minutes and Tommy Clay

Tommy Clay joined Spurs from Leicester Fosse in January 1914 and went on to make over 350 senior appearances despite losing four seasons to World War One. He gained four England caps and skippered Tottenham on their return to Division One in 1920.

Jimmy Cantrell tussles for the ball with a Southend United defender at the Kursaal ground in February 1921. Spurs won the third-round FA Cup-tie 4-1 with Cantrell scoring one of their goals.

converted a penalty given for a foul on Seed 12 minutes later. Smith got the third from a corner, Walden the fourth from Bliss' centre and by half-time the match was over. Spurs eased up in the second half, further goals from Cantrell and Bliss being cancelled out by two efforts from the visitors. Bradford City were next to visit White Hart Lane and left well and truly beaten 4-0. Little Fanny Walden was injured and Jimmy Banks, usually an inside-forward, was asked to replace the magical right-winger. In the first half he appeared totally lost but in the second found his feet to give a fine performance, but the man of the match was Jimmy Seed. Two minutes after the interval he latched on to a defensive error to put Spurs one up and 30 seconds later made it two. Banks got the third from a corner before Seed completed his hat-trick with a shot from 25 yards.

Spurs were expected to have no problems in the third round – Third Division Southend United away, but their poorest showing of the competition saw them behind for almost 60 minutes. Spurs seemed content to let the home team make all the running, waiting for them to wear themselves out before trying to win the game. Southend took the lead after ten minutes when George Nicholls scored from close in but Spurs were soon level, Banks' corner being headed home by Cantrell. Ten minutes before the interval Bert Smith was adjudged to have fouled Joe Dorsett and a penalty was awarded. Albert Fairclough went to take the kick but was put off when the referee decided it was not on the spot, moved it and refused to let Fairclough touch it again. When he did take his shot, he put it wide – that little bit of luck all Cup-winners' need? For the first 15 minutes of the second half the pattern was identical, Southend on top, Spurs defending but never seriously in danger of conceding another goal. Sure enough, Southend tired and in the last half-hour Spurs took control. Cantrell put Banks through for the second and the same player then scored with a ferocious free-kick from the edge of the box before Seed finished the scoring. Cup holders Aston Villa were next with almost 52,000 people packing White Hart Lane to

Jimmy Dimmock, a star of the Tottenham team throughout the 1920s. Dimmock's left-wing wizardry was a major factor in Spurs winning promotion in 1920 and the FA Cup a year later when he scored the only goal of the Final.

General view of the 1921 FA Cup Final between Spurs and Wolves at Stamford Bridge. The attendance was 72,805.

see if Spurs could avenge the previous season's defeat. They witnessed the best Cup-tie of the season and a match that was talked about for years. The only goal came in the 23rd minute. Heavy pressure on the Villa area saw the ball cleared to Jimmy Dimmock who began a run on goal. After dummying his way past a defender he centred across goal where Seed and the Villa full-back, Bert Smart, both went for the ball. It broke to Banks whose shot into the far corner gave the Villa 'keeper no chance. Try as Villa might they could not get the upper hand and Sam Hardy was called upon to make three tremendous saves to keep them in the game. The second half saw a terrific struggle but Spurs always seemed in command with Charlie Walters providing great protection to Alex Hunter who had replaced the injured Bill Jacques.

The semi-final took place at Hillsborough with Preston North End providing the opposition. Spurs won 2-1 but with a better referee the scoreline would have truly reflected Spurs' dominance of the game, they should have had three or four more goals. Jimmy Banks had a goal disallowed in the first half after latching on to a loose ball and giving Arthur Causer no chance. It was disallowed, said the referee, because Seed had been fouled and instead of a goal he gave Spurs a free-kick. When Spurs did get the ball in

the net from a goalmouth scramble again the referee gave a free-kick, this time to Preston, but refusing to explain why. On the one occasion they could have scored with no excuse for the referee to disallow it Jimmy Dimmock, only a few yards out, almost broke the cross bar with the goal at his mercy. It really looked like the fates were against Spurs when, early in the second half, Banks was clearly brought down in the box. A blatant penalty, but no, play on, said the referee. Eventually Spurs got their reward, a brilliant bout of inter-passing between Grimsdell and Dimmock ended with Grimsdell suddenly cutting the ball back to Bert Bliss who hooked it home. A second goal was not long in coming with Grimsdell again involved before putting Bliss through.

Preston got their consolation near the end after a mix up in the Spurs defence allowed Frank Jefferies to get in a shot. The ball was covered by Hunter but a deflection off Tommy Clay's knees took it out of his reach. Inspired to seek an equaliser Preston were surprisingly ineffective and Spurs had the better chances to add to the score. In the other semi-final at Anfield, Wolverhampton Wanderers and Cardiff City fought out a goalless draw with Second Division Wolves winning the Old Trafford replay 3-1. The Final took place at Stamford Bridge with King George V and the Duke of York in attendance. A

Fanny Walden had the misfortune to miss the latter half of Spurs' successful 1920-21 FA Cup campaign because of injury. Walden, at 5ft 2in one of the smallest League players ever, played in 236 games for Spurs and won two England caps, eight years apart because of World War One.

Wolves goalkeeper Billy George dives too late to stop Dimmock's winning goal.

Arthur Grimsdell receives the FA Cup from King George V. It was the first time a southern club had won the trophy since Spurs' last success 20 years earlier.

'keeper was only called upon to make two serious saves and Walters was even able to find time to help his attackers.

The only serious threat to Spurs goal came from Sammy Brooks, a Fanny Walden clone later to sign for Spurs. The few chances that did arise fell to Spurs but only one was converted. That was in the 54th minute when Dimmock, who overall had a quiet game, took a pass from Bliss and advanced on the Wolves' goal. His attack was stopped by Maurice Woodward, but the full-back was slow to clear and Dimmock recovered possession to fire in a low angled drive from the corner of the box that skidded in at the far post. When Arthur Grimsdell, who had replaced Clay as captain, went up to collect the Cup it was the first time it had been back in the South since Spurs first success 20 years earlier. The Cup-winning team contained few changes from the promotion winning team.

Alex Hunter, ex Queens Park, was persuaded to join the professional ranks in May 1920 and got in the team when Jacques was injured in February 1921. Daring, per-haps a little too so at times, he grabbed his chance when it came along but could not maintain his form and left little more than a year after collecting his Cup winners' medal. At left-back Bob McDonald had emerged to displace both Pearson and Brown. Originally a right-back he had little hope of replacing Clay but when tried on the left his hard-tackling style proved complimentary to Clay. Centre-half Charlie Walters, like McDonald and Hunter, another capture from the amateur ranks, this time Oxford City, was an effective destroyer in the 'stopper' mould. Fast and determined Spurs had such faith in his ability they let Charlie Rance move to Derby County. Jimmy Banks was called up early in the Cup campaign to replace injured Fanny Walden having lost his place at inside-forward

torrential downpour that had lasted for hours and only abated long enough for the presentation of the teams turned the pitch into a quagmire, with pools of water everywhere and barely a blade of grass in sight. Eventually the rain subsided but never enough for the pitch to dry out and right to the end players were slipping and sliding. These were not the conditions for Spurs' cultured passing game but they did suit the more direct, robust, Wolves style. Not surprisingly clear cut chances were few and far between with the defences dominating.

The whole Spurs' defence was superb but centre-half Charlie Walters was the star. Totally in charge of the opposing forwards he gave such excellent protection to Alex Hunter that the with the signing of Jimmy Seed. Seed, discarded by Sunderland after being gassed during the war, had resurrected his career with Mid-Rhondda and was probably Peter McWilliams' most important signing for Spurs. The mastermind behind Spurs' success he was the complete inside-forward, combining well with his half-back, always looking to set his winger free and a regular goalscorer. His release in August 1927 to join Sheffield Wednesday ranks alongside the sale of Pat Jennings to Arsenal 50 years later as the worst transfer decision in Spurs' history.

Pre-war Ups and Downs

TWO years of success looked unlikely to be followed by a third when Spurs began 1921-22 in disappointing fashion as injuries took their toll and age began to show, particularly with Jimmy Cantrell. Indeed, it was not until Christmas that they began to display any really consistent form, embarking on a run that saw them finish second in the table, the highest placing of a London club since the League's formation. They were six points behind champions Liverpool and had never really been in with a chance of taking the title, but there was always the Cup to defend and again that looked the best bet for glory.

Third Division Brentford and Watford were seen off in the first two rounds and in the third round Spurs were drawn with Manchester City. As home and away League games were then played on consecutive Saturdays, the teams met three weeks on the trot, drawing 3-3 in the first League encounter at White Hart Lane, Spurs winning the return 3-1 and then taking the Cup-tie back in London by the odd goal of three.

Cardiff City were the next opponents and on a mudheap of a pitch at Ninian Park it took a last-minute equaliser for Cardiff to force a replay. Almost 54,000, with as many locked out, saw goals by Dimmock and Charlie Wilson, who had replaced Cantrell, give Spurs a 2-1 victory in another match that lived long in the memory of those present.

Through to the semi-final, could Spurs become the first club to retain the Cup since Blackburn Rovers in 1891? As in 1921, Spurs were paired with Preston at Hillsborough, the Lancashire club this time gaining revenge for their earlier defeat in another match clouded by controversy. In the first half Spurs were well on top, a single goal from Seed far from adequate reward for their territorial dominance. The story goes that during the interval the Preston players were given champagne. True or not they were a different team in the second half, taking the game to Spurs and fully deserving their equaliser.

A battle royal ensued which Spurs looked to have won when a typical thunderbolt drive from Bliss gave the Preston goalkeeper no chance. But the goal was not allowed to stand, the referee claiming that before the ball crossed the line he had blown his whistle to allow a Preston player, lying in the centre-circle and who it turned out was not even injured, treatment. The decision knocked Spurs right back and before they could recover Preston snatched the winner.

The great team of 1920 and 1921 now began to deteriorate rapidly. Clay, Dimmock, Grimsdell, Seed and Smith were still there but while Spurs bought in many players, both from other clubs and through the ranks, the quality was not the same. There were exceptions: inside-forward Jack Elkes, signed from Southampton in May 1923 for £1,000, was recognised as one of the best in his position and unlucky not to win international honours. He added good passing and dribbling skills to the midfield and scored more than his fair share of goals before moving into the centre-half berth where his physical strength allowed him to handle the most difficult of opponents but still gave him room to display his creative talents.

South African-born Frank Osborne was signed from Fulham for £1,500 in January 1924. Equally good on the wing or at centre-forward, his versatility is evidenced by the fact that he won two caps in his Fulham days, one in each position and did the same in his seven years with Spurs. When he played at centre-forward he could be relied on to get a few goals, but the lack of top quality forwards forced Spurs to play Osborne on the wing far too often. It was no good having a goalscorer if there was nobody setting up the chances.

Spurs still had the nucleus of a strong team but it matters not how great one or two may be if the rest are not good enough. That was Spurs' problem. The directors came in for a great deal of criticism from newspapers and fans alike for refusing to sign players but they steadfastly

In March 1923, Spurs met a Variety Artists' XI at White Hart Lane in aid of charity. Here are some of the Tottenham team, wearing fur hats and false beards.

refused to pay 'ridiculous transfer fees, running into several thousands of pounds, asked for ordinary players', preferring to develop local youngsters. It was all very laudable but the fact was that the local talent, decimated by the war, was not good enough.

The major weaknesses were in goal and at centre-forward. Herbert Blake, Geordie Maddison, Fred Hinton, Jock Britton, Bill Kaine and Jimmy Smith were all tried but none of them provided the last line of defence needed by a club that seriously wanted to challenge for the League championship. Alex Lindsay, Bill Lane, Harry Hargreaves, John Blair, Tommy Roe, Arthur Sanders and Albert Evans were all given a chance at centre-forward but only Lindsay ever looked a likely answer to the problem and only then in 1923-24 when he had Seed, Dimmock and Walden setting up the chances.

Only once did Spurs' supporters have cause to dream of great success and that dream was shattered by injury to only one player. At the beginning of October 1925 Spurs were joint leaders of the First Division, the first time they had reached such a lofty perch. On the last day of

Crystal Palace clear their lines in the FA Cup first-round tie against Spurs at Selhurst Park in January 1924. Tottenham went down 2-0.

the month Arthur Grimsdell broke his leg at Leicester and from then on it was all downhill with Spurs finishing 15th.

A lower mid-table position seemed acceptable to the directors and their lack of ambition was clearly shown with the departure of Peter

Spurs goalkeeper Hinton punches clear punches clear from a Bolton attack at White Hart Lane on the first day of the 1924-25 season. Tottenham won 3-0 but at the end of the season could manage only 12th place.

McWilliam. On a salary of £850 a year, paid weekly so that he could be sacked with only a week's notice, he was approached by Second Division leaders Middlesbrough in December 1926 and was offered £1,500 a year to become their manager. McWilliam was happy with Spurs and did not want to leave; he had taken the club to top spot again only a month earlier, but when he asked the board to increase his salary to £1,000 a year they refused. Not surprisingly he handed in his notice, giving three months, still time enough for the directors to change their mind, but they would not.

McWilliam had done a splendid job, taking a demoralised club back into the First Division, on to FA Cup success, second in the League and still near the top with an aging team desperately in need of investment. It was another sad error of judgment on the part of the board. Billy Minter, who had retired from playing in 1920 and taken on the role of trainer, was given the task of replacing McWilliam, assuming responsibility in February 1927. Deeply committed to Spurs he had an almost impossible job but did not make

life easy for himself with his decision to sell Jimmy Seed.

One of Minter's first decisions was to promote 20-year-old Taffy O'Callaghan from the reserves to replace Seed, who had been injured in the third round FA Cup-tie with West Ham in January 1927. O'Callaghan's youthful enthusiasm certainly gave the team, and supporters, a badly needed lift after McWilliam's departure. Full of energy but with bags of skill and able to pass or shoot with either foot and equal success, he performed so well that when Seed was fit he could not win back his place.

Seed was not happy at the thought of reserve-team football and successfully applied for the manager's job at Aldershot, but Spurs would not release him so he could take up the post, preferring to sell him to Sheffield Wednesday in August 1927. In the long term Minter's decision was probably correct, O'Callaghan was ten years younger and clearly had a fine career in front of him, but it was too much to expect the youngster to fill such an experienced player's boots so quickly.

Jimmy Seed leads the team for the FA Cup-tie against Northampton Town at White Hart Lane in January 1924. Spurs won 3-0, then overcame Bolton in a replay but in the next round lost at Blackburn in another replay.

High kicking in the Spurs-Bolton FA Cup-tie at White Hart Lane in January 1925.

Arthur Grimsdell heads away from danger as Blackburn Rovers press at White Hart Lane in October 1925. Spurs won 4-2.

Jimmy Dimmock challenges Arsenal goalkeeper Harper at White Hart Lane in January 1926. The North London rivals drew 1-1.

Spurs looked reasonably safe in 1927-28 with Dimmock, Grimsdell, Harry Skitt, and Darkie Lowdell, signed from Sheffield Wednesday in part exchange for Seed, providing a solid base, and O'Callaghan and Osborne the attacking genius. Victories over Bristol City, Oldham Athletic and Leicester City took them to the sixth round of the FA Cup but on one of those days when just about everything that could go wrong does go wrong, Spurs were hammered 6-0 at Huddersfield.

The real disappointment, though, came in the League. Just before Easter, 35 points from an equal number of games saw Spurs lying in seventh place. Sheffield Wednesday, two games in hand but 11 points behind were bottom of the table and looking doomed. The clubs met twice over Easter with Wednesday winning 3-1 at White Hart Lane and 4-2 at Hillsborough, Seed scoring in both games and playing better than he had ever done. Still there was no cause for concern, especially when two O'Callaghan goals defeated Arsenal 24 hours after the game in Sheffield.

Spurs picked up only one point in the last four games, finished the season early and departed for a four-game tour to Holland. On their return they found they had been relegated. Inspired by Seed, Wednesday had collected 17 points from their last ten games to finish 14th, leading a cluster of clubs on 39 points, one more than Spurs and two more than Middlesbrough.

To underscore the irony and frustration of it all, while Spurs were struggling to escape Division Two, Seed was leading Wednesday to successive League titles.

One might have expected relegation would have jolted the club into opening the cheque book but nothing could be further from the truth. Perhaps it was felt a team so unluckily relegated would prove far too strong for Second Division teams, or just that the fees demanded were far too high. Whatever the reason new signings were few and of poor quality. Former England centre-forward Tom Roberts arrived from Preston for £1,000. He started well with two goals on his debut, but was injured in his next match and made only two more appearances before being released at the end of one season.

Another centre-forward, Randolph Galloway, discarded by Coventry and unable to find another

Tottenham's Blair scores his side's first goal against West Bromwich Albion at White Hart Lane in September 1926. Spurs went on to win 3-0.

Forster and Clay tangle with Arsenal's Charlie Buchan at Highbury in December 1926, when Spurs won 4-2.

Taking risks to see the big game. Part of the 47,296 crowd at Filbert Street who saw Spurs beat Leicester City 3-0 in the fifth round of the FA Cup in February 1928. In the quarter-finals, however, Tottenham were hammered 6-1 at Huddersfield.

club, was signed after a month's trial. He also began well – two goals in three games at the start of the season – but then dropped into the reserves. Joe Scott from Barnsley, was a winger expected to challenge Dimmock but never in the same class. Thirty-four-year-old centre-half Harry Wilding arrived from Chelsea in November 1928 and played 12 games before it was realised he was well past his best.

Clay and Grimsdell had reached the end of their great careers but it was only in February 1929 that steps were taken to strengthen the team, too late for promotion but at least providing hope, in the form of full-back Edwin Herod from Charlton Athletic and another former England centre-forward, Ted Harper from Sheffield Wednesday. Harper, who cost £5,500, had an immediate effect, scoring 11 goals in the same number of games to help Spurs finish tenth.

Billy Cook from Aston Villa and Tom Meads from Reading were the only new signings for 1929-30, but with Harper missing the start of the season due to injury only 12 points were taken from 15 games. For the first time relegation to Division Three became a real concern, the pressure began to affect Billy Minter's health and in November 1929 he resigned.

The Bury manager Percy Smith, a former Preston and Blackburn Rovers player, was appointed in his place. Ted Harper's goals enabled Spurs to finish 12th in Division Two, still the club's lowest ever League placing, but at least it gave Smith time to look at the playing staff and decide where it needed strengthening.

Whether it was the fear of failure or Smith's persuasive tongue is not clear, but at last the board were persuaded to relax the purse strings. Dick Rowley, Southampton's Irish international centre-forward, and Aston Villa's Welsh international Willie Davies were Smith's first signings, arriving in February 1930. In the summer they were joined by full-backs Bert Hodgkinson from Barnsley and Bert Lyons from Clapton Orient, and the Reading centre-half Tom Messer.

Another new arrival was a 20-year-old from Chesterfield, George Hunt. With Harper and Rowley expected to compete for the centre-forward position, and only a season's experience, Hunt was very much 'one for the future', snapped up from under the nose of Arsenal's Herbert Chapman who was keen but had decided to leave it a while before making his move.

A lot of money was laid out and for most of the

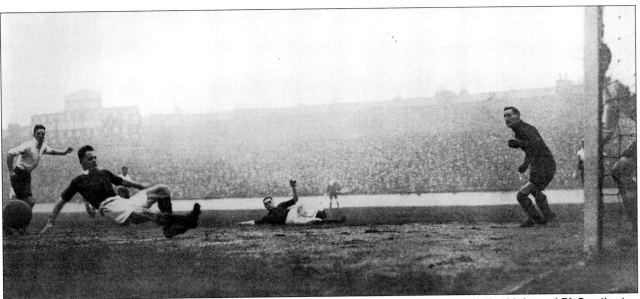

A cross goes begging in Tottenham's penalty area as Manchester City fail to take advantage in the third-round FA Cup-tie at White Hart Lane in January 1930. The game ended 2-2 but City won the replay 4-1.

In March 1931 Spurs were battling with Everton and West Brom for promotion to the First Division. West Brom gained a vital point at White Hart Lane and went on to win promotion and the FA Cup that year. Here, Spurs' George Hunt shoots straight at the Baggies' goalkeeper.

season it looked to have been well spent. Everton were the outstanding team and led the table from almost start to finish, but by the new year the second promotion place had become a straight fight between Spurs and West Bromwich Albion, with Spurs the favourites.

Taffy O'Callaghan provided the bullets for Ted Harper to fire and in 28 games Harper found the target 34 times. A goalscorer pure and simple with great strength and bravery, he had built a big reputation with Blackburn Rovers and Sheffield Wednesday but enhanced it in his time at White Hart Lane. This made him a target for a lot of harsh treatment and it was not unusual for him

take the field heavily bandaged. On 21 March, Harper scored at Swansea before being crippled by a serious leg injury which put him out for six games. He returned for the last two games, scored twice but was far from fit and was forced to depart the action early.

George Hunt was given the task of replacing Harper and scored five goals in eight games but he lacked Harper's experience and perhaps thought more was expected of him than was the case. In Harper's absence Spurs managed only four draws, allowing Albion to pip them for second spot by three points. It was a great disappointment and one that heralded further changes.

Heads up in the Southampton goal during the Second Division game at White Lane in October 1932. Spurs won 5-0 and at the end of the season were promoted as runners-up.

Cook, Skitt, Dimmock, Herod and Osborne were all allowed to move on, David Colquhoun was signed from St Mirren, Jack Moran from Wigan Borough and several youngsters were promoted from the club's Northfleet nursery club.

An embarrassing 4-0 defeat at Wolves in the first match of 1931-32, followed by a 4-0 defeat of Preston at home, sums up the whole season – inconsistent. George Hunt was installed as first-choice centre-forward and the experienced Jimmy Brain signed from Arsenal to provide the right kind of support. Harper and Rowley were allowed to join Preston in December 1931. Moran and Jimmy Smailes, signed from Huddersfield in March 1931, were given their chance but then discarded along with Alf Messer. Former England full-back Bill Felton was signed from Manchester City but no matter how much Smith changed the team they could not string together a decent run of results and eighth place was a major let-down for a side that had gone so close to promotion 12 months earlier.

But every cloud has its silver lining and for Spurs that was the discovery of several stars of the future – all of them, no doubt much to the pleasure of the directors, home-produced. As the season wore on, more and more youngsters were given their opportunity. Wally Alsford, who had looked like replacing Skitt until Colquhoun's arrival, was given another chance, Allan Taylor replaced Cyril Spiers for long spells, Joe Nicholls was called up for the last two games of the campaign and Tom Evans finished the season a regular at half-back.

But most promising was the trio of Arthur Rowe, George Greenfield and Willie Evans. Rowe, born within a crowd's roar of White Hart Lane and called into the team in October 1931, played centre-half but not in the 'stopper' fashion then so popular. He was a throwback to the footballing half-backs of the 1900s, as effective starting attacks from deep as in defending his own goal.

Inside-forward Greenfield, another local lad, was an exceptional talent, tipped for international honours after no more than 20 League outings.

George Hunt puts the Bradford City goalkeeper under pressure at Tottenham in April 1933 as Spurs close in on promotion, although they dropped a point in this game which ended 1-1.

Sadly he sustained a serious leg injury in December 1932, never fully recovered and was forced to retire. Evans made his debut on his 19th birthday and immediately captivated Spurs' fans with his pace and shooting.

Promise in abundance there may have been but it was not apparent at the start of the following season. After playing Oldham on 1 October 1932, Spurs were fourth from bottom with only six points from eight games, the nearest they had ever been to the Third Division. Four of those points came from an opening day 4-1 defeat of Charlton Athletic and a 6-1 thrashing of Manchester United, but all four away games had been lost.

Another home-produced player, Bill Whatley, had replaced Cecil Poynton at full-back but David Levene had not done so well and Percy Smith decided to ring the changes. Levene, Willie Davies and Jimmy Brain were dropped, Greenfield and Meads recalled, Les Howe reintroduced after only three games two years earlier.

The turnaround was astonishing. Preston were

beaten 6-2 at Deepdale, Burnley 4-1 and Southampton 5-0 at home, Millwall 4-1 away and Port Vale 4-0 at home. The 'Greyhounds' had arrived. Speed combined with precision, skill with confidence, trickery with determination, football of this quality had not been seen by Spurs regulars for over ten years.

For almost five months few could hold Tottenham as they surged up the table. The only setback was in December when George Greenfield broke his leg at Fulham. Spurs had lost the outstanding young inside-forward of the season, but Percy Smith was quick to respond, immediately securing the transfer from Notts County of the only player capable of replacing Greenfield, Willie Hall. Greenfield's loss cost Spurs five points, points that almost proved decisive come the end of the season.

Stoke had led the table from the start and Spurs were rarely able to climb above them. Bradford City, Bury, Manchester United, Nottingham Forest and Swansea Town all took it in turn to challenge for second place but the real threat came with a late run from Fulham. In mid-March, Taffy O'Callaghan and Les Howe were injured and Jimmy McCormick was signed from Chesterfield, but Spurs had to scrap for every point and too often had to settle for one when two were needed.

In the penultimate match Spurs lost at West Ham, only their third defeat in 34 games, but it looked as if promotion would depend on the last match of the season. Surprisingly though, Fulham also lost, at home to Grimsby, and Spurs were up. A 3-1 win over Notts County left Spurs one point behind Stoke and five ahead of Fulham but it had been much closer than the final table suggested.

Taffy O'Callaghan had scored 14 goals but the real stars were Willie Evans with 28 and George Hunt with 33.

Evans was a revelation, his exceptional speed down the wing too much for most full-backs, his bullet-like shooting too hot for most 'keepers. He was the right wing regular until sustaining a serious knee injury at Villa Park on his 24th birthday. An operation could not cure the problem and at only 25 he was released. Fulham took him on but a second operation was no more successful and he was forced to retire.

George Hunt really justified the faith Percy Smith showed in him. Solid muscle and everlasting energy he never gave defences a moment's peace and even when the ball was at the other end of the pitch defenders could not take their eyes off him for a second. His speed off

Spurs and Newcastle players observe two minutes' silence at White Hart Lane on Armistice Day 1933.

the mark and willingness to chase even a lost cause gave him many goals.

No major changes in personnel were made for the return to the top flight, a few juniors were promoted from Northfleet, Alan Hall was signed for a modest fee after scoring 56 goals in only two years with Lincoln City but the critics were not impressed. The defence might be safe enough but the forward line was thought lightweight, First Division defences would soon knock them out of their stride. This view was understandable: McCormick and Hall were 5ft 7in, Hunt and O'Callaghan 5ft 8in and Evans only 5ft 6in. But Spurs' game was based on speed; quick interpassing, movement off the ball and acceleration leaving opponents for dead; if they were quick enough defenders would not even be able to get to them.

The season began better than even Spurs could have imagined. By the end of November they were top of the table, leading defending champions Arsenal and Huddersfield Town and looking to have a real chance of their first League title. The turning point came at Christmas when

two games against Huddersfield produced two defeats. Even a 3-1 victory at Highbury at the end of January was not enough to get Spurs back in the race and come the final reckoning they had to be content with third place, ten points behind Arsenal and seven behind Huddersfield.

The 'Greyhounds' was a nickname given to Spurs as they raced up the Second Division, but greyhounds are delicate animals known for speed not stamina and so it proved with Spurs. A quick burst up the League could not be sustained and was followed by an equally rapid decline. They started 1934-35 badly and it was not until the fifth game that a win was recorded, and things just went from bad to worse. The style of football had not altered in any way, Spurs still tried to play their fast, flowing, inter-passing game, but suffered one injury after another, were rarely able to field the same team twice and often finished a game with only nine or ten men, some of them carrying injuries.

And it was not only the established first-teamers that suffered, the reserves were hit just as badly. Spurs' strength had lain in their teamwork,

George Hunt beats Everton's Ted Sagar for Spurs' first goal in their 3-0 win over the Toffees in the third round of the FA Cup in January 1934.

Spurs goalkeeper Nicholls punches clear against Aston Villa at White Hart Lane in February 1934, but Villa won this fifth-round FA Cup-tie with the only goal of the game.

players familiar with each other knowing what a colleague was going to do without thinking and making a pass without the need to look first. That strength was undermined as no less than 36 players were used in the season.

Every area of the team was affected but the biggest losses were undoubtedly Arthur Rowe and Willie Hall. Rowe was the backbone of the team and after he was injured early in December 1934, Spurs managed only one win in 20 games. Hall

Spurs trainer George Hardy welcomes a bowler-hatted Harold Hardinge to White Hart Lane as Tottenham's reserve-team manager in January 1935. Hardinge, a former Sheffield United player, was a double international, having been capped once for England at soccer and once at cricket, when he played for Kent.

was injured a month earlier and without him the midfield lost its way. Hall was rushed back in the last six weeks of the season but was far from fit and anyway it was too late, Spurs' fate was already decided.

Again the directors came in for a lot of criticism for not signing players but the same old problem was blamed – exorbitant fees demanded for players no better than those already on the books.

Even when players were secured – Sam Bell from Luton Town, Andy Duncan from Hull City – it was not long before they fell to Spurs' injury jinx. Spurs finished rock bottom, three points

adrift of partners in relegation, Leicester City, while that club from down the road were winning their third successive title and fourth in the last five years.

A struggling club is a dispirited club and when spirits are low everybody looks for a scapegoat. Throughout the season there were stories that the Spurs' directors had interfered in Percy Smith's team selections and it was no surprise when Smith handed in his resignation late in April 1935, citing just that as the reason. His allegations were denied but hastened his departure, with Jack Tresadern of Crystal Palace, remembered as West

Tottenham scout Ben Ives points out something to new Spurs manager Jack Tresadern after he took over in July 1935. Trainer George Hardy is on Tresadern's left.

Ham's captain in the first Wembley FA Cup Final, Smith's replacement.

Tresadern had three years in charge, three unsuccessful years with little to enthuse about. Only early in 1935-36 did Spurs look as if they might return to the First Division. Prior to the start of the Christmas games they were second to a Leicester City team inspired by the promptings of Taffy O'Callaghan, who had surprisingly been allowed to leave Spurs for the Midlands club the previous March. Spurs lost three of their four games over the holiday period and although they remained near the top, Charlton Athletic and Manchester United proved the more consistent and Spurs had to settle for fifth place. The deciding factor was Spurs' home form, only two of the last nine home games were won, one was lost and six drawn. The lost points proved crucial in the final reckoning.

The only bright spots came with the FA Cup. For the first time since 1928, Spurs got through to the sixth round, beating Southend United, Huddersfield Town and Bradford before going out to Sheffield United, and the emergence of Johnny Morrison, a great goalscoring centre-forward following in the footsteps of Ted Harper and George Hunt.

Spotted playing for Callenders Athletic, Morrison joined the professional staff at White Hart Lane in July 1933, after only a year at Northfleet, but it was three years before Tresadern gave him a real chance. He replaced Hunt in September 1935 and responded with 25 goals in only 32 games. An opportunist goalscorer, quick off the mark, brave and eager to get in a shot at goal, he was very similar to Hunt and therein lay a problem – they were so alike they could not play in the same team without getting in each other's way.

Eventually Tresadern was forced to choose between the two and in October 1937 allowed Hunt to move to Arsenal. Hunt was still a crowd favourite and letting him leave was bad enough, but to join Spurs' nearest neighbours was not a popular decision and one that was always held against him.

Spurs dropped to tenth the next season and finished fifth in 1937-38, but never seriously entertained thoughts of promotion. Again it was only the FA Cup that provided any distraction

On the eve of the 1935-36 season Spurs' washing is pegged out to dry at White Hart Lane. A groundsman lends the club's laundress a hand.

Morrison of Spurs and Barrett of West Ham in a heading duel at Upton Park on the first day of the 1936-37 season. Morrison later scored but Spurs lost 2-1.

Skipper Arthur Rowe welcomes Bradford full-back Ralph Ward to White Hart Lane in March 1936. Ward, a former England schoolboy international, had impressed in two FA Cup-ties against Tottenham that season and he went on to play in 118 League games for the club and, including wartime games, turned out nearly 400 times overall.

from mid-table drudgery. Each season Spurs managed to get as far as the sixth round, but no further, although 1937 did see two of Spurs' finest performances for many a year. In the third round they were drawn away to First Division Portsmouth, a team in a rich vein of form and odds-on favourites, but Spurs pulled off the

surprise of the round not only winning but scoring five without reply.

After a hard-fought one-nil victory over Plymouth Argyle, Spurs earned a creditable draw in the fifth round at Goodison Park but with only six minutes of the replay remaining, Everton were 3-1 up and coasting. It looked to be all over when

Barnsley goalkeeper Ellis about to save from Spurs' Miller in the Second Division game at White Hart Lane in September 1937. Spurs won 3-0, Miller scoring one of their goals, and ended the season in fifth place. In the FA Cup they were beaten in the quarter-finals by Sunderland, the eventual winners of the trophy.

Everton were awarded a penalty but play was called back because of a foul throw by Joe Mercer. Morrison promptly pulled one back, Joe Meek grabbed an equaliser and with the last kick of the game Morrison snatched the winner.

Preston North End were the visitors in the sixth round and were comfortable 3-1 winners, although Spurs played most of the game with Morrison hobbling on the wing and Rowe injured in the second half.

In 1938 Blackburn Rovers, New Brighton and Chesterfield were defeated before a record White Hart Lane attendance of 75,038 saw Sunderland ruin Spurs' dreams with a 1-0 victory in the sixth round. Top scorer in the Cup run was the amateur Jackie Gibbons, an RAF aircraftsman equally effective at inside or centre-forward and a great acquisition for Spurs, especially as he did not cost a penny.

With Morrison and winger Fred Sargent, Spurs looked to have the makings of an excellent forward line for 1938-39 and they were very disappointed when Gibbons signed amateur forms for Brentford in July 1938. Spurs' transfer market policy remained unaltered during Tresadern's time as manager; few recruits were signed, all of them from the cheaper end of the market, and most did little to improve the team. Ralph Ward and Joe Meek, who were both signed from Bradford in March 1936 after impressing Tresadern with their performances against Spurs in the FA Cup, were exceptions.

Ward, a solid, tough-tackling full-back, was signed to partner the highly promising Fred Channell but ended up replacing him when Channell was so badly injured in their one game together that he had to retire. Meek, a 5ft 5in inside-forward with a cannonball shot, did well for just over a season but when Willie Hall moved to inside-right, Meek was out in the cold. Les Miller from the French club, Sochaux, and Colin Lyman from Northampton Town, both left wingers, looked promising at times but neither were an adequate replacement for Willie Evans.

Tresadern was not a success, not only were Spurs unable to get out of the Second Division but the standard of performance had dipped and for a crowd brought up on the highest quality football that was not acceptable. His dealings in the transfer market were criticised but how much that was down to him and how much his hands were tied by the board is not clear. Rumours were circulating well before the end of the 1937-38 season that it would be Tresadern's last in charge and Peter McWilliam would return. Tresadern decided to jump before being pushed and handed in his resignation after a successful last-minute application for the manager's job at Plymouth.

Three days later it was announced McWilliam was indeed returning. McWilliam inherited a squad that was simply not up to achieving promotion but apart from England full-back Bert Sproston, he started his first season back with the same team that had failed Tresadern. Sproston was signed from Leeds for £9,500, a big fee and a sure sign of McWilliam's desire to secure only the best, but left after only nine League outings. Selected for the match on 5 November 1938, he had already made it clear he could not settle in London and on the morning of the game was transferred to Manchester City – and played for City against Spurs that afternoon.

Spurs started the season as they were to continue it – inconsistently. A good win would be followed by a bad defeat, no more than three wins could be strung together and they occupied a mid-table position throughout the campaign. The defence was conceding more goals but the real weakness was in attack where Almer Hall was top-scorer with only ten goals and Johnny Morrison even failed to reach double figures. Before the season was over McWilliam was looking to the future, introducing young talent developed at Northfleet such as Ron Burgess, Bill Nicholson, Freddie Cox, Albert Tomkin and Arthur Hitchins.

It was in the early 1920s, and at McWilliam's instigation, that Spurs had adopted Northfleet as

On his first day back as Spurs manager, Peter McWilliam (right) renews acquaintance with Billy Minter, a great servant to the club and the man who succeeded McWilliam at the end of his first term in charge.

New Spurs manager Peter McWilliam (wearing hat) in the recreation room at White Hart Lane on the eve of the 1938-39 season.

Bert Sproston takes the ball from Arnold of Fulham during Spurs' 1-0 home win over the Cottagers in October 1938.

Morrison scores for Tottenham in the 3-3 FA Cup fourth-round draw at Upton Park in January 1939. West Ham eventually won a second replay at Highbury and Spurs' interest in the FA Cup was over for seven years.

their nursery club. The first player to progress to the White Hart Lane staff was Harry Skitt in 1923, and it proved a valuable training ground, undoubtedly saving the club a fortune in the transfer market. It was a sad day when they were forced to abandon the nursery after World War Two.

There was a particularly rich vein of talent emerging from Northfleet in the late 1930s and after Spurs had finished eighth in 1938-39, McWilliam promoted several further youngsters – Les Bennett, Ted Ditchburn, George Dorling and Les Medley. He knew that youth alone would not be enough and added some experience with the signing of former England inside-forward Ronnie Dix from Derby County, but was not to see how his team would shape up due to the outbreak of World War Two.

In September 1939, after only three games, the League season was abandoned, players returned home or joined the forces and for six weeks there was uncertainty as to what would happen to football. For two weeks no matches were played, but when the government made it clear football

could continue, subject to severe restrictions on attendances and providing unnecessary travel was avoided, friendly matches were arranged until the Football League could organise emergency competitions.

Spurs participated in two Football League South competitions, winning the second, and in a two-legged cup tournament, going out to Crystal Palace in the first round. It was apparent from the outset there would be problems getting together a full team for matches and Spurs, like all clubs, were soon forced to call up juniors and guest players. The outlook was not promising, all clubs were losing money, players' availability was unlikely to improve and travel was increasingly difficult.

In March 1940 the Football League suggested shutting down for the duration but the clubs were against this, knowing they would lose more money and many might not even survive. For some clubs the problems were even worse, for they had nowhere to play. When Highbury was commandeered for use as a First Aid post and Air-Raid Precaution centre, Spurs willingly

Spurs goalkeeper Ted Ditchburn tips a shot over the bar during a wartime Football League South game against Reading in February 1944.

allowed them the use of White Hart Lane, returning the favour from World War One. For 1940-41, a further Football League South was run, decided on goal-average as there was no chance of the clubs meeting each other twice, and a cup tournament, again on a two-legged basis. These competitions did not provide the London clubs with a full fixture list but they persuaded the FA to sanction a London War Cup.

Spurs' director George Wagstaffe-Simmons was given the job of drafting the rules and provided for two initial league competitions giving the four semi-finalists. Spurs lost to the eventual winners, Brentford in the one-legged semi-final at White Hart Lane. Fielding a full team was not the only problem which faced London clubs this season. Many games had to be abandoned or stopped because of air raids and one Spurs' match in particular was stopped after 15 minutes and not resumed for another 80.

In 1941-42 the League was totally restructured; the goal-average method of deciding places was scrapped and the 70 competing clubs were to play in North and South Divisions with the clubs sub-divided into groups. In theory this seemed fine, but when the London clubs received their fixture lists they realised it would be almost impossible to

make many of the journeys expected of them and even harder to find players for some away games. Playing football was no longer a job, players not in the services had 'proper' jobs to do, and like all other workers were expected to help with the war effort on Saturday mornings. Those serving could never be sure of getting leave. Minor adjustments were made but the Football League would not make the wholesale changes the London clubs insisted were necessary so they decided to form their own London War League and run a cup competition, contending that resolutions passed by the FA in 1915 allowed them to do so.

The 11 London clubs were joined by Aldershot, Brighton and Hove Albion, Portsmouth, Reading and Watford, but immediately ran into conflict with the Football League. By forming their own competition the 16 clubs had ceased to be members of the League. The actions of both sides came in for a lot of criticism with the 'rebels' appealing for public support on the grounds they were trying to comply with government wishes. Efforts were made to heal the rift but when some of the London clubs announced they would rather close down than bow to the Football League's demands, it became insurmountable. Sanction for their competitions was given by the

FA and proceeded with the London clubs also appealing against their 'expulsion' from the Football League. Their appeal was never decided, the FA suggesting the clubs and League should settle the matter between themselves, which they did and which resulted in the Football League South for the next three seasons proceeding very much along the lines the London clubs had proposed.

Spurs finished second in 1942-43 and won the League for the next two years but only in 1944 did they get past the league stage of the Cup, losing in the semi-final to Charlton Athletic. Unlike many clubs, Spurs not only fulfilled all their fixtures but put a full team in the field each time, although not always without difficulty. In September 1944 they arrived at Reading with only four men – goalkeeper Harry Dukes ran all the way from the station to make kick-off and players from the crowd were called upon to make up the numbers. Juniors were frequently called upon and guest players became the rule rather than the exception. Among the many guests Spurs called on were ex-players, Doug Hunt and Taffy O'Callaghan, past internationals, Frank O'Donnell, Pat Beasley, Jakey Jackson, Bobby Browne and Tommy Pearson and future stars, Jack Rowley, Bobby Flavell and Wilf Mannion.

If anything good came of the war, in a football sense, it was the opportunities given to young players. Sonny Walters, Les Medley, Sid Tickridge, Les Bennett, Jack Chisholm, Les Stevens and Arthur Willis all gained valuable experience playing against seasoned professionals with Ron Burgess, Bill Nicholson and Ted Ditchburn even playing in wartime internationals.

With the war over it was originally planned to return to the pre-war League set-up for 1945-46 but clubs realised transport problems would continue and players would only be released from the services slowly. It was decided the top two divisions would again be run on regional lines and nine wins in the last ten games helped Spurs finish ninth in the Southern Section. As the season progressed, players returned but Peter McWilliam did not, deciding he was too old to continue in management. Charles Roberts had died in 1943, so Spurs lost both their guiding lights within two years. Former Arsenal winger Joe Hulme was appointed to replace McWilliam and soon set about preparing for the return to normal football, signing George Foreman and Charlie Whitchurch from West Ham United, Charlie Rundle from St Blazey and unsuccessfully trying to persuade Major Roy White, a wartime discovery, to sign professional.

'Make it Simple, Make it Quick'

IN 1946-47 football reverted to it's pre-war format but the quality of play was far from the same, although that was perhaps to be expected. A whole generation had been ravaged by war and players had gone the best part of seven years without proper training. Many players were unfit or past their best and inexperienced youngsters were called upon. Not that football struggled to make a mark at a time when the public was demanding entertainment after so many years of war. Attendances were large as the game kicked-off into what many regard in retrospect as a 'golden age' of great players performing before sometimes huge crowds throughout the 1940s.

Spurs were more fortunate than most, at least the majority of their players were young and promising, had come through from Northfleet together and knew each other's play. And like all Spurs' teams they played attractive football, passing the ball, relying on skill not brawn and trying to give crowds the entertainment they craved.

Tottenham finished sixth in 1946-47, eighth in 1947-48 and fifth in 1948-49; always in the top half of the table, sometimes hovering for while in a promotion spot but never near enough when it really mattered. The high point of Hulme's reign came in 1948 when Spurs progressed to a Villa Park FA Cup semi-final against First Division Blackpool. In the third round they pulled off a fine 2-0 win at struggling First Division Bolton Wanderers and followed that up by beating three Second Division rivals, West Bromwich Albion 3-1 at home, Leicester City 5-2 at home, and Southampton 1-0 away.

Blackpool's path to the last four had been comparatively easy with successive home victories over Leeds United, Chester, Colchester United and Fulham. With players of the calibre of Stanley Matthews, Stan Mortensen and Harry Johnston, Blackpool were clear favourites but Spurs pushed them to the limit and got to within four minutes of their first Wembley appearance. The first half was goalless but with 19 minutes of the second period played, Len Duquemin emerged from a goalmouth scramble to put Spurs one-up.

There was nothing special about the goal, but then there had been nothing special about the game, two teams struggling to get the upper hand with defences dominating. There were only four minutes remaining when Mortensen took a pass from Matthews and set off on a 30-yard run past four defenders that took him to the touch-line. There seemed no danger but somehow he managed to beat Ditchburn with a shot from an almost impossible angle. The goal totally devastated Spurs and in extra-time Mortensen scored twice more to wrap the game up.

His goal did more than win one match though, it knocked the heart out of Spurs for the rest of the season. They failed to score in their next four matches, dropped points continually and slipped out of the promotion race. In March 1949, Joe Hulme returned to White Hart Lane after a short illness to be told that if he was unfit to continue as manager, then he could resign. He turned down the invitation, only to be sacked a month later. Hulme had done a good job under difficult circumstances in his three years at White Hart Lane but this is perhaps only appreciated in hindsight. He may have failed to get Spurs out of the Second Division but he had taken them to within a few minutes of Wembley and built a team that, with one addition, was soon to set new standards of excellence.

And he had almost secured that one addition

Ted Ditchburn, pictured here in 1944, was a product of the pre-war Northfleet nursery. He went on to make 453 peacetime appearances for Spurs which included 247 consecutive League games.

Welsh international wing-half Ron Burgess made his Spurs debut in 1938-39 and one can only imagine how many appearances he would have added to his 328 League and FA Cup games for the club, had it not been for World War Two and those missing seven seasons.

Charlton's Sam Bartram clears from Les Bennett of Spurs in the First Division match at The Valley in September 1950. Alf Ramsey's penalty earned newly-promoted Tottenham a 1-1 draw.

himself. In March 1949, Spurs had tried to sign Southampton's transfer-listed right-back Alf Ramsey but were unable to complete a deal before the transfer deadline. Ramsey was to prove the missing piece in the jigsaw every football manager strives to put together.

Immediately on his return from military duty, Ted Ditchburn had established himself as undisputed number-one choice between the posts. Charlie Withers had, if only for the time being, won his battle with Arthur Willis for the left-back slot and Hulme had seen that Bill Nicholson would be far more valuable to the team at right-half than in the centre of defence.

Centre-half had proved a bit of a problem with Horace Woodward and Vic Buckingham unable to do the job Hulme wanted, so in March 1949 he signed Harry Clarke from Lovell's Athletic. At left-half he had Ron Burgess, one of the finest half-backs of his or any generation. On the flanks were Sonny Walters and Les Medley. Walters, a local lad who had gone through the ranks with Tottenham Juniors, Walthamstow Avenue and Finchley to sign professional during the war, had displaced Freddie Cox on the right and Medley, another local player who had emigrated to Canada but returned in January 1948 had taken Ernie Jones' place on the left. Eddie Baily and Les Bennett were well established in the inside-forward positions and up front was the Channel Islander, Len Duquemin, a centre-forward whose all round team play was as important as his goalscoring ability.

Hulme may not have achieved anything in terms of honours, but he certainly left his successor with the players who could satisfy the fans' demands for a return to the First Division. That successor was Arthur Rowe, Spurs' former centre-half who had gone to coach in Hungary on retiring in April 1939, returned on the outbreak of war and in four years turned Chelmsford City into the most exciting non-League team in the country. His impact back at the club that always flowed through his veins was to be even more immediate. His only change in personnel was to sign Ramsey. The real change he brought about was in the minds of players. He convinced them of the simplicity of football, when you had the ball you attacked, when you lost the ball you defended. And that meant everybody, whether nominally attacker or defender.

Ted Ditchburn may have been the last line of defence; but he was also the first line of attack. Len Duquemin may have been expected to score goals, but he was also expected to stop them. But more important even than that, you could only score when you had the ball and only concede goals when the opposition had it. That meant retaining possession – simple in theory, not so simple in practice. Football was still a game where players tried to dribble their way past their markers, where passes were played in front of the man for him to run on to but where an opponent had just as much chance of cutting out the pass. Rowe knew that to retain possession his players had to have control, passing ability and, most importantly, accuracy. The ball had to be moved around quickly with players moving into space, taking a pass, laying the ball off and moving on again to receive another pass.

Push the ball to a teammate, run into space – 'Push and Run'. To achieve accuracy the play had to be simple but it also had to be quick, thus Rowe's famous maxim, "Make it simple, make it quick". Keep the passing short, two passes of 20 yards had more chance of reaching their target than one of 40. The idea was all very good, but would it work in practice?. Could players resist the temptation to take on an opponent, could they keep running for 90 minutes? In short, could they keep it quick and simple?

Rowe's first games in charge provided the answer, a 4-1 win at Brentford and a similar scoreline at home to Plymouth Argyle. Blackburn Rovers were the next visitors and dented Spurs' confidence when they pinched the points with a 3-2 win, but Spurs then went to the end of the year unbeaten, only four points dropped in 22 games. Top of the table from first match to last, their lead over their most serious challengers, the two Sheffield clubs, simply increased as the weeks went by.

Promotion was secured with a 2-0 win at Queen's Park Rangers on 1 April 1950, with six games left, the Second Division championship was confirmed on Easter Friday with a goalless draw at home to Hull City. Spurs could have equalled their 1920 record of 70 points but eased up, perhaps practically stopped would be a more apt description, in their last five matches. They lost four and drew the other to finish nine points ahead of Sheffield Wednesday, Sheffield United and Southampton who were only separated on goal-average.

Rowe's tactics had worked better than even he could have expected and set a new standard for English football to try to follow. Would it work in the First Division? There was no reason why it should not. After all, some of Spurs' best performances of the season had come against First Division opposition in the FA Cup. At Stoke City in the third round the home team was so totally outclassed that Spurs should have scored eight goals instead of the solitary effort from Eddie Baily that gave the scoreline a false impression. In the fourth round Sunderland, Ivor Broadis and Len Shackleton included, were given a footballing lesson as they were thrashed 5-1 before an all-ticket 66,000 crowd at White Hart Lane. Spurs were very unlucky to go out of the competition to an early Everton penalty in the next round at Goodison Park.

Back in the top flight, Spurs' first game was at home to Blackpool. They got a nasty shock, losing 4-1 to the team that had finished seventh the previous season. The tactics were the same but while they were simple, they were not quick enough. Spurs were now up against the best teams in the country – if they wanted 'Push and Run' to succeed at the highest level they had to step up a gear, move the ball around more, at pace and keeping it away from the opposition.

After 35 minutes of the next game, at Bolton, Spurs were a goal down. New signing Peter Murphy, in for the injured Les Bennett, then set out on a 50-yard dribble, totally against Rowe's principles, before scoring with a great cross-shot. It turned the game in Spurs' favour and three second-half goals gave them the confidence that 'Push and Run' could more than hold its own in the First Division.

It took another seven games before Spurs really got to grips with the more accomplished opposition they had to face, but a 3-2 win at Villa Park at the end of September set them off on a run of eight victories on the trot that moved them from mid-table to second place behind Arsenal. This run included successive home defeats of Stoke City 6-1, Portsmouth 5-1 and second-placed Newcastle United 7-0.

That last performance was probably Spurs' best since the 1930s. A great Newcastle team including Joe Harvey, Jackie Milburn and George Robledo were humbled as every move from Spurs paid dividends. Newcastle did not play badly – indeed, they played well enough to have beaten almost anybody else – it was just that Spurs were on a different plane. Even without their inspirational captain Ron Burgess, Spurs' attack, particularly Eddie Baily and three-goal Les Medley, ripped the Newcastle defence to pieces, while at the other end their defence barely gave Milburn and his colleagues a sniff of goal.

If Spurs thought they had now made their mark they were soon brought down to earth with a 3-2 defeat at mid-table Huddersfield Town and a 3-3 draw at home to the new second-placed team, Middlesbrough. December proved a good month, though, with four wins and three draws, and at the end of the year Spurs stood proudly top of the Football League, the first time they had occupied that exalted position for 25 years.

January's heavy grounds slowed them down, and contributed to their going out of the FA Cup to Huddersfield at the first hurdle, but in the League they managed to stay ahead of the chasing pack led by Manchester United. On 14 April 1951 Huddersfield visited White Hart Lane and were expected to surrender the two points that would practically guarantee Spurs the title, but for the third time that season Town played well above themselves to pull off a shock victory over Tottenham.

A draw at Middlesbrough was followed by Sheffield Wednesday's visit in the penultimate game of the season. A minute before half-time Len Duquemin scored the goal that proved enough to secure the points; and give Spurs the Football League championship for the first time in their history.

In only two years, and at minimal expense, Arthur Rowe had moulded a group of talented players, most of them home-produced, into the most exciting and effective combination in the country, leading them from the wilderness of Second Division football to the very peak of the English game. He had put to them a simple philosophy of how the game should be played and, whilst fortunate to have players who could adapt to his thinking, had instilled in them a belief and confidence without which his ideas could never have been put into practise.

He built a team in the truest sense of the word. Certainly, there were outstanding individuals, but they all worked together knowing no one player could succeed without the help of his teammates. From Ditchburn in goal to Medley at outside-left, football flowed through the team, each member playing his part and helping his colleagues do likewise.

For many the 'Push and Run' team remains the best in Spurs' history. In goal was the evergreen Ted Ditchburn, tall, athletic, a great shot-stopper and as accurate with his kicking as his throwing. The best right-back in the country was Alf Ramsey, stylish, composed, starting attacks from deep in his own half. Partnering Ramsey, Arthur Willis, who replaced Charlie Withers after only two games, was as reliable a defender as any team could hope for.

Between them was Harry Clarke. At 6ft 3in his command in the air was almost total, yet he was as comfortable with the ball at his feet as most wing-halves. At half-back lay the real strength of the team with Bill Nicholson, solid, hard-tackling, always playing the simple ball, and Ron Burgess, the captain, a non-stop dynamo, defending one minute, supporting the forwards the next.

On the right wing, the fast, direct Sonny Walters, on the left the equally fast but trickier Les Medley. At centre-forward was the tireless Len Duquemin, a goalscorer in his own right but the perfect example of the team player, dragging his marker out of the middle and creating chances for his fellow forwards.

Pulling the strings in midfield was the ideal pair of inside-forwards, Les Bennett, tall, long-striding, unorthodox, always likely to score, and

Tottenham Hotspur, the League champions, a team for a practice match pictured just before the start of the 1951-52 season. Back row (left to right): Ramsey, Nicholson, Clarke, Ditchburn, Duquemin, Willis, Walters. Front row: Castle, Bennett, Burgess, Baily, Medley.

Eddie Baily, a player for whom 'Push and Run' could have been invented.

For two years nobody – with the unfathomable exception of Huddersfield Town – was able to work out a way to contain Spurs fast flowing football. Defensive solidity allied to accurate passing, swift interchanging of positions and continual support made it almost impossible to tie Spurs down. Movement was the main weapon, players always creating or looking for space, even if it took them away from their usual positions, moving around, providing support wherever it was needed.

It was quite normal for Duquemin to move out wide to collect a pass before cutting the ball back for Walters or Medley, who had wandered into the middle, to have a go at goal. Indeed, the goals were spread right around the forward line with Medley leading scorer in 1949-50 and Walters taking the honours in 1950-51.

It would have been fascinating to see if top continental teams could have coped with the 'Push and Run' style but, sadly, competitive European football had yet to arrive. Spurs did meet European opposition, winning four and losing only one of their matches on a tour to Germany and Belgium in 1950 and twice defeating Copenhagen XIs on their 1951 end-of-season tour, drawing the third game. During the course of 1950-51 they beat a Liege XI and Racing Club de Paris in friendlies and Borussia Dortmund in a Festival of Britain match. Their only defeat at the hands of continental opposition that season was to FC Austria in another Festival of Britain game played two days after Spurs had collected the League championship trophy.

Transition to Greater Glories

AT THE start of 1951-52, Arthur Rowe announced he did not expect Spurs to retain their title, but that they would finish in the top six. This may have been an attempt to take some pressure off his team but it is more likely he had realised that Spurs' luck with injuries could not last for ever. For two years they had relied on a nucleus of only 13 players. Others had been used, of course, but only one, Billy Rees, had taken his number of appearances into double figures.

That soon changed. With Harry Clarke injured in pre-season training, his deputy Brian Farley crocked in the first match of the season and third-choice Derek King side-lined after only two outings, Bill Nicholson had to revert to his old centre-half position. Sonny Walters and Eddie Baily also missed early games and Len

Middlesbrough goalkeeper Ugolini punches clear from Sonny Walters of Spurs with 'Boro wing-half Dicks in close attendance. The game at White Hart Lane in December 1951 ended in a 3-1 win for Spurs.

Duquemin was omitted after a poor start to the season.

Results were not too bad, three wins in the first four games, but the magic was missing and never was this more apparent than in the fifth game when Newcastle United extracted revenge for their humiliation of ten months earlier by thrashing Spurs 7-2 at St James' Park. A place near the top of the table was maintained but five defeats in the month culminating in the Christmas fixtures left Spurs with too much to do if they were to overtake Manchester United, Arsenal and Portsmouth. A fourth round FA Cup exit at home to Newcastle in February 1952 sandwiched between League defeats at Manchester United and at home to Arsenal left Spurs with little to play for as the season neared its end.

Heavy grounds and persistent injury problems did not help as Rowe shuffled the team, particularly the forward line, in an effort to improve results. Towards the end of the season Spurs did manage to rediscover some of their form of the previous campaign. Unbeaten in their last 12 games they overtook Portsmouth and Arsenal to finish second to Manchester United.

With the season over, Spurs embarked on their most extensive tour to date playing – and winning – ten games in North America. Manchester United were touring there at the same time and two matches between them were arranged to show the locals the very best of English football. The first took place at the University Stadium in Toronto and, with both teams at almost full strength, Spurs put on a wonderful display to run out 5-0 winners. The second was only a day later at the Yankee Stadium, New York. After both sides had paid homage to the legendary 'Babe' Ruth, an early goal for United showed how much their pride had been dented by the first defeat but Spurs then turned on the style to score seven goals without reply. United may have been League champions but Spurs demonstrated they were still more than a force to be reckoned with.

Sadly it was perhaps the swan-song of 'Push and Run'. Three years of great attacking football had taken Spurs to the pinnacle but as quickly as a team develops a new style of play, so opponents fathom out a way to counter it. Spurs' great strength lay in their desire and ability to attack from any part of the field; always looking to go forward with quick, short-passing committing defenders and continual movement dragging players out of position. Other clubs realised that if they were to stop Spurs they had to stop the passing: mark tightly, stand off instead of diving into the tackle and only tackle when they were sure to win the ball.

Ted Ditchburn rarely kicked downfield, preferring to throw the ball out to one of his full-backs, so a winger tight on the full-back would stop that ploy. Nicholson, Burgess and Baily were the link between defence and attack so if they were tightly marked, unable to receive the ball or lay it off, the attack would be left isolated and unable to do its job.

The 1952-53 season proved to be the final fling for the 'Push and Run' side that had served Spurs so well. The players were not getting any younger, slowing down, taking longer to recover from injury and not backed up by reserves of equal quality. In the League early results were disappointing as Spurs occupied a lower-mid table position and any dreams of another title were soon forgotten. Only in mid-November, with the coming of the heavier grounds that had proved so troublesome in the past, did their football began to exhibit its old prowess – just in time for the FA Cup. In the third round they had to fight hard to gain a 1-1 draw at Tranmere Rovers but in the replay outclassed their brave Third Division North opponents 9-1 with debutant Roy Hollis, Duquemin and Baily each scoring twice and the ever-reliable, but underrated, Sid McClellan grabbing a hat-trick.

For the fourth round trip to Preston, Spurs were deep in an injury crisis and Charlie Withers was pressed into service on the left wing. He surprised supporters, journalists and teammates alike with both goals in a 2-2 draw, the only goals he scored in over 200 appearances for Spurs.

A single goal from Len Duquemin in the replay was enough to give Spurs a fifth round visit to Halifax Town, conquerors of First Division Cardiff City and Stoke City in the previous rounds, but even a snow covered pitch, blue dye being used for the markings, could not prevent Spurs securing an easy 3-0 victory.

In the sixth round Spurs had to travel again, this time to Birmingham City's St Andrew's ground where Les Bennett's goal was enough to earn an injury-ravaged Spurs' team yet another replay. Clarke and Nicholson were both unable to take their places in a 2-2 draw at White Hart Lane, nor for the second replay decided by Sonny Walters' solitary strike at Molineux.

Just like 1948, Spurs' semi-final opponents were Blackpool, surprise sixth-round conquerors of champions-elect Arsenal, and again Villa Park was the venue. Five years earlier Spurs had got to

Les Bennett (out of picture) scores against West Brom at White Hart Lane on the opening day of the 1952-53 season but Albion went on to win 4-3.

within four minutes of their first visit to Wembley. They got almost as close again. Bill Perry gave Blackpool a first-half lead but Spurs gradually got the upper hand with Duquemin getting the equaliser early in the second half after Walters jumped over Bennett's pass to leave 'The Duke' with only George Farm to beat. Extra-time approached with Spurs the better team and confident they would be heading towards the Twin Towers. There were only ten seconds of injury time left when Eddie Baily was adjudged to have handled the ball.

As he stood disputing the decision, Blackpool took the kick quickly but even then there appeared no danger as Ramsey dispossessed Bill Perry. Instead of belting the ball into touch, however, Ramsey hesitated, decided to play it back to Ditchburn but slipped as he did so. Jackie Mudie nipped in and nudged his shot past the helpless 'keeper. There was time for Spurs to restart but that was it, the referee's whistle went and again Spurs had missed out on the greatest day in the football calendar.

Ramsey was not the first Spurs' full-back to make the mistake that saw them knocked out of

a Cup competition – remember Tommy Clay in 1920 – and was not to be the last. Of course, if it had not been for Ramsey's fatal error then Stanley Matthews may never have collected the Cup winners' medal that had eluded him for so long. Not that this was any consolation for Spurs.

The 'Push and Run' era was over now, Rowe's great team had passed its peak and was on the downward slope. The manager knew this, but arresting the slide was not easy. Great players are hard to replace at the best of times but when a great team grows old, the task becomes almost impossible. Rowe has been accused of being too loyal to the players that had served him so well. There may be some truth in this, but there was no point in discarding players unless suitable replacements were available and therein lay Rowe's major problem. He had some good youngsters on the books, Tony Marchi, Tommy Harmer, Alfie Stokes, Ralph Wetton, Ron Reynolds, Colin Brittan, but none of them were as experienced or as good as the old guard.

Les Medley was the first of the 'Push and Run' team to depart, returning to his wife's home in Canada in the summer of 1953. An unwanted

Bill Nicholson in action against Newcastle United at White Hart Lane in January 1953, when Spurs beat the Magpies 3-2.

Manchester United's Jack Rowley is under pressure from Alf Ramsey at White Hart Lane in September 1953. The game ended 1-1.

loss, but Spurs were at least able to secure a more than adequate replacement in the brilliant England amateur international, George Robb; at last persuading the schoolteacher to turn professional.

In other positions they were not so fortunate. Although results at the start of 1953-54 were reasonably good, performances were poor and the need for new blood was obvious. The defence was slow and always under pressure, the midfield too concerned with defence to attack, the forward line, Robb excepted, lacking in penetration and ponderous. The entire season was spent with Spurs in the lower half of the table, rarely in

Spurs' team which lost 5-2 at Bramall Lane in November 1953. Back row (left to right): Ramsey, Nicholson, Ditchburn, Burgess, Clarke, Withers. Front row: Baily, Walters, Bennett, Brooks, Robb.

danger of relegation but a pale shadow of a once-great team. The only relief came with the FA Cup when, Robb for Medley, the championship side of three years earlier fought its way to the sixth round.

Rowe knew changes had to be made, ageing stars discarded, youngsters given their chance. If not, he might be remembered not as the man who led Spurs to their first League title and laid the foundations for a glorious future but the man who built a great team and then presided over its demise.

Ron Burgess was allowed to move to Swansea Town, where he was joined by Arthur Willis; Colin Brittan, Dave Dunmore, Mel Hopkins, Alan Woods and Ralph Wetton were all given their chance. The transition was not painless, though. At the end of September 1954, a 5-1 defeat at Blackpool left Spurs one point off a relegation spot. Les Bennett was dropped and soon joined West Ham United,

Bill Nicholson was recalled, Johnny Brooks installed as creator-in-chief, Tony Marchi given his chance, Johnny Gavin signed from Norwich City.

Alas, there was little improvement and by mid-November only Sheffield Wednesday were below Spurs. Two successive victories eased the nerves but Rowe knew he had to find a successor to Nicholson. The man he wanted was Danny Blanchflower of Aston Villa but he had competition from an equally desperate Arsenal who were favourites to secure the Irishman's signature with both clubs having offered £28,000. A 3-1 defeat at home to Everton provided the ammunition Rowe needed to persuade the board to make more money available. Spurs upped their offer by £2,000, Arsenal failed to match it and Rowe secured one of the most important players in Spurs' history.

It was also Rowe's last major act as Spurs' manager. Blanchflower's impact was immediate

Tottenham Hotspur staff on the eve of the 1953-54 season. Back row (left to right): Nicholson, Robb, King, Farley, Marchi, Brittan, Ward, Ditchburn, Reynolds, Burgess, Clarke, Bennett, Duquemin, Rawlings. Middle row: Walley, Wilmot, Cliss, Gibbins, Ramsey, McClellan, Withers, Wetton, Willis, Brooks, Spivey, Laurel. Front row: Harmer, Hutchinson, Baily, Baker, Stokes, Pitcher, Dulin, Dowsett, Walters.

Sheffield United goalkeeper Ted Burgin and full-back Graham Shaw don't appear to have the ball, but neither does Spurs' Eddie Baily. This game at White Hart Lane in April 1954 ended in a 2-1 victory for Tottenham.

Spurs' first-team squad at the start of the 1955-56 season. Back row (left to right): Duquemin, King, Hopkins, Ditchburn, Reynolds, Marchi, Baker, Clarke. Front row: Gavin, Withers, Walters, Blanchflower, Bailey, Brooks, Stokes, Robb.

and despite going out of the FA Cup to Third Division North giantkillers York City, the corner looked to have been turned. A new team was taking shape.

But the strain had taken its toll on Rowe's health and when he fell ill in April 1955, his assistant Jimmy Anderson was put in temporary charge. Rowe's contract was due to run out in January 1956 but he knew it would be some time before he could return and rather than leave Spurs in limbo he resigned. Anderson was given the job on a permanent basis. He had joined Spurs as a groundstaff boy in 1908 but failed to make the grade as a player, working behind the scenes and on the training and coaching staff before his appointment as Joe Hulme's assistant after World War Two.

He could not have had a worse start to his managerial career – one draw and five defeats in his first six games, only six points out of the first 30 and rock bottom of the First Division. The defence leaked goals, the forwards struggled to

find rhythm. The situation was desperate, relegation more a certainty than a threat.

The basis of a good team was there – Blanchflower, Clarke, Robb, Brooks, Hopkins and Marchi – but a replacement for the departed Alf Ramsey had not been secured, outside-right was proving a problem position and, crucially, Spurs did not have a regular goalscorer. Little Alfie Stokes had started the season at centre-forward but while he showed promise he was not physically suited to the role and Anderson tried Dave Dunmore, who was even less successful. The turnround came in November 1955 when Ron Reynolds replaced the injured Ted Ditchburn and Anderson's scouring of the transfer market at last paid dividends with the signing of Maurice Norman, then a right-back, from Norwich City.

The defence strengthened, Anderson was able to turn his attention to the forward line and just before Christmas, Bobby Smith arrived from Chelsea. The dependable Len Duquemin was recalled with Eddie Baily the man to make way

Spurs goalkeeper Ron Reynolds looks stranded on a snowy pitch at White Hart Lane but Maurice Norman has things under control, taking the ball away from Birmingham's attackers in February 1956. Spurs lost 1-0 though.

for Smith, but at last Spurs had two men up front and they immediately hit it off. Slowly Spurs edged their way up the table and from the turn of the year it was clear the relegation places would be filled by any two from Spurs, Huddersfield Town, Aston Villa and Sheffield United. The fixtures had decreed the two Yorkshire clubs should visit White Hart Lane for the last two games of the season but unexpected FA Cup success caused Spurs' visit to Cardiff to be postponed and rescheduled for the intervening Monday.

When Huddersfield pulled off a surprise 2-1 win the nerve ends were still exposed but a dour goalless draw at Ninian Park saw Spurs safe. A Bobby Smith hat-trick condemned Sheffield United to the Second Division and the season ended with Spurs in 18th place.

It was in the FA Cup that Spurs unexpectedly made an impression. Midland League Boston United – who, fielding six ex-Rams players, had scored a sensational 6-1 win at Third Division North club Derby County in the previous round – were dispatched in the third round, and Second

Division Middlesbrough in the next, both at White Hart Lane.

The fifth round draw gave Spurs a visit to Third Division North Doncaster Rovers and immediately invoked all too fresh memories of the previous season's crash at York City. They need not have worried, a fourth-minute goal from Smith and another from Brooks ten minutes later dispelled any fears of another major upset and although Doncaster had the better of the second half, Spurs' new defence stood the test.

West Ham United were the next hurdle and, even though a Second Division side, they provided a much sterner test, not surprising when they had already accounted for First Division Preston North End and Cardiff City and won a fifth-round replay at Blackburn Rovers.

Almost 70,000 people made their way to White Hart Lane for a quite superb game of attacking football and saw a Tottenham team which had now discovered a belief in itself that had been sadly lacking only six months earlier. John Dick gave the visitors a deserved lead after 20 minutes and Spurs looked to be in real trouble two minutes later when he got a second. Tommy Harmer put Spurs back in the game with a penalty awarded for handball by John Bond but only two more minutes had passed before Dick completed his hat-trick. The first-half scoring was not over, though, as a George Robb header gave Spurs fresh hope.

Spurs were well on top in the second half but Bobby Smith had pulled a muscle in the first 45 minutes, was only operating at half-speed and spent much of the half on the right wing. There were only 15 minutes left when Duquemin headed an equaliser from Robb's centre but Spurs were not satisfied. Smith missed two chances he would have converted if fully fit and it took two good saves from Ernie Gregory to force a replay.

Another capacity crowd assembled five days later and if the second game did not reach the heights of the first, they still had nothing to complain about. End-to-end football saw both teams have good chances but the only goal of the first half came a few minutes before the break when Harmer got his head to a cross missed by Gregory under pressure from Smith. Billy Dare's headed equaliser straight after the change of ends inspired West Ham, but again Spurs defence did it's job and 20 minutes from the end Duquemin snatched the winner.

Unlike 1948 and 1953, Spurs' semi-final opponents were not Blackpool, this time it was Manchester City, although again the venue was Villa Park. Outside-right was still proving a great problem and for the fifth-round tie with Doncaster Jimmy Anderson had called up Tommy Harmer, asking him to play not as an orthodox winger but more as a wide midfielder. The tactic had paid dividends, particularly in the two games with West Ham, but the week before the semi-final the tough tackling Portsmouth defenders had completely shut Harmer out of the game and Anderson was worried that Manchester City's fiery Welsh international Roy Paul would do the same.

He decided that somebody more physically equipped to withstand Paul's challenges was needed and so dropped Harmer and gave the job to Dave Dunmore. The balance of the team was disrupted; Spurs' passing well below standard, but Anderson's decision could have been vindicated in the first few minutes when only a goal-line clearance by Bill Leivers prevented Dunmore giving Spurs the lead. Both defences played well but City's attack always looked more dangerous, although Spurs were first to get the ball in the net, Bobby Smith's 30th minute effort being ruled

offside. Ten minutes later Bobby Johnstone got what proved to be the only goal of the game, heading in a left wing cross.

City had the better of the second half especially in the last 20 minutes when Danny Blanchflower sent Maurice Norman forward in a desperate attempt to grab the equaliser. Even then Spurs created few chances, although newspaper photographs later showed they should have had a penalty when Bert Trautmann dropped Dunmore's cross and wrapped his arms around Robb's legs to prevent him reaching the loose ball until a defender could clear. Within a fortnight Harmer was recalled and was rarely left out again for the next four years.

Anderson's first season in charge had been difficult; the highs of a good FA Cup run combined with the lows of a season long struggle in the League. There were undoubtedly signs that Spurs fortunes were changing but even Anderson must have been surprised at how quickly candidates for relegation could be turned into a title-chasing side. In the summer Terry Medwin, equally good on the wing or at centre-forward, was signed from Swansea Town to solve the right wing problems and had an immediate impact with five goals in his first four games. An early-season injury deprived Spurs of Maurice Norman's services but Peter Baker took the opportunity to prove himself a more than adequate replacement.

Not that the defence was a major concern. The forwards were flowing, at times it was as if they were able to find the net at will with the goals spread round and no less than six players getting into double figures. Pulling the strings in midfield was little Tommy Harmer, one of the most talented individuals to play for Spurs. Hackney-born 'Harmer the Charmer' had joined the professional staff in 1948, made his debut in September 1951, but played only a handful of games each season until Anderson at last gave him a regular place. The concern had always been that, at only 5ft 8in, Harmer was not not big or strong enough for League football. Small and slight he may have been but every ounce of his 8½st was packed with a magical talent that few others possessed and given the chance he showed that skill would always prevail.

Under Harmer's promptings, Spurs were soon in second place but that was to be where they spent practically the whole season. There was one outstanding team in the First Division, Manchester United's 'Busby Babes', and Spurs were rarely able to get close to them. They

Bobby Smith's illustrious Tottenham career took off in the 1957-58 season when he equalled Ted Harper's 36 League goals in a season.

Manchester United. While Tommy Harmer caught the eye up front, behind him Tony Marchi realised the rich potential he had shown as a youngster so much that at the end of the season he became the target for the Italian club, Lanerossi. Spurs could not refuse the Italian's £42,000 bid and Marchi could not afford to turn down the rewards on offer in his father's homeland.

Anderson secured Jim Iley as his replacement but the loss of Marchi proved greater than many expected. A poor start to the 1957-58 season saw Portsmouth, twice, and Manchester City put five goals past Ron Reynolds, Wolverhampton Wanderers and Nottingham Forest each scored four times. Iley, a more attacking half-back than Marchi, was finding it hard to compensate for the departed captain, while centre-half John Ryden was missing Marchi's steadying influence.

Anderson recalled the veteran Ted Ditchburn, switched Ryden to left-half and reinstated Maurice Norman in the centre-half position he had occupied for a few games towards the end of the previous season. The improvement was immediate. With Danny Blanchflower no longer needed to cover for his defenders and able to push forward where he was at his most effective, Spurs gradually climbed up the table, five successive victories at the end of the season enabling them to finish third. Bobby Smith scored 36 League goals to equal Ted Harper's 1931 record and Blanchflower was elected Footballer of the Year. According to the club handbook it 'set the seal on his distinguished career'.

However, hopes of greater things to come were dashed even before the new season got under way. George Robb had been struggling with the serious knee injury that was to finish his career

finished the season eight points behind United, scoring one goal more and conceding only two less.

The only low point in the season was in February when, after easily seeing off Leicester City and Chelsea, Spurs went out of the FA Cup to a Third Division club for the second time in three years, this time at Bournemouth & Boscombe Athletic, managed by former Spurs' winger Freddie Cox.

That one defeat had a lasting effect, only seven points collected in the next eight League games extinguishing any hopes Spurs had of catching

John Hollowbread is beaten by a Roy Vernon header at Ewood Park in August 1958, when Spurs were thumped 5-0, their third successive defeat from the start of the season with 12 goals conceded.

and in February 1958 Anderson signed Swansea Town's flying young winger Cliff Jones for a record £35,000. A member of the Wales' World Cup finals squad that year, he was expected to make a big impact in his first full season in Division One but broke his leg in pre-season training. If that was not bad enough Ron Reynolds lost the tip of a finger in an accident at home.

Yet again Spurs started the season in miserable fashion, no amount of changes would improve results and Anderson, having just completed 50 years service to the club, began to feel the pressure. In October 1958, he resigned. Three years in charge may not have produced any major honours but Anderson's teams had continued to give Spurs' fans the attractive, attacking brand of football they demanded. He had introduced several home-produced players such as Peter Baker, Ron Henry and Terry Dyson, and made some good forays into the transfer market with signings like Bobby Smith, Maurice Norman, Cliff Jones and Terry Medwin.

The foundations for success laid, the job of building upon them was given to Bill Nicholson, assistant manager and coach. Nicholson's first game in charge was against a struggling Everton side on 11 October 1958, when a 10-4 victory provided a glimpse of the great days to come.

Not that those days were just around the corner. For the rest of the season Spurs loitered just above the relegation zone, finished in 18th place and again suffered the embarrassment of going out of the FA Cup to a Third Division side, this time Norwich City.

Nicholson knew that if Spurs were to be a power new blood had to be signed and by the end of the season Dave Mackay had arrived from Heart of Midlothian, to be joined in the summer by goalkeeper Bill Brown. Tony Marchi also returned to White Hart Lane, despite keen interest from Arsenal. His transfer to Italy had sensibly contained a clause that if he was to leave the Italian League then Spurs would have first option on his services.

For once Spurs opened a new season in good

form and it was not until match 13 that they surrendered both points. Of the previous dozen, six had been drawn, four of them at home, and it was the points dropped at White Hart Lane that were to prove crucial come the end of the season.

In early October, Spurs were top of Division One, leading Wolverhampton Wanderers on goal-average, but well as the team was playing Nicholson was not satisfied, there was still room for improvement and he swooped to buy Falkirk's John White for a bargain £20,000, one of the best signings he was to ever make.

Two successive defeats at the beginning of November knocked Spurs back and things looked to take a turn for the worse when Mel Hopkins broke his nose playing for Wales, but Ron Henry deputised and by Christmas Spurs were back on top. Reinforced by the signing of Les Allen from Chelsea, out-of-favour Johnny Brooks moving in the opposite direction, Spurs retained top spot until the end of March but the pressure was beginning to tell. Successive home draws with Fulham and Luton Town, coupled with defeats at Bolton Wanderers and Everton, saw Wolves as favourites but on Good Friday Spurs pulled off a fine 3-1 win at Chelsea with Bobby Smith getting a hat-trick.

Four games left, three of them at home. Spurs were back in the race, but Easter Saturday and Monday saw first Manchester City and then Chelsea leave White Hart Lane with one-goal victories under their belts. Those results virtually killed off any hopes Spurs had of taking the title but it might have been different but for the meticulous timekeeping of referee Gilbert Pullin. On the stroke of half-time against Manchester City he awarded Spurs a penalty. Cliff Jones shot was saved by Bert Trautmann but the ball bounced back to Jones for a simple tap-in. 1-0 to Spurs, but no, Pullin had added on time for the penalty to be taken, but that was all, the goal was disallowed.

Wolves were now odds-on favourites to take their third League title on the trot and complete the first leg of the fabled 'double'. Spurs penultimate game of the season was at Molineux and with the pressure off they turned in one of their best performances of the season to win 3-1.

It was the end of Wolves' golden era, and the beginning of Spurs 'Glory, Glory Days'. Wolves beat Blackburn Rovers to capture the FA Cup in a dreadfully tedious Final, but Burnley won their last game at Manchester City to pip Stan Cullis' team for the League championship. In less than two years Nicholson had built a team capable of challenging for the title, and now they had experienced the pressure of battling for football's top prize. All they had to do was go out and win it. And win it they did; in a style and with a panache that nobody before, or since, has matched.

The Double, Europe – and the Cup Again

THE 1960-61 season started with a 2-0 home win over Everton, a match that was not particularly outstanding, the teams evenly matched until Les Allen and Bobby Smith scored in the last five minutes. Nothing spectacular and little to indicate the joys to come. Two days later, at Bloomfield Road, a poor Blackpool side that was to spend all season fighting relegation was beaten 3-1 by an exhibition of fast-flowing football that threatened a Spurs' goal every time they crossed the half-way line and set the superlatives flowing.

Blackburn Rovers, Manchester United, Bolton Wanderers, Arsenal, Leicester City and Aston Villa all succumbed to the 'Super Spurs'. The first 11 matches were won, the last of them a 4-0 thrashing of Wolves on their own Molineux pitch that had Stan Cullis announcing, "Spurs are the finest club team I've ever seen in the Football League."

It was Manchester City who brought Spurs' incredible opening run to a halt, pinching a 1-1 draw at White Hart Lane in a game which Spurs totally dominated. City's goal was scored by Clive Colbridge and Spurs claimed that it should have been disallowed for handball. The referee would have none of it. The official in question? None other than Mr Gilbert Pullin, who had denied Spurs a vital goal the previous season.

Spurs responded to this setback in the only way they knew, playing even better football to beat Nottingham Forest and Newcastle United away

Maurice Norman sees his shot hit the back of the Sheffield Wednesday net at Hillsborough on 12 November 1960, but it was the Owls who emerged victorious, winning 2-1 to end Spurs' astonishing start to the season. The next week, though, Spurs were back on course, beating Birmingham City 6-0.

Danny Blanchflower and Dave Mackay, Spurs' magnificent wing-halves, close in on Birmingham City outside-left Brian Taylor and it is Blanchflower who clears the ball.

and Cardiff City and Fulham at home. With Spurs having dropped only one point in 16 games, there was only one team looking remotely capable of providing any sort of challenge, Sheffield Wednesday, five points behind but with a game in hand. In 24 visits to Hillsborough Spurs had only once returned victorious, in 1937, it had been the scene of their first defeat of 1959-60 and was to prove the graveyard of their unbeaten run again. Winners of their previous eight home games, Wednesday had no intention of surrendering their record to Spurs.

With both teams determined to attack, play ebbed and flowed from one end to the other, but with Wednesday on top, their defence never in real trouble, their forwards proving a handful for Maurice Norman and his defenders. With half-time only five minutes away, a bad back pass by Peter Swan let Les Allen in for what should have been an easy goal but Wednesday's reserve 'keeper, Roy McLaren, pulled off a brilliant save. The ball was instantly cleared downfield where Billy Griffin converted Bobby Craig's cross.

Spurs hit back within two minutes, Maurice Norman rising above a cluster of defenders to head home Dave Mackay's free-kick. And they had the better of play early in the second half, but Wednesday forced their way back into the game and midway through the second period John Fantham smashed home a loose ball in the box and, despite all Spurs' attempts, that proved the winning goal.

There is never a good time to lose but, truth be told, Spurs were probably relieved their great run had come to an end, for the pressure was beginning to tell. A week later any hangover from the Hillsborough defeat was well and truly banished with a 6-0 hammering of Birmingham City. Another seven matches were played before the end of the year, only champions Burnley taking a point and that in one of the most outstanding games for many a year. After 36 minutes Spurs were 4-0 up but Burnley fought back superbly to force a 4-4 draw.

As the new year arrived Spurs were ten points ahead of second-place Wolves, the title was well within their grasp and it was time to turn their attention to the FA Cup. Charlton Athletic provided the third-round opposition at White Hart Lane and certainly made Spurs work hard before they could progress courtesy of a 3-2 victory. Two Les Allen goals in the first half-hour, both created by Danny Blanchflower, looked to have set up an easy win, but Stuart Leary pulled one back before Terry Dyson, with Blanchflower again the architect, restored Spurs' two-goal lead. Charlton reduced the deficit through Sam Lawrie within 30 seconds of the restart but despite the balance of play being in their favour were unable to force the replay they probably deserved.

In 1960 Spurs had drawn 2-2 with Crewe Alexandra at Gresty Road in the fourth round before thoroughly outclassing their opponents 13-2 in the replay. They were now drawn to meet the Fourth Division club at home. Crewe were given no chance of pulling off a shock but were determined there would be no repeat of their earlier drubbing, even if it meant resorting to the crudest of tactics. Terry Dyson's header gave Spurs a fifth-minute lead and Bobby Smith added a second but Terry Tighe shocked Spurs with a goal for the visitors.

Crewe's tactics were certainly upsetting Spurs' rhythm, John White in particular suffering, but in Dave Mackay and Bobby Smith Spurs had players capable of mixing it with the best and from a Les Allen corner it was Mackay who nodded in the third. Spurs were totally in control and it was only the heroic performance of Brian Williamson in the Crewe goal that limited Tottenham to second-half goals from Cliff Jones and Les Allen.

Spurs travelled to Villa Park in the fifth-round seven days after reaching 50 League points in record time with a 2-1 win on the same pitch. For 15 minutes they probed Villa's defence before suddenly turning on the style and displaying their football at its brilliant best. In the half hour before the break they overran Villa, zipping the ball around with close, first-time passing, spreading the play wide with long wing-to-wing passes, running at the Villa defence with mazy dribbles. At the centre of it all was Dave Mackay, having an outstanding game even by his remarkable standards.

The first goal came after 18 minutes following a five-pass move started by John White's dribble

We're not quite ready! Tottenham's 1960-61 double-winning team can't compose themselves for this photograph taken in November th
campaign. Back row (left to right): Hills, Smith, Ryden, Norman, Hopkins, Baker, Mackay. Middle row: Jones, Marchi, Brown,
Hollowbread, Henry, Allen. Front row: Harmer, Cecil Poynton (trainer), Blanchflower, Bill Nicholson (manager), Dyson.

At White Hart Lane in mid-April 1961, Spurs gained revenge over Sheffield Wednesday, winning by an identical 2-1 scoreline. Here, Bobby Smith hammers a goal past Ron Springett.

down the left wing. Cliff Jones hit a vicious volley that debutant 'keeper Geoff Sidebottom had little chance with, especially when it clipped full-back John Neal and rocketed into the top corner. The second goal arrived five minutes before half-time, Jones hitting another unstoppable shot after a sweeping move involving the whole forward line. The match won, Spurs cruised through the second half, nothing Villa could do posing any threat.

Sunderland away in the sixth round was never going to be easy but a tenth-minute goal from a Cliff Jones header lulled Spurs into a false sense of security. Totally in command in the first half, they had the chances to kill off the game but preferred to take things easy, indulging themselves with an exhibition of delicate skills. They almost paid the ultimate penalty, the Second Division side equalising through Willie McPheat early in the second half, and for the rest of the game submitting Spurs' defence to the type of thorough examination few First Division sides could manage.

The lesson learned, Spurs made no mistake in the replay. It took almost half an hour for Les Allen to get the first, hammering the ball home after John White's shot had been deflected to him, but three minutes later Sunderland 'keeper John Wakeham made a great save from Cliff Jones,

only to see the ball drop at Bobby Smith's feet for an easy second. Terry Dyson scored either side of half-time and Dave Mackay added a fifth to set up a semi-final with Burnley, who had beaten Sheffield Wednesday the previous night in their replay.

Burnley held no fear for Spurs, their only concern was the venue – Villa Park, graveyard of their Wembley dreams three times since the war. Every jinx has to come to an end though, and certainly Spurs would never have a better chance to put theirs to rest. A bone-hard surface and gusty wind deprived spectators of the great game hoped for with both teams struggling to overcome the elements as well as each other for the opening half hour.

Cup winners' luck then smiled on Spurs as Burnley centre-half Jimmy Adamson totally missed Allen's flick to allow Smith an easy run on goal and Spurs' opener. Burnley had looked to be getting the upper hand but now Spurs were in control, the only moment of concern coming two minutes into the second half when Burnley looked to have equalised but Jimmy Robson's header from an Alex Elder free-kick was disallowed for a push on Norman. Just two minutes later Smith volleyed his second, only moments after three Burnley efforts had been cleared off the line. Spurs then shut up shop, only

Scottish international John White, in action against Leicester City at White Hart Lane, was an ever present in the League and Cup double team, along with Les Allen, Danny Blanchflower and Ron Henry.

breaking out in the last minute for Jones to round off the scoring with a third goal. Bobby Smith was chaired off the pitch by delirious supporters, at last Spurs were going to Wembley.

The FA Cup had to take a back seat now, seven points dropped by Spurs in the League since starting on the road to Wembley had allowed Sheffield Wednesday to get within four points. Newcastle United, third from bottom, were expected to prove easy prey but every bit of bad luck possible struck Spurs, and every bit of good luck went Newcastle's way. Totally outclassed the Magpies could not have complained if Spurs had hit double figures but they scored only one, and Newcastle got two.

A draw at Fulham followed and the cynics were quick to appear: "Spurs are crumbling, the pressure had got to them, the 'double' is beyond them".

Spurs responded the only way the critics would understand, four straight wins leaving them with only two more points needed to clinch the title. On 17 April, some 61,205 spectators crammed into White Hart Lane ready to hail the new champions but first Spurs had to overcome their only remaining challengers, Sheffield Wednesday. Both clubs had four games left, Spurs six points ahead. Just as in 1951, victory and the championship would be theirs. And not only that, but they would get revenge for their first defeat of the season.

For eight months Spurs had enthralled the

Although Spurs lost their last League game of the 1960-61 season, 2-1 at home to West Brom, they were already Football League champions. Danny Blanchflower, one hand steadying the League trophy, addresses the 52,000 crowd.

Acrobatics in front of the Leicester City goal during the 1961 FA Cup Final as Spurs attackers Cliff Jones and
Terry Dyson go flying.

country with a brand of football nobody could hope to match, but on a tense, nerve-jangling night, skill and flair had to be set aside, it was now a time for passion, determination and courage. The pressure was intense for all concerned, none more so than the referee Tommy Dawes who made some strange decisions including the free-kick he awarded the visitors after 29 minutes when centre-forward John Fantham went down with Norman two yards away. Don Megson's shot was blocked by the defensive wall but rebounded back to him and his second effort gave Bill Brown no chance.

The silence was deafening, but not for long as the crowd urged Spurs forward. They were well on top but could not get past the well-marshalled Wednesday defence and always had to watch for the sudden counter-attack. Three minutes from the break Keith Ellis headed against Brown's post, but 50 seconds later Terry Dyson outjumped Megson to nod on Peter Baker's 40-yard clearance. Bobby Smith showed unexpected skill

to flick the ball over Peter Swan's head and smashed his shot past Ron Springett. The cheers had not died down before Maurice Norman met Danny Blanchflower's free-kick to set up Les Allen for a right-footed winner and the Football League title.

Spurs lost two of their last three League games but all that mattered now was Wembley, the Cup Final, part two of the 'Impossible Dream'. Certainly they were not playing as well as they had earlier in the season but perhaps the expectation, the strain of living up to the title 'Team of the Century' was taking its toll. A great deal was expected against a Leicester City side that had taken three games to overcome Sheffield United in their semi-final, possibly too much, and the Final proved a disappointment.

Spurs were clearly nervous, although if John White had taken an easy chance in the third minute they may have turned on the style. As it was the opening play was fairly even, Spurs if anything having the better of it, but the turning

Leicester defenders watch thankfully as a header from Dyson skims their crossbar with Gordon Banks well beaten.

point came on 19 minutes. Les Allen caught Len Chalmers with a clumsy tackle and as the Leicester full-back went down he wrenched his knee so badly he was left a virtual passenger for the rest of the game.

No substitutes were allowed in those days so Chalmers moved to the left wing with Leicester forced to reshuffle. As is often the case, ten men fight harder than 11 and for 50 minutes Leicester kept Spurs at bay. Cliff Jones did get the ball in the net once, five minutes before half-time, but, as pictures subsequently proved, it was wrongly disallowed for offside. As the game wore on Leicester tired and Spurs assumed greater control, the first goal eventually arriving in the 69th minute.

A sweeping move finished with Terry Dyson passing to Bobby Smith on the penalty spot. In an instant Smith killed the ball, turned past his marker and rifled the ball past Gordon Banks. The tension lifted from Spurs like a veil and at last they began to play like the champions they were. Seven minutes after the first goal Smith escaped down the right, crossed to the far post and there was Dyson flying in to plant a firm header past

Banks. Leicester had given their all, they had nothing left and for the last few minutes Spurs were able to indulge in the football that had taken them to the peak.

When referee Jim Kelly blew the final whistle Spurs had achieved the feat that several great teams, Arsenal, Manchester United, Wolves included, had come close to but could still only dream about, the first League and FA Cup 'double' since 1897.

Bill Nicholson had been an essential component of Arthur Rowe's 'Push and Run' side, so it is no surprise his team played football in the same basic style. On the floor, short-passing, possession retained and with the best possible use made of every inch of the pitch. It may not have been as fast and there was a bit more of the long ball for, in Danny Blanchflower, Spurs possessed a player whose passes over 40 yards could be as accurate as many over ten but it was more controlled, and for that perhaps deadlier.

Rowe had been fortunate that the players in his team, with the exception of Alf Ramsey, had developed together at Spurs. They had played with each other for some time, knew each other's

Banks is beaten again and this time Dyson's effort finds the net for the second Tottenham goal.

Danny Blanchflower leads his triumphant team down the steps from the Royal Box after collecting the **FA** Cup from the Duchess of Kent to complete a historic double.

Blanchflower and the FA Cup, held aloft in front of Tottenham's adoring fans at Wembley.

Tottenham Hotspur manager Bill Nicholson listens to a point from Inter-Milan official Bruno Passalacqua as the two discuss the transfer of Jimmy Greaves to Tottenham in November 1961. In the middle is Signora Simonetta Cattazso, wife of Inter's assistant trainer, who acted as interpreter during the negotiations.

style. Nicholson had not been so lucky, he had taken over a struggling team, signed players to fit the style he wanted them to play, built a totally new team. It was a team constructed around four exceptional footballers, Blanchflower, Mackay, Jones and White, but just like all great teams they were supported by more-than-average teammates.

Goalkeeper Bill Brown was a great successor to Ted Ditchburn, quiet, safe, confident and with great positional sense that made his job look easy. Full-backs Peter Baker and Ron Henry, the only home-grown players in the team, were the unsung heroes. Baker, protege of Alf Ramsey, had many of his predecessor's attributes if not his presence. Fast and strong in the tackle, he never wasted the ball, always looking to make progress rather than just clear the danger. Henry on the left, determined, never beaten, a shade slow but what he lacked in pace he more than made up for with his knack of being in the right place at the right time.

As with the 'Push and Run' team, Spurs great strength lay at half-back. At the centre the tall,

commanding Maurice Norman, winning everything in the air, long legs snaking out to take the ball on the ground. It was Norman's reliability at centre-half that allowed his half-back partners to make so many forays in support of the forwards.

And what half-back partners! On the right the captain Danny Blanchflower, immaculate in all he did, whether directing play, dribbling past an opponent, playing the ball long or short, but most importantly inspiring his colleagues by example, turning Nicholson's ideas into reality. On the left, the never-say-die Dave Mackay, the heart of the team, all action and dynamism, ferocious in the tackle and never beaten.

Leading the attack was underrated Bobby Smith, the epitome of a typical English centre-forward, brave, strong, hard working but with more skill than he was given credit for. Supplying the ammunition for Smith from the wings were the totally contrasting Cliff Jones and Terry Dyson. Jones was without doubt the best winger in the country, great acceleration, electric pace,

Dave Mackay and Feyenoord's Kraay lie injured after colliding during the European Cup second-round second-leg match at White Hart Lane in November 1961. The sides drew 1-1 and Spurs went through 4-2 on aggregate.

particularly adept at suddenly changing direction and bravery that bordered on the reckless. Dyson was, perhaps, not the most talented of players but what he lacked in skill he more than made up for in effort. A non-stop worker for every second of the 90 minutes, opposing defenders never got a moment's rest with his persistent harrying and chasing.

Inside-left Les Allen, little more than a reserve at Chelsea, had been the final piece in Nicholson's jigsaw. A great team man, unselfish and hard working he made an excellent foil for Bobby Smith, taking some of the goalscoring weight off Smith's shoulders. At inside-right Spurs had John White, one of the finest inside-forwards the game has ever produced. A graceful, artistic player, delicate in possession but with endless stamina, White was not the type that took the eye, working quietly, probing for an opening, keeping the play flowing, but most importantly making his teammates play – a sure sign of a true footballer.

Nicholson had built the best team in the country but it was not yet a great team. To merit that mantle the initial success had to be sustained, more trophies won, and not only at home. Competitive club football was now established at European level, could Spurs take a brand of football that had swept all before it at home and repeat the feat against the top clubs on the continent?

Tottenham certainly thought they could and

embarked on their European Cup campaign with tremendous confidence, confidence that was soon to be shattered. Their opponents in the preliminary round of the European Cup were the Polish champions, Górnik Zabrze, with the first leg played before a 70,000 crowd in the dour mining town.

Spurs treated the match as they would an ordinary Cup-tie, going at their opponents, seeking to impose their style. Within eight minutes they were a goal down, two minutes after the break they were four behind. A late rally saw them pull two goals back but they returned to London having been taught a very harsh lesson. The fact was Spurs just had no idea how to play matches over two legs, they thought they could play their usual attacking game away from home. It had not occurred to them that they first had to defend, contain their rivals, quieten the crowd, then look to attack. Spurs pride had not merely been dented, it had been shattered.

A week later it was rediscovered in the first of many famous nights under the White Hart Lane floodlights. Playing with an intensity that frightened the Poles, Spurs hit the post within the first 30 seconds, were level on aggregate after 20 minutes and 7-5 ahead overall when the half-time whistle blew. Three more goals in the second half secured an 8-1 result and one of the most famous victories in Spurs' history.

Feyenoord were next, the first leg again away from home. Spurs, without Mackay, Smith and

Terry Dyson scores Spurs' goal with a fine close-range header in the second game against Feyenoord.

Allen, showed they had learned their lesson, resisting the temptation to push forward too soon, holding the Dutch and striking just before and after half-time to take control and eventually run out 3-1 winners. The hard work done Spurs settled for a 1-1 draw in the second leg and then took a rest for three months before the second round clashes with Dukla Prague.

By the time of the trip to Czechoslovakia for the first leg, Jimmy Greaves had been signed but he would not be eligible until the next round. On a snow-covered pitch Spurs adopted the sort of defensive attitude so well known in European football now but totally alien to their natural instincts. It worked well, a single-goal defeat leaving them confident of making the semi-final. In the return leg Spurs really turned on the power, two goals apiece from Dave Mackay and Les Allen seeing them through on a 4-2 aggregate.

Spurs were fortunate with the semi-final draw, again they were drawn away in the first leg. They were not so lucky, though, with their opponents, the European Cup holders, Benfica. In the Stadium of Light, Benfica played at the peak of

their powers and were a goal up within five minutes, getting a second midway through the first half. Spurs were sadly below par, but even then they had their chances and with a little more luck could have reached the interval on level terms.

A goal by Greaves only a minute after Benfica's first was disallowed for offside and both Greaves and Cliff Jones had chances they would normally have snapped up. Ten minutes after the break Bobby Smith pulled a goal back and for a spell Spurs looked good for a draw, but Benfica snatched a third and hard as Spurs tried they could not get another, at least not one that counted. In the last minute Bobby Smith did find the back of the net again but his effort was ruled offside, even though two Benfica defenders were standing on the line.

If Spurs had an uphill job on their hands after the first leg it became almost 'Mission Impossible' after 15 minutes under the White Hart Lane floodlights when Benfica captain Aguas strode through to score for the visitors. Spurs had to score three just to force a replay in Brussels. They

Bobby Smith turns on the ball to shoot home Spurs' first goal against Dukla Prague in the second-leg of the European Cup quarter-finals in February 1962.

Dukla goalkeeper Kouba looks upfield. In the net behind him is the ball, hammered home by Bobby Smith for Spurs' third goal.

minute Smith did drive home John White's cross but even then it seemed too late. Two minutes into the second half, though, Danny Blanchflower coolly converted a penalty for a foul on White to signal the most sustained onslaught possible on Benfica's goal – and 43 minutes of the most courageous defending.

Spurs threw everything they could at the Portuguese, but the nearest they got to that all important third goal was a shot from Mackay that hit the bar. Spurs were beaten but they had shown they were more than able to live with the best in Europe, all they needed now was another chance to prove it.

There was no UEFA Cup in the early 1960s. To qualify for Europe a club had to win either the League or FA Cup, and in 1961-62, Spurs came

thought they had got one only eight minutes after Aguas' stunner when Jimmy Greaves slipped Bobby Smith's pass beyond the 'keeper. The referee gave the goal but then saw the linesman's flag was raised and after consulting his colleague gave Benfica a free-kick for offside. In the 35th

Spurs goalkeeper Bill Brown gets in line to save a flying header from Aguas of Benfica in the European Cup semi-final second-leg match at White Hart Lane in April 1962.

Jimmy Greaves sends the ball into the Benfica net but the goal was disallowed.

This time Aguas is on target for his goal. Brown cannot get across to save the day, Norman can only watch in anguish.

Bobby Smith volleys home for Tottenham who won 2-1 on the night but lost 4-3 on aggregate and so watched Benfica take their place in the 1962 European Cup Final.

Jimmy Greaves joined Spurs from Inter-Milan in December 1961 for almost £100,000 and went on to become the greatest goalscorer in the club's history with 266 goals in 380 senior games.

Ron Henry watches as Burnley's Ray Pointer fails to drive the ball into an empty net at Turf Moor in March 1962.

close to winning both again. In the League they did not start as well as in the 'double' season – indeed, nobody has ever done so since – suffering with a problem they rarely faced in 1960-61, injuries to key players, and their obvious exertions in Europe.

Burnley were soon top of the table, but not too far ahead to be caught. Spurs were playing as well as ever but Bill Nicholson was always looking to improve the team and when he heard Jimmy Greaves was anxious to return from Italy moved quickly to sign the greatest goalscorer in Spurs' history. Match by match Spurs drew closer to the Lancashire club but the real threat emerged from an unexpected quarter, Ipswich Town. Guided by former Spurs' star Alf Ramsey, the newly-promoted club did not reach top spot until the end of March but held on to take the title by three points from Burnley.

In the FA Cup, two goals from Jimmy Greaves and one from Cliff Jones in a quite stunning first half gave Spurs a comfortable lead against Birmingham City at St Andrew's in the third round. Jimmy Harris pulled one back before the break and only four minutes into the second period the same player reduced the deficit even further.

Spurs were under the cosh and when Ken Leek, dropped from Leicester's team on the eve of the 1961 Final, stabbed home the equaliser after Bill Brown had failed to hold Stan Lynn's free-kick, Spurs were just grateful to cling on for the draw. In the replay, that man Harris gave Birmingham a 50-second lead but it was just the signal for another stunning Spurs' performance. Before a capacity crowd Terry Medwin got an equaliser 15 minutes later and in the second half Jimmy Greaves, Medwin and Les Allen added to the score with Birmingham's only reply coming from Leek. It was a rampaging second 45 minutes from Spurs and the perfect answer to Birmingham manager Gil Merrick's jibe after the first game that Spurs were 'only a first half team'.

Plymouth Argyle's Home Park was packed solid for the fourth round but there was never any hope of a giantkilling as Spurs treated the locals to an exhibition of top-class football. Greaves, twice, Medwin, Jones and John White scored to give Spurs an easy 5-1 win. An early Bobby Smith goal at The Hawthorns put Spurs in control against West Bromwich Albion and when he got a second on the stroke of half-time the game looked over. Albion did not agree, though, and only four minutes into the second half Keith Smith pulled one back. Albion took control and had their chances to equalise but Derek Kevan did not get their second until Greaves had added Spurs' third. Another Greaves' effort in the last

Danny Blanchflower watches Burnley skipper Jimmy Adamson toss the coin before the start of the 1962 FA Cup Final.

Bobby Smith restores Spurs' lead against Burnley at Wembley.

minute rounded off an exhilarating performance.

Having put out two 'Second City' clubs, the sixth round draw gave Spurs the chance to complete the set with Aston Villa called on to visit White Hart Lane. The midlanders opted for a physical approach but two goals in five minutes from Blanchflower and Jones gave Tottenham a comfortable victory.

Spurs dominated the semi-final against Manchester United at Hillsborough from the fourth minute when Bobby Smith nodded Blanchflower's free-kick into Greaves' path and the goalscorer supreme nipped through a static defence to prod the ball past David Gaskell. Midway through the first half Cliff Jones added the second with a typical soaring header and even when David Herd scored for United, it did not knock Spurs out of their elegant stride. The setback was treated with disdain as Medwin restored Spurs' two-goal lead within two minutes. On Grand National day, Tottenham's thoroughbreds totally outclassed the also rans from Manchester to set up a Final with Burnley.

In modern times only Newcastle United had managed to successfully retain the FA Cup and as

Burnley had finished the League campaign one point ahead of Spurs, they went into the Final slight favourites. The match was all that a Cup Final should be, two sides with great individuals playing within team frameworks, committed to open, attacking football, putting on a feast for the climax of the season and suitable fare to place before the Queen and Duke of Edinburgh.

Barely three minutes had elapsed when Jimmy Greaves collected Bobby Smith's nod down to home-in on the Burnley goal pursued by desperate defenders. As if he knew he would be caught, Greaves stopped dead in his tracks, but as the defenders passed him turned and placed the ball perfectly out of Adam Blacklaw's reach.

Spurs continued to look the more dangerous but both teams had their chances and it was surprising that the second goal did not come until five minutes after half-time. Ray Pointer passed out to Gordon Harris on the left wing, his low centre to the near post was met by Jimmy Adamson and the ball went between Bill Brown's legs for the one 100th goal in Wembley FA Cup Finals.

If this success gave Burnley heart it was soon

knocked out of them. From the resumption Danny Blanchflower put the ball through to John White in midfield, he passed to Cliff Jones, ran past the full-back to take the return pass, and without looking up crossed low towards the penalty spot. Bobby Smith controlled the ball

before swivelling to hammer his shot past Blacklaw.

The final goal arrived ten minutes from the end when Blacklaw failed to hold a cross under Cliff Jones' challenge. Terry Medwin's shot was a certain goal until Tommy Cummings, standing on

Tottenham Hotspur with the FA Cup which they retained in 1962. Back row (left to right): Baker, Norman, Brown, Henry, Mackay. Front row: Medwin, White, Blanchflower, Smith, Greaves, Jones.

the line, stuck out an arm to deflect the ball away. There was no doubt about the penalty and no doubt about the outcome as Blanchflower sent the 'keeper the wrong way.

The Great Cup Fighters

SPURS may not have qualified for Europe's premier competition in 1962-63 but they were in the European Cup-winners' Cup and in the first round were drawn against Glasgow Rangers in what was billed as the 'Championship of Britain'. For the first time Spurs had the disadvantage of playing the first leg at home – at least it might be regarded as a disadvantage these days – but to Spurs such matters meant little, it was just another match to be won. And won it was in a game that really did show British football at its absolute best.

In only the fourth minute a Jimmy Greaves corner exposed the Scots' great fear, big Maurice Norman. Three of them moved to cover the threat, leaving John White totally free to head Greaves' pin-point centre home. Willie Henderson scored from five yards to level the scores, but when Greaves swung another corner towards the near post, White was there to nod over the line, although the goal was originally credited to Greaves.

In the last 12 minutes of the first half, the game really came to life. First, Les Allen got his head to

John White heads Spurs' first goal in their 5-2 win over Glasgow Rangers at White Hart Lane in the first-round first-leg European Cup-winners' Cup-tie in October 1962.

Northern Ireland international Danny Blanchflower, arguably the best-known of all Tottenham Hotspur players and certainly one of the greatest. He joined Spurs from Aston Villa in 1954 for almost £30,000. Blanchflower, of course, skippered the double-winning side and made 382 senior appearances as one of the finest attacking wing-halves the game has ever seen.

Dave Mackay, at left-half the perfect foil for Blanchflower. Spurs equalled the British transfer record when they paid £30,000 for his signature from Hearts in March 1959 and he went on to make 318 appearances and score 51 goals, sharing in all those glory days of the 1960s.

Bobby Smith gets the better of Slovan Bratislava goalkeeper Schroif and defender Popluhar in the European Cup-winners' Cup second-round second-leg game at White Hart Lane in March 1963. Spurs won 6-0.

Cliff Jones cross, then, nine minutes later, Allen's shot from Medwin's cross looked to be covered but deflected off Rangers captain, Bob Shearer, past Bill Ritchie. Only a minute later Jimmy Millar's header made it 4-2 at the break. The second half was not so dramatic. Spurs should have scored two or three more but had to settle for only one, ten minutes from the end when another Greaves corner was thumped home by Norman.

Rangers believed they still had a chance of taking the tie but those hopes were effectively killed off after only eight minutes of the second leg. That was all it took for Greaves to outpace three defenders and put Spurs ahead. Early in the second half Ralph Brand equalised, but two minutes later Bobby Smith put Spurs back in control. Dave Wilson scored Rangers' second and at least it looked as if they would save pride by not losing both games, until four minutes from the final whistle when the recalled Smith headed home the winner.

Slovan Bratislava were next and on a muddy pitch Spurs were fortunate to escape with only a two-goal defeat. In what was undoubtedly their worst European performance of the time, it was only thanks to the heroics of Bill Brown that they returned with any hope of making the next round. The White Hart Lane crowd had a reputation for lifting the team on European nights and were said to be worth a goal start, but nine days later even they had their work cut.

For 30 minutes Spurs bombarded Villem Schroif's goal but it was all passion and physical effort, Spurs had forgotten the football that had served them so well, the football that Slovan were now playing, and were it not for Brown, and on one occasion the post, the Czechs may well have secured a semi-final place for themselves.

Continual high balls seemed to be getting Spurs nowhere but when White's cross was poorly headed out, Dave Mackay was on hand to drill the ball home. It was as if the shackles had been taken off. Greaves and Jones sliced their way through for Greaves to level the overall score and only a minute later Smith got himself on the end of a Frank Saul cross to put Spurs ahead. In the second half it was Schroif's turn to keep his team in the game but in a nine-minute spell of magnificent football goals by Greaves, Jones and White finished the contest.

In the semi-final Spurs met OFK Belgrade, a talented team but not really in the same class. With the first leg in Belgrade, the Yugoslavs decided their best chance of success lay in adopting an aggressive approach and the match proved the most physical of Spurs early European adventures. If OFK thought they could muscle Spurs out of their stride, they could not have been more mistaken. Spurs were not a team easily intimidated, indeed such tactics just made them even more determined to show that skill would win, and in Dave Mackay and Bobby Smith they possessed players who relished a hard battle.

For 25 minutes Spurs allowed OFK to do their best (or worst!) before striking. A brutal foul on Smith by Maric gave Spurs a free-kick just outside the box. Before it could be taken Maric was out cold in the area, Smith was surrounded by a mob of Belgrade players and the referee had to move quickly to prevent a free-for-all developing. When Marchi took the kick, Smith laid it off for White to rifle home from 20 yards. The lead only lasted ten minutes, an equaliser coming from a harshly-awarded penalty when the ball ricocheted on to Mackay's arm.

Ten minutes into the second half the Yugoslav's tactics looked to have paid dividends. Jimmy Greaves foolishly kicked out at his marker when the ball was nowhere near and got himself sent off, the first Spurs player to be dismissed for almost 35 years. As is so often the case, the remaining ten men just worked that bit harder to compensate. Spurs continued to dictate and it was no surprise when Terry Dyson whipped in the winner with 20 minutes left. It may not have been an emphatic victory but showed Spurs at their fighting best.

The second leg proved a disappointment. Spurs won it comfortably enough but the events of a week earlier had not been forgotten and as referee Sorensen said, "In the second half both teams seemed more interested in each other than the ball." Thankfully the cool-headed Danny Blanchflower was available again, after being injured in the second match against Rangers, and made sure there was no repeat of Greaves' first-leg foolishness. Dave Mackay was moved up to replace Greaves but he still found time to cover every inch of the pitch. After 23 minutes he got on the end of Blanchflower's cross to slide the ball home and, after OFK had equalised after another five minutes play, chested down White's cross to set up Cliff Jones for the second three minutes before the break. The final goal, a diving header by Smith from White's cross, came four minutes after the break and made sure of Spurs place in the Final against holders Atlético Madrid in Rotterdam on 15 May.

Spurs' build-up to the Final was not what they would have wanted. They were defeated in the League at Maine Road four days earlier, Dave Mackay and John White were doubtful with injuries and Danny Blanchflower not fully recovered from the injury sustained at Ibrox in November. This was not the great team that had won the 'double' and they knew that the Final was their last chance to become the first British club to win a European trophy and leave another indelible mark on British football history.

Their opponents, Atlético Madrid, desperate for the money another season in Europe would provide to finance the building of their new stadium, were struggling to escape the considerable shadow of their great rivals, Real, and on £360 per man bonus to retain the trophy.

Even though a more than capable deputy was available in Tony Marchi, Spurs' confidence took a nasty knock when Mackay failed a fitness test. He was such a crucial part of the team, it's inspiration, and his loss was particularly felt by Bill Nicholson. His team talk concentrated on the strengths of the Spaniards and it was left to Danny Blanchflower to lift his teammates and

Bobby Smith is foiled by the OFK goalkeeper in the European Cup-winners' Cup semi-final first-leg game in Belgrade in April 1963.

convince them that Atlético had more cause to worry about Spurs than Spurs did about them.

The skipper's pep talk worked a treat. Spurs started the match as if they were determined to finish it in 30 minutes, not 90, and right from the start went at the Spanish defence. Early on a Greaves header from Terry Dyson's corner hit the post, but it took only 15 minutes for the first goal to come. Blanchflower to White, on to Smith and out to the flying Cliff Jones on the right wing. He beat full-back Rodriguez for speed before sending over a perfect cross for the incoming Jimmy Greaves to half-volley home.

Twenty minutes of concentrated Spurs attacking elapsed before the second goal arrived. Dyson retrieved a Greaves centre that had been allowed to go right across the goal and laid it back for John White to calmly pick his spot from the edge of the box.

The holders started the second half knowing that if they were to have any chance of collecting their win bonus they had to get an early goal, and within two minutes they did just that. Ron Henry saved a certain goal, but only by punching the ball off the line, and Bill Brown had no chance with Collar's penalty. For the next 15 minutes Atlético took charge and after the brilliance of Spurs' attacking play it was now the turn of the defence

to show their resilience. The rearguard passed the test with full marks and then Terry Dyson, playing the match of his life, struck to settle the result. There appeared no danger as he cheekily beat his marker and lobbed the ball towards the near post. A cross or a shot? It matters not. If a cross the 'keeper made a hash of cutting it out, if a shot he fluffed the save. The ball drifted over his head and under the bar, 3-1, the Spaniards knew they were beaten.

For the last 25 minutes Spurs strolled through the game, Greaves getting his second from another Dyson centre and the little winger piling on the humiliation with a 40-yard run through the centre before firing home from 25 yards with only three minutes left. Another glorious chapter in Spurs' history had been written.

Spurs had to beat Atlético if they were to have another crack at European football. Burnley had extracted revenge for their FA Cup Final defeat with a shattering 3-0 win at White Hart Lane in the third round and Everton had taken the League title. Spurs had matched Everton stride for stride until the Easter period, successive defeats at Sheffield Wednesday and Liverpool sandwiched between home draws with Burnley and Fulham effectively handing the title to the Goodison club.

Tottenham Hotspur with the European Cup-winners' Cup trophy they won by beating Atlético Madrid in Rotterdam in May 1963. Back row (left to right): Jones, Henry, Hopkins, Norman, Hollowbread, Brown, Bobby Smith, White, Greaves, John Smith. Front row: Saul, Baker, Mackay, Blanchflower, Marchi, Allen, Dyson, Clayton.

Alas, the defence of the European Cup-winners' Cup lasted only two matches. Drawn against Manchester United in the first round, Spurs' 2-0 home win set up the prospect of a great second leg at Old Trafford. It was a great game but not in the way hoped for. United took an early lead

through David Herd but the contest was turned upside down after only eight minutes when Dave Mackay went into a typically hard challenge with Noel Cantwell and broke his left leg. Substitutes were still a thing of the future so Spurs had to fight a rearguard action for the rest of the game.

They put up a fantastic battle, even United captain Bill Foulkes admitting that after the loss of Mackay, Spurs ten men were the better team, but against a side of United's quality it was asking too much to expect them to hold on.

Herd pulled the aggregate score level in the 53rd minute but within 60 seconds Greaves had headed home from a White cross. Bobby Charlton got United's third but with only two minutes left Spurs looked to have held on for a third match (away goals did not count double in those days) until Charlton scored a decisive fourth.

Viewed in isolation, the loss of Mackay was bad enough but it was not the first injury setback Spurs had suffered. On the summer tour of South Africa Terry Medwin had broken a leg and did not play again before retiring. Danny

Jimmy Greaves (extreme right) crashes a shot past Manchester United's David Gaskell in the European Cup-winners' Cup first-round first-leg game at White Hart Lane in December 1963, but the referee has blown for offside. Spurs still won 2-0 but lost the away game 4-1.

Blanchflower never fully recovered from the knee injury he suffered against Glasgow Rangers and was to retire at the end of the season.

Bill Nicholson, meanwhile, was quick to realise that if he was to avoid the problems Arthur Rowe had faced when the 'Push and Run' team went into decline, he had to start building a new side quickly. Alan Mullery, Laurie Brown and Jimmy

Bill Brown parries this shot at Ewood Park in September 1963, but it was Blackburn Rovers who emerged victors with a remarkable 7-2 scoreline against Spurs.

Jimmy Greaves beats Bolton Wanderers goalkeeper Eddie Hopkinson and Spurs are on the way to a 3-1 win at Burnden Park in December 1963.

Robertson were the first arrivals and were joined in the summer of 1964 by Pat Jennings and Cyril Knowles.

With Jimmy Greaves, Ron Henry, Terry Dyson and John White, the nucleus of a promising team combining youth and experience was there but just before the start of the season Nicholson's plans were dealt a shattering blow. John White, 'The Ghost' of White Hart Lane, was killed when the tree he was sheltering under on Crews Hill Golf Course was struck by lightning. He was only 27, not yet at the peak of his career, but recognised as one of the finest inside-forwards in Britain. It was a tragic blow and one from which Spurs did not recover for some time.

With Blanchflower and White gone, the entire creative heart had been ripped out of Spurs and, if that was not enough, two months later Dave Mackay again broke his leg in a reserve match.

Spurs went through a difficult two or three years. A place near the top of the table was always maintained but a serious championship challenge never materialised. The FA Cup provided little more than short-lived distraction. The fans had grown used to success, they wanted more, they demanded more and, although they knew a new

team had to be built, patience is a virtue few football fans possess. At the same time football was changing. Alf Ramsey's England won the World Cup in a style more competent than spectacular, systems were becoming more important than players, work-rate more important than flair and winning more important than entertaining. To Spurs fans and Bill Nicholson alike winning alone was not enough, it had to be achieved playing the stylish, attacking football that had become Spurs' hallmark.

That it took only four years for an almost totally new team to be built and another major trophy to find a place in the White Hart Lane boardroom is testimony to Nicholson's managerial skill. He showed great courage in discarding players who had brought to Spurs a level of success no other club in the country had experienced and in securing replacements, often risking considerable sums of money on the transfer market.

Apart from Jennings, Knowles, Mullery and Robertson, he signed Alan Gilzean and Terry Venables and promoted Joe Kinnear and Phil Beal from the reserves. His new team was completed with the signing of Mike England from Blackburn Rovers in August 1966. The best

Frank Saul's goal against Sheffield Wednesday at White Hart Lane in November 1965. The Owls won 3-2

centre-half in the country, he was desperately needed to replace Maurice Norman, another star of the 'double' side whose career was finished by a broken leg.

With Dave Mackay back to his best and Jimmy Greaves finding the net again after missing much of the previous season, and in consequence the World Cup Final, due to hepatitis, Spurs started the 1966-67 season well. The only disappointment came with an early exit from the Football League Cup, a competition they had previously refused to enter, at West Ham.

Midway through October they were top of the table but five of the next six games were lost, the other drawn, and by the end of the year Manchester United, Law, Best, Charlton and co, were far enough ahead to be out of reach. Only the FA Cup was left and when Spurs were drawn at Millwall in the third round even that looked a hopeful target; for Millwall had been undefeated for 59 League games at The Den. As luck would have it Plymouth ended the Lions record a week before the Cup-tie but Millwall still made Spurs battle hard for a draw and did almost as well in the replay, a lone Alan Gilzean goal proving decisive.

A Portsmouth side apparently with no higher ambition than a draw were comfortably beaten 3-1 at home in the next round with two goals from Gilzean and one from Greaves but against Bristol City in the fifth round Spurs had that slice of fortune so well known by Cup winners. Jimmy Greaves gave Spurs the lead but a surprisingly determined City side never gave up and, when they were awarded a penalty, looked like getting the draw they merited. Pat Jennings saved Tony Ford's effort but the referee ruled he had moved and ordered the kick be retaken. Chris Crowe stepped up – and blasted the ball wide. In the last minute Greaves showed how it should be done, netting Spurs second from a penalty given for handball.

The Second Division again provided the opposition in the quarter-final, Birmingham City at St Andrew's. In a poor game both teams seemed reluctant to attack and a goalless draw

Mullery (4) and Mackay (6) hang their heads. Spurs have just conceded a goal at Deepdale in March 1966. They went down 2-1 to Preston in the fifth round of the FA Cup before a crowd of 36,792.

Pat Jennings makes a diving save against Manchester United in the First Division game at White Hart Lane in September 1966, when Spurs won 2-1.

Alan Gilzean is celebrating but it's Frank Saul (in the net) who has scored against Burnley at Turf Moor in September 1966.

Pat Jennings makes a vain bid to save a shot from Ian Hamilton, Chelsea's 16-year-old debutant, at White Hart Lane in March 1967. Jimmy Greaves scored against his old club in the 1-1 draw.

Jimmy Robertson (far right) has just scored Spurs' first goal in the 1967 FA Cup Final against Chelsea.

was hardly surprising. In the replay Spurs had to take the initiative and a 6-0 victory demonstrated that a more positive attitude in the first game and a replay would not have been needed. Greaves and Venables grabbed two each, Gilzean and Saul the others.

The semi-final at last pitched Spurs against First Division opposition – second-in-the-table Nottingham Forest at Hillsborough. With Forest on top, a typical piece of Greaves opportunism gave Spurs the lead in the 33rd minute. A Mike England clearance was nodded down to Greaves by Alan Gilzean. In a flash he turned and hit a half volley along the ground and in off the post. What was not so typical was that the goal came from 25 yards, for Greaves usually saved his shooting until he was inside the box.

Forest had been the pre-match favourites and they certainly had the upper hand until Frank Saul robbed Terry Hennessey midway through the second half to grab Spurs' second. Hennessey pulled one back nine minutes from time and Forest threw everyone forward in search of the equaliser, but Spurs' defence stood firm and,

indeed, Forest's Peter Grummitt was called on to make three excellent saves at the death.

In the other semi-final Chelsea needed three games to overcome Leeds United to give football its first all-London FA Cup Final, at least in modern times. The Final itself was not the most memorable of games, not that Spurs were to blame, they were just so superior to their younger opponents. They dictated the game from the start, passing the ball around, probing for weaknesses, never threatened by a Chelsea team content to soak up the pressure and hope to get a goal on the break. Even then it took Spurs until a minute before the interval to opening the scoring. Alan Mullery, playing one of his best games in a Spurs' shirt, ran at the Chelsea defence before unleashing his shot. Alan Harris blocked it but the ball spun to Jimmy Robertson who rifled it home from the edge of the box.

Little changed in the second half, Spurs looking for a second, Chelsea unable to mount an attack of any note. A second goal always looked on the cards and it came in the 66th minute. Dave Mackay hurled a long throw into the Chelsea

Spurs, 1967 FA Cup winners with their trophy. Back row (left to right): Kinnear, Knowles, England, Jennings, Gilzean, Mullery. Front row: Robertson, Greaves, Mackay, Venables, Saul.

area, Robertson touched it on and there was Frank Saul, swivelling to hit it home. The result beyond doubt, Chelsea's heads down, Spurs relaxed – and let Chelsea back in. With four minutes left John Boyle hit a hopeful cross into the centre, Pat Jennings missed his punch and the ball hit Bobby Tambling's head to ricochet into the net. Chelsea rallied and for the only time in the game Spurs were under pressure but Chelsea knew it was not to be their day when Jennings came out to pluck a wickedly curling cross out of the air with one hand, as if he was playing in a practice match.

Dave Mackay collected the trophy and, with it, the passport to another assault on Europe. The Cup winning team contained an ideal mixture of youth and experience and should have been capable of going on to win further trophies.

In goal was Pat Jennings, only 21 years old but already displaying all the attributes – coolness, quick reactions, strength and positional sense – that were soon to make him the best 'keeper in the world.

The full-back pairing of Joe Kinnear and Cyril Knowles was perfectly balanced. Kinnear, first and foremost a hard-tackling defender but quite happy to push up when safe to do so; Knowles, the epitome of an attacking full-back, always looking to overlap and hit over pinpoint crosses that created many a goal, but still capable of handling the most difficult of wingers.

In the centre of defence was the outstanding Mike England, big and strong, he was almost unbeatable in the air. To either side were Alan Mullery and Dave Mackay. Mullery had a difficult time when he first arrived, taking over the number-four shirt worn for so long by Danny Blanchflower, but Spurs supporters eventually realised that while he did not possess the same brilliant skills of the popular Irishman, he more than made up for that with his never-ending hard work and enthusiasm. As for Mackay, a man who never knew the meaning of defeat, the mere fact he was still playing after twice breaking his leg was an inspiration.

Mike England made almost 400 senior appearances for Tottenham after joining them from Blackburn Rovers for £95,000 in the 1966 close season.

Jimmy Pearce (9) wheels away in delight after scoring for Spurs in the 2-2 draw at Turf Moor in March 1969.

On the right wing was Jimmy Robertson. A bargain £25,000 buy from St Mirren, he was not merely an orthodox winger but loved to cut inside and go for goal himself. On the opposite wing Frank Saul had won the battle with Cliff Jones for the number 11 shirt. Hard working, capable of playing anywhere in the front line, Saul had played six games in the 'double' season and, although he never really lived up to his early promise, still scored some crucial goals. Alan Gilzean wore the number-nine shirt but he was not a bustling type of centre-forward, more an artist relying on subtlety and skill rather than physical presence to score goals himself or set up chances for his colleagues.

From inside-left former Chelsea star Terry Venables provided the probing passes for his forwards to feed on. And up front with Gilzean, ever alert to finish off the hard work of his teammates was the master goalscorer, Jimmy Greaves. After the campaigns of the early 1960s, Spurs had missed playing in Europe for three years and hopes were high that the 'Glory, Glory Nights' would now return.

Those hopes looked well founded in the first round when Spurs beat Hajduk Split 2-0 away in the first leg. In the return Spurs were three up by half-time and coasting through. They eased up in

the second half, allowed the Yugoslavs to pull two goals back in the space of 60 seconds only ten minutes from time, responded with a fourth but then let the visitors round off the entertainment with a last-minute penalty.

The warning was obvious, they had to be more ruthless and finish off their opponents when they had the chance. In the second round Spurs were drawn against Olympique Lyonnais. The first leg in France was a battle, Spurs facing tremendous intimidation and receiving no protection from a Czech referee who seemed to regard tackling as illegal but bodychecking and physical assault as legitimate.

The match exploded after half an hour when the French centre-forward, Guy, responded to a Mullery tackle by kicking the Spurs skipper in the face. A free-for-all lasting eight minutes ensued before the referee sent both Guy and Mullery for an early bath. After that Spurs were just glad to escape without serious injury and a one-goal deficit to make up.

Even without the suspended Mullery and injured Mike England, Spurs were 2-0 up and coasting by half-time in the second leg. Twice the French pulled a goal back, but each time Spurs immediately responded by restoring their overall lead. They had ample opportunities to wrap-up

Alan Gilzean, 133 goals in 439 appearances for Spurs after signing from Dundee for £72,500 in December 1964.

the tie but failed to take them and paid the penalty ten minutes from the end when Bouassa grabbed a third for the visitors who then pulled everybody back.

Try as they might Spurs could not break through again and went out on the away-goals rule. Only Lyonnais were more surprised to find themselves in the next round than Spurs.

Out of Europe, attention returned to the domestic competitions where Spurs were in the upper reaches of Division One but looking unlikely to offer a serious challenge to Leeds, Liverpool and Manchester United. Extra power was needed up front and Nicholson again broke the British transfer record agreeing a £125,000 deal to sign Martin Chivers from Southampton. Chivers made a great start, scoring the winner on his debut at Sheffield Wednesday and then grabbing both goals in a thrilling draw at Old Trafford in the third round of the FA Cup, but struggled to really settle in and could not stop Spurs going out of the FA Cup in a fifth-round replay at Liverpool or help them finish higher than seventh in the League.

Over the next two years Spurs struggled to make any sort of impression and Bill Nicholson rang the changes. Dave Mackay, not getting any younger, was allowed to join Derby County for a nominal fee and inspired Brian Clough's young team to the Second Division title. Cliff Jones, the last link with the 'double' winners, was likewise rewarded for his great service with a cut-price transfer to Fulham. Jimmy Robertson and Terry Venables moved to Arsenal and Queen's Park Rangers respectively. They were replaced by home grown talent and promising youngsters such as Phil Beal, Peter Collins, Ray Evans, Jimmy Pearce, Steve Perryman and John Pratt. The one major signing was Roger Morgan from Queen's Park Rangers but injury cut his career all too short.

The nearest Spurs got to adding to their list of honours was in 1968-69 when they reached the semi-final of the League Cup, going out to Arsenal in two violent games that did neither club any credit.

All the time football continued it's trend towards defensive domination. Avoiding defeat became more important than winning and entertainment was sacrificed in the search for victory. The demands on players changed; hard work, stamina and ability to fit rigid systems took priority to flair and basic skills. This was totally the opposite to the way Spurs, supporters included, wanted to see football played but it could not be ignored. Much as Nicholson was determined to uphold the entertaining football on which Spurs' reputation was built he realised that if further success was to be achieved, they would have match their rivals for hard work and commitment before superior skills could hope to prevail.

Easy in theory but not so easy in practice, matters came to a head in January 1970. Having struggled to overcome Bradford City in a third-round FA Cup replay, a poor performance in the next round against Crystal Palace was followed by an even worse showing in the Selhurst Park replay. It was an embarrassing defeat, Palace were not in the same class as Spurs for skill but they made up for their shortcomings with sheer commitment.

Nicholson felt let down by his 'star' players, if they were not willing to put in the effort needed he would promote players who were. Wholesale changes were made with Greaves, Gilzean, Kinnear and Knowles dropped. Results may not have noticeably improved but all the players knew exactly where they stood – reputations counted for nothing if the job was not being done.

Only Jimmy Greaves failed to get his place back, the greatest goalscorer in Spurs history joining West Ham as part of the record £200,000 deal that saw England World Cup hero Martin Peters move to White Hart Lane. Peters was just the sort of player Nicholson needed – experienced and hard working but skilful too, in many respects a modern day John White. With Alan Mullery and the tenacious young Steve Perryman beside him in midfield, Peters brought out the best in Martin Chivers who soon developed into the best centre-forward in the country.

Defensively Spurs may not have been strong enough to sustain a challenge for the League title, and consistency was always a problem, but in the one-off arena of Cup football Spurs were always able to raise their game. And so it proved with four Cup Finals and two semi-finals reached in four years. Spurs had little time for the Football League Cup, when it first started in 1960-61 – had they entered they could well have achieved that still elusive 'treble' – considering there were already enough demands on players.

It was not until 1966 that they first went into the competition but even then they opted out in 1967-68 when they qualified for the European Cup-winners' Cup. The competition gained credibility, first with the decision to stage the Final at Wembley and then when the Football

Alan Mullery won an FA Cup winners' medal with Spurs and skippered the side to success in the League Cup and the UEFA Cup. In all he made 374 senor appearances for Spurs, scoring 30 goals.

Alan Gilzean in action in the 3-0 win over Blackpool at White Hart Lane in September 1970.

League announced the winners would be one of England's entrants in the Fairs Cup (later to become the UEFA Cup). Any route to the riches and glory of Europe had to be taken seriously.

Like all First Division clubs Spurs were exempt from the first round. In the second they easily beat Third Division Swansea City 3-0 and followed that with a hard fought 2-1 defeat of Sheffield United, grateful that the match was in London and not Sheffield where the Second Division side had pulled off the performance of the second round in disposing of Leeds United.

In the fifth round the odds were on Spurs drawing a lower division side as no less than 14 First Division clubs had already been knocked out, but the draw pitted them against West Bromwich Albion, uncomfortably near the bottom of Division One. A 5-0 victory may look easy but Albion put up a spirited performance and it was four goals in the last 20 minutes that gave the result such a flattering scoreline. Coventry City were next and returned to the Midlands beaten 4-1 in what was a bruising contest.

The line-up for the semi-finals was Aston Villa,

Bristol City, Manchester United and Spurs. Of the three, Bristol City were certainly the weakest and the luck that had seen Spurs drawn at home in all the previous rounds held when they were drawn against the Second Division strugglers, with the first leg away. Spurs were surprised by the quality of City's football at Ashton Gate but a 1-1 draw made them clear favourites for the Final.

However, if Spurs thought the hard work had been done they got a nasty shock in the second leg. City not only battled but played in a way many bigger clubs would have envied. It was only in extra-time that Martin Chivers and Jimmy Pearce got the goals that finally overcame their brave challenge. In the other semi-final, Villa beat Manchester United and went to Wembley as underdogs although on the two previous occasions Third Division clubs had made it to League Cup Finals under the Twin Towers they had beaten First Division opposition, Queen's Park Rangers overcoming West Bromwich Albion in 1967 and Swindon Town accounting for Arsenal in 1969.

Villa very nearly emulated their predecessors. In the first 20 minutes Spurs were in command

In March 1970, Spurs broke the British transfer record when Martin Peters joined them from West Ham United with Jimmy Greaves going in the opposite direction, Peters being valued at £200,000. At White Hart Lane, Peters gained two League Cup winners' tankards and a UEFA Cup winners' medal, took his tally of full England caps to 67 and took over as captain when Alan Mullery left.

Spurs parade the Football League Cup after their 2-0 victory over Aston Villa at Wembley in February 1971.

but for the next hour Villa took control and with few chances being created it was obvious the first goal was going to be all important. That goal very nearly came on the hour. As Villa centre-forward Andy Lochhead went for a high ball he gave reserve centre-half Peter Collins, standing in for injured Mike England, a little nudge. It was enough to send Collins crashing into Pat Jennings and as all three fell to the ground, the former Burnley star hooked the ball towards an empty net. Lochhead was about to start the celebrations when Steve Perryman appeared from nowhere to hook the ball clear but it was only when referee Jim Finney awarded Villa a throw-in that they realised they had not scored.

There were only 11 minutes left when the first goal finally arrived. Alan Gilzean found Jimmy Neighbour as the winger cut in from the left, John Dunn parried his shot but the ball fell perfectly for Chivers to slot home. Three minutes later the game was all over. Chivers controlled an awkward pass, twisted and turned past three defenders and blasted the ball home.

Two months had elapsed between the disposal of Bristol City in the semi-final and the success at Wembley, and during that time Spurs embarked on their FA Cup campaign, disposing of Sheffield Wednesday, Carlisle United and Nottingham Forest. They went to Wembley knowing that if they could overcome Liverpool in the sixth round a week later, the prospect of reaching the two major Cup Finals would become a real possibility.

Spurs had not won at Anfield for 59 years, the best they could hope for was a draw, and that was just what they got. In a real backs-to-the-wall performance they not only prevented Liverpool from scoring but had the best chances themselves. A year longer than Spurs' atrocious record at Anfield was their record in FA Cup replays. Not since Blackburn Rovers in 1911 had they lost at home but that record fell to Liverpool, or more accurately Liverpool 'keeper, Ray Clemence, who single-handedly kept Spurs out after Steve Heighway had scored a breakaway goal.

To the good Cup runs Spurs could add third place in the League but the gloss was taken off the season when five days after beating Spurs 1-0 at White Hart Lane to win the League, Arsenal beat Liverpool in the FA Cup Final to complete the 'double'.

Spurs had thus lost the honour of being the only club in modern times to take both major honours in the same season, but entry to the UEFA Cup, successor to the Fairs Cup, gave them the chance of becoming the first British club to engrave their name on two top European trophies. To this day the UEFA Cup contains a variety of talent; fading teams on the way down, improving teams on the way up and minnows one might be forgiven for thinking were there just to provide shooting practice for the bigger clubs.

Spurs' first opponents, the Icelandic outfit Keflavik, were one of the latter clubs as was shown by Spurs far from flattering 15-1 aggregate victory. Nantes were next and while Spurs were fortunate to return from France with a goalless draw they should have scored many more than Martin Peters' one effort in the second leg.

There were some famous sides in the last 16, including Real Madrid, Juventus, AC Milan and Ferencváros, but Spurs drew a relatively unknown quantity in Rapid Bucharest with the first leg at home. The match was over after only 20 seconds when Martin Peters scored from a Chivers' long throw, and from then on it was just a matter of how many Spurs would get. They could have had plenty but settled for two more against a dispirited team whose only real contribution to the evening's entertainment was the comic antics of their 6ft 5in goalkeeper, Raducanu.

In Arctic conditions the Romanians took the second leg far more seriously, throwing everything at Spurs in the first half but resorting to violence after Jimmy Pearce had scored. Pearce was only on the pitch for 12 minutes, replacing Alan Gilzean early in the second half, but he had a goal disallowed, scored and then got sent off after exchanging blows with the home full-back, Pop. Spurs showed great discipline to finish the game without further losses and after Chivers had

got a second goal could even afford a Peters penalty miss.

In the fourth round Spurs had to return to Romania, this time to face the factory side, Unizale Textile Arad. A hard-fought 2-0 win should have put the tie beyond doubt but, still suffering from going out of the FA Cup to Leeds in the sixth round only three days earlier, Spurs gave probably their worst-ever European performance in the second leg. It was only thanks to an Alan Gilzean goal nine minutes from the final whistle that they preserved their record of never having lost a home European game.

There would have to be a vast improvement if they were to beat AC Milan in the semi-final. The first leg was Spurs' eighth match in 19 days and the strain was telling. Injuries left Nicholson short and he was forced to recall Alan Mullery from a loan spell with Fulham. The club captain had been missing since October with a pelvic injury and had returned to his old club in an effort to convince Nicholson of his fitness. Now he had the opportunity to do that at first hand.

Milan had some great players – Schnellinger, Benetti and Rivera – but like so many Italian teams of the time were all too happy to hide their talent beneath a packed defence and cloak of brutality. From the opening minutes it was obvious Spurs were in for a painful night and they were not helped by a Spanish referee who somehow contrived to award more free-kicks to Milan than against them. The main hatchet-man was Romeo Benetti and it was ironic that on the one occasion he choose to show his skill he should rocket home a half-clearance to give Milan a 25th minute lead.

That Spurs managed to raise their game was a tribute to their character and the tireless cajoling of Mullery, who played like a Trojan, but the Italians' defence held firm and it was hard to see where a goal might come from. It came from one of the youngest players in the team, Steve Perryman being set up by Gilzean and Peters to drill the ball home from the edge of the box 12 minutes before the break.

Just on the hour Sogliano was sent off after one assault too many on Mullery and four minutes later Perryman got a second from about the same range when a corner was only half cleared. After that Milan pulled ten men behind the ball,

Spurs could not get another and they were left to hope their defence would survive the battering it was bound to get in the return leg.

The early 1960s had seen some great Spurs performances in Europe but they were surpassed

AC Milan goalkeeper Cudicini is an unhappy man because Spurs' Alan Mullery has just scored against him in the San Siro Stadium. The goal ensured that Spurs would contest the 1972 UEFA Cup Final against Wolverhampton Wanderers.

by that in Milan. After only seven minutes, the 80,000 crowd in the San Siro were stunned into silence. A Chivers shot, following a great cross from Knowles, was blocked, the ball broke to Perryman and he laid it back for Mullery to crack a 20-yard shot into the top corner of the net. For the next hour Spurs had few scares but when Knowles missed his tackle on Bignon, Phil Beal was adjudged to have brought the man down. Rivera blasted the spot-kick home. Milan then went at Spurs with a vengeance but the defence held firm and a memorable performance saw Spurs through to the Final.

After trips to Iceland, France, Romania and Italy, Spurs' growing band of travelling fans were hoping for a visit to Hungary in the Final but were disappointed they had nothing more strenuous than a trip up the motorway to take on Wolverhampton Wanderers, conquerors of Ferencváros. A European trophy may have been at stake but with two English clubs competing the first leg took on the atmosphere of an ordinary League game.

Both teams were set on attacking, but they were equally determined not to concede a goal and it was not until 12 minutes into the second half that the deadlock was broken. Mike England took a free-kick from deep inside his own half, launched the ball towards the Wolves box and Martin Chivers got in front of his marker to power a majestic header past Phil Parkes.

Fifteen minutes later Wolves drew level in controversial fashion. Fouled on the edge of the box, John Richards took a quick free-kick as Spurs were still lining up the defensive wall and Jim McCalliog had an easy job to slip the ball past Pat Jennings. Spurs expected the kick to be retaken but referee Bakhramov, forever famous as the linesman who allowed Geoff Hurst's goal in the 1966 World Cup Final, merely pointed to the centre spot.

Content with a draw, and an away goal, Bill Nicholson pulled off Ralph Coates and sent on John Pratt to close the game down. The extra defender was needed as Wolves poured forward in search of the winner but, as so often happens,

Wolves' David Wagstaffe scores with a 30-yard drive four minutes from half-time in the second leg of the 1972 UEFA Cup Final at White Hart Lane.

Alan Mullery heads home for Spurs in the 1972 UEFA Cup Final second leg. A crowd of 54,303 saw Tottenham take the trophy on aggregate, 3-2.

Martin Chivers (9) has the Wolves defence in a tangle in the second leg of the 1972 UEFA Cup Final.

they left themselves open to the 'sucker punch'. Only three minutes remained when Alan Mullery picked up the ball on the edge of Spurs' box and laid it forward to Chivers, just inside the Wolves' half and almost on the touch-line. He pushed the ball forward, advanced a few paces and then thundered a 40-yard shot into the top corner. It was a goal of rare quality deserving to win a Cup Final, not just a first leg.

Needing only to avoid defeat to secure the trophy, Spurs' confidence was high for the second leg, an early goal all that was needed for the party

to begin. It came after 30 minutes, Alan Mullery hurling himself full length to meet Martin Peters' free-kick before crashing into the Wolves 'keeper and knocking himself out.

Confident before, Spurs really relaxed now – and let Wolves back in. Just four minutes of the first half remained when David Wagstaffe cut in from the left to hit a wickedly swerving shot past Jennings. Inspired by their success, Wolves emerged for the second half a different team, dominating play, forcing Spurs back and looking ever more likely to grab the goal that would force

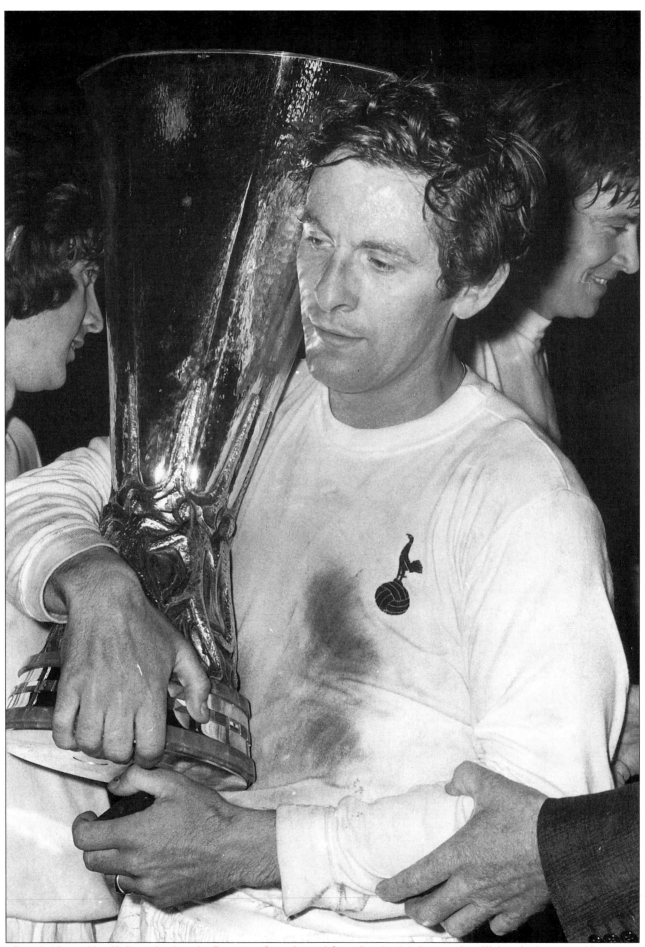

Proud skipper Alan Mullery clutches the European Cup-winners' Cup after the 1-1 draw against Wolves in the second leg gave Spurs the trophy.

Alan Gilzean stabs the ball into an empty Everton net at Goodison Park in February 1972, in the fifth round of the FA Cup.

Martin Peters' goal against Everton which helped Spurs to a 2-0 win and a quarter-final tie at Leeds, where they lost 2-1.

extra-time. Spurs were hardly able to get out of their own half, Mullery, Perryman, even Peters, forced to fall back to help out their hard-pressed defenders, but they hung on and when the final whistle went thousands of youngsters flooded on to the pitch. Alan Mullery, in his last match for

the club, was left to do a lone lap of honour, alone that is save for thousands of fans and one big trophy.

Spurs had certainly lived up to their reputation as a Cup team in 1971-72. Apart from winning the UEFA Cup they reached the sixth round of the FA

Spurs with the UEFA and Anglo-Italian League Cup-winners' Cups, pictured before the start of the 1972-73 season. Back row (left to right): Beal, Evans, Knowles, Collins, Jennings, England, Chivers, Gilzean, Naylor. Front row: Coates, Kinnear, Pearce, Peters, Perryman, Pratt, Morgan, Neighbour.

Comedy duo Peter Cook and Dudley Moore pictured with Tottenham Hotspur players in 1972.

Martin Chivers steams through the Lyn Oslo defence in the home leg of the 1972-73 UEFA Cup first-round tie which Spurs won 6-0 to complete a 12-3 aggregate victory over the Norwegian part-timers.

Cup, the semi-final of the League Cup and beat Torino in the two-legged Anglo-Italian League Cup-winners' Cup. They seemed able to raise their game for one-off Cup competitions but found the bread and butter of League football too much of a chore, and that was how it continued for the next two years.

In 1972-73 they went out of the FA Cup to Derby County in a fourth-round replay that provided one of the most dramatic Cup-ties witnessed by a White Hart Lane crowd for many years. 3-1 down with only five minutes left, Derby forced the match into extra-time and then scored twice more without reply.

The defence of the UEFA Cup began with a 12-3 aggregate demolition of Lyn Oslo and continued with a 4-0 first-leg hammering of Olympiakos Piraeus that made the second leg a formality. It got tougher with the visit of the technically adept Red Star Belgrade. Goals by Chivers and Gilzean gave Spurs a first leg advantage but it took another great defensive performance to limit the Yugoslavs to only one goal in the return.

In the fourth round Spurs really had their backs to the wall after a 1-0 victory over Vitória Setúbal in the first leg was secured only thanks to an 81st-minute goal from substitute Ray Evans, a full-back thrown on up front by Bill Nicholson in a desperate attempt to crack the Portuguese defence. Only 20 minutes of the second leg had gone when Vitória restored parity and Spurs looked to be out when the home team grabbed a second 20 minutes into the second half. Only four

An exchange of pennants as Tottenham play host to Vitória Setúbal in the UEFA Cup fourth-round tie and went through on the away-goals rule

minutes later, however, Chivers blasted home a 35-yard free-kick to see Spurs through on the away-goals rule.

The semi-final paired Spurs with Liverpool and when they returned from Anfield only one goal down – and that a lucky rebound off Alec Lindsay as he got in the way of a clearance – they were favourites to go on and meet Borussia Mönchengladbach or Twente Enschede in the Final. It took Spurs until three minutes into the second half to equalise through Peters but as they pushed forward looking for the winner they allowed the League champions elect to snatch a breakaway goal through Steve Heighway. Peters got a second 20 minutes from time, but Ray Clemence would not be beaten again and now it was Spurs turn to sample the bitter taste of defeat on the away-goals rule.

It was again the League Cup that provided the ticket to continued European competition. Huddersfield Town were comfortably disposed of in the second round but Middlesbrough proved far more difficult opponents in round three. After a 1-1 draw at Ayresome Park, the Second Division side were outplayed in the replay but their defence showed a stubborn streak which some of Spurs' more illustrious visitors from Europe would have envied and prevented Spurs scoring in two hours of play. 'Boro forced extra-time in the second replay, too, but an Alan Gilzean goal three minutes from the end gave Spurs victory and a meeting with Millwall only two days later, when early goals from Perryman and Peters made sure any tiredness was not allowed to affect the result.

After accounting for three lower division clubs,

Spurs go close in the 1973 Football League Cup Final against Norwich City at Wembley Stadium. The game, one of the most tedious Cup Finals in memory, was settled by a Ralph Coates goal.

in the fifth round Spurs were drawn at League leaders Liverpool and they got within 12 minutes of their first victory at Anfield since 1912 before a typical Emlyn Hughes screamer forced a replay. Such were the demands caused by their Cup successes that Spurs were again in action only two days later, and again they decided to get the game over early. In driving rain they launched a ferocious onslaught on Ray Clemence's goal and 15 minutes of brilliant attacking play was rewarded with two goals from Chivers and one from John Pratt. As the rain eased off, so did Spurs. Ian Callaghan got a consolation goal four minutes from the end but as Bill Shankly admitted, after such a devastating opening Liverpool's only hope lay in a floodlight failure.

The semi-final gave Wolves the chance to avenge their UEFA Cup Final defeat of the previous season but again Spurs decided to get the first-leg match over and done with in double-quick time. Peters netted after only three minutes and another John Pratt special from 25 yards on the quarter hour put Spurs in command with a Kenny Hibbitt penalty on the stroke of half-time the only reply.

Spurs approached the second leg at White Hart Lane in far too casual a mood and it was only when Wolves scored five minutes from the interval that they realised another trip to Wembley was by no means a certainty. Wolves' goal had a tinge of good fortune about it, an Alan Sunderland shot bouncing off Jennings' knees, on to Terry Naylor's head and into the net, but they all count.

A 72nd-minute goal from Peters should have finished Wolves off but in the last minute they scored again through John Richards to send the tie into extra-time. Spurs controlled the extra half-hour and it was no less than they deserved when Chivers drove home a Ray Evans cross with six minutes left.

Norwich City beat Chelsea in the other semi-final to earn a first visit to Wembley but disappointingly appeared to go into the Final concerned only to avoid a heavy defeat. Nine or ten men back in defence for most of the time, they provided little of the afternoon's entertainment but it must be said that Spurs were unable to impose themselves on the game.

In one of the most tedious of Wembley Finals the only goal came after 72 minutes. A long throw by Chivers was back headed by Peters, Gilzean

nudged the ball towards England, but David Cross just managed to nick it away from him. It rolled invitingly to Ralph Coates, on for the injured John Pratt, and from the edge of the box he drove the ball out of Kevin Keelan's reach. It was not a Final to remember, but three Cups in three years was better than most clubs could boast.

Spurs parade the League Cup after their Wembley win over Norwich City.

Faltering in the League – But More Cup Joy

GOOD Cup runs are all well and good but the true test of a team's ability lies in League competition where consistency, discipline and organisation are the bywords of success. Those vital commodities have rarely been high on the list of Spurs' attributes but in the early 1970s they had become even more important and their absence had much to do with Spurs' failure to have any say in the championship battle, indeed their gradual decline as a League force.

This inability to impress in the world's oldest League competition was made all the more frustrating by the way Spurs could raise their game for the really important Cup–ties and never was this more apparent than in the 1973–74 season. Exit from both FA and League Cups at the first hurdle and a mid–table position in the League would have been viewed as disastrous most seasons, but these failures were forgotten as Spurs basked in the glory of another run to the UEFA Cup Final, not that such progress could have been expected after the first round of the competition.

Spurs returned from Zurich 5–1 victors over

Spurs on the eve of the 1973-74 season with the Football League Cup. Back row (left to right): Dillon, Gilzean, Collins, Chivers, Jennings, Daines, England, Knowles, Evans, Naylor. Front row: Coates, Kinnear, Pratt, Perryman, Peters, Beal, Pearce, Neighbour, Holder.

Grasshoppers but three of their goals had arrived in the last 15 minutes and, had it not been for an outstanding performance by Pat Jennings, they would have been hard pressed to escape with a draw. The story was the same in the second leg, only now it was Barry Daines, in for the injured Jennings, saving Spurs' blushes, and four goals in the last 16 minutes that gave Spurs a 4–1 victory.

A 1–1 draw at Aberdeen was a definite improvement but it took two goals in the last ten minutes from young Chris McGrath to see off the Scots 4–1 in the second leg.

The third round gave Spurs their longest European journey, 2,500 miles to deepest Georgia to face Dinamo Tbilisi. A Ralph Coates goal and another superb performance by Jennings secured a 1–1 draw, but in the second leg Spurs at last turned on the style to win 5–1. 1FC Cologne had lost only one of 31 European ties at home but Spurs gave their performance of the season to inflicted a second defeat. With another youngster, Matt Dillon, called up to reinforce the defence it was obvious Spurs were going to pull everyone back and rely on the odd counter-attack for a crucial away goal. With England and his co-defenders soaking up the German's attacks like a sponge, Nicholson's tactics worked to perfection, goals in each half from McGrath and Peters more than cancelling out the sole success of the home team. Two early goals in the second leg set up a comfortable 3–0 win and Spurs third successive UEFA Cup semi-final.

Nicholson abandoned the defensive tactics that had worked so well in Cologne for the first leg of the semi-final against Lokomotive Leipzig, deciding instead to surprise the East Germans by attacking them on their own ground. Again his decision was vindicated with a 2–1 win and although the visitors had the best of the first half in the return leg goals from McGrath and Chivers gave Spurs a comfortable 4–1 aggregate win and a Final against Feyenoord.

The luck that had seen Spurs drawn away in the first leg of each previous round deserted them for the Final, and probably made the difference between winning and losing. The new Dutch champions, full of internationals, were pushed back from the start but their defence stood firm and it was six minutes from the break before the breakthrough came, Mike England getting his head to a Ray Evans' free-kick to glance the ball home. The joy lasted only four minutes, van Hanegem curling a 20-yard free-kick around the defensive wall and out of Jennings' reach to equalise. They say that just before half-time is the best time to score and certainly the draining of Spurs' confidence was visible.

The Dutch began to take control but just after the hour England's presence in the visitors' box again proved crucial. He did not get his head to another Evans' free-kick but panicked van Daele into slicing the ball into his own net. Spurs had the opportunities to increase their lead but equally the elegant Dutch had some good chances of their own. It looked as if Spurs had settled for taking a one-goal advantage to Rotterdam when, with four minutes left, de Jong got on the end of a long pass to slide the ball past Jennings.

Returning to the scene of their 1963 Cup-winners' Cup triumph Spurs were always facing an uphill struggle but they looked to be in with a chance until midway through the first half when what appeared to be a good goal by McGrath was disallowed for offside. It was not the effect the referee's decision had on the players that turned the game but the reaction of the Spurs' supporters. They were segregated from the home fans by little more than flimsy fencing and a mass brawl broke out which developed into a full-scale riot with the intervention of baton-welding police.

It was impossible for those on the pitch to ignore the happenings on the terraces but Spurs still held out until three minutes from the break when Jennings failed to gather a free-kick and Rijsbergen nodded home. Half-time is crucial for any manager, particularly one whose team has just gone a goal behind, but Bill Nicholson had no opportunity to influence his team; he was needed to appeal over the public address system for an end to the fighting.

With most Spurs' supporters cleared from the ground the team did their best to get back in the game, but Feyenoord were adept at retaining possession and Spurs were left chasing their tails most of the time. Six minutes from the end the Dutch tied up the game, Ressel scoring from an acute angle. Spurs had lost their first major Final but the loss of that fine record was nothing compared to the shame brought upon the club by its so-called fans.

Dragged before UEFA, Spurs were ordered to play their next two home European games at least 250 kilometres from White Hart Lane but the penalty was never enforced. It was to be another seven years before the club qualified for Europe and in 1980, as part of UEFA's 25th anniversary amnesty, the punishment was lifted.

The events of Rotterdam, though, had a far greater impact than any penalty UEFA could

Mike England (5) celebrates his goal against Feyenoord in the 1974 UEFA Cup Final first leg at White Hart Lane. But Spurs could only draw 2-2 and in the second leg they lost 2-0.

Spurs' Chris McGrath is beaten to the ball by Feyenoord goalkeeper Eddy Treytel in the first leg of the UEFA Cup Final in 1974.

impose. They destroyed, thankfully not for too long, Bill Nicholson's love for the game. Disenchantment had been building for some time; football was no longer the entertainment he believed it should be, avoiding defeat all that mattered. Off the pitch money was taking over, players no longer happy just to play the game but wanting more and more, demanding a transfer if left out, loyalty a thing of the past.

Four Finals in four years, three of them won, could not disguise the fact that Spurs were on a downward slope and Nicholson knew he could not arrest the slide. Unable to sign the new players he wanted, partly, as he later revealed, because he would not agree to demands for under-the-counter payments, he introduced some of the club's youngsters, Chris Jones, Matt Dillon, Keith Osgood, Chris McGrath, Jimmy Neighbour.

But while the promise was there experience was lacking and when Spurs lost the first four matches of 1974–75 he decided the time had come to resign. It was the end of the most glorious and successful period in Spurs' history and a sad end at that, for Nicholson was merely thanked for his services and allowed to walk away from the club to which he had given so much. Perhaps a total break was for the best, but it left a bitter taste, particularly when he was not even consulted on who his successor should be.

It was public knowledge Nicholson favoured Danny Blanchflower, forever remembered as captain of the 'double' winning side and a man whose football philosophy mirrored that of Nicholson, but Blanchflower had a reputation for being his own man and the board wanted someone more restrained than the articulate Irishman. Anyway, he did not apply for the job and, so the board thought, if he could not even bother to seek out one of the most prestigious jobs in football, then why should they approach him?

The board announced they wanted somebody like Nicholson, a man who would get on with the job quietly and effectively, not someone who would rock the boat. In appointing Hull City manager Terry Neill they chose a man more like Blanchflower than Nicholson, a manager who welcomed media attention and was just as at home with members of the press as he was on the training ground. It was not a popular decision, particularly with the supporters who remembered Neill as a long–serving, former Arsenal captain. How could a man so closely linked to their bitter rivals have the commitment to Spurs that was necessary, that Bill Nicholson had shown?

Publicly, Neill exhibited a relaxed attitude to Spurs' problems and tried to impart that attitude to the players. It seemed to work at the start, his first two games in charge were won, but three successive defeats followed and Spurs were soon back in trouble at the foot of the table. John Duncan and Don McAllister were signed, Alfie Conn given his chance, Martin Peters and Mike England allowed to move on, but performances improved little and one point from eight games in the new year left Spurs favourites for relegation.

When the situation looked desperate the team at last began to find some rhythm and four wins in six games left Spurs needing to beat Leeds United at White Hart Lane in the last game of the season to survive. Leeds were through to the European Cup Final but with almost 50,000 fans behind them Spurs battled to a 4–2 victory to escape and sent Luton Town down instead.

After coming so close to Second Division football, any position above the relegation zone had to be an improvement but in finishing ninth the next season Spurs did better than many expected especially as they also managed to reach the semi–final of the League Cup before going out to Newcastle United.

Another year of struggle seemed probable early on with results almost as bad as 12 months earlier but the signing of Willie Young proved crucial. A big, ungainly, centre–half he was far from elegant but had great determination and his arrival allowed Keith Osgood to operate alongside the pivot, where his more accomplished defending could be put to better use.

Neill also showed he was not afraid to give youth its chance, Neil McNab, Glenn Hoddle and several others being given the opportunity to show what they could do. While Neill certainly improved results he was still having a difficult time off the pitch. No matter what he said the fans still doubted his loyalty to Spurs but his real problem lay in his relationship with the board; Neill was not another Nicholson and both sides found it hard to come to terms with that. In June 1976, with Bertie Mee announcing his retirement as Arsenal manager, Neill resigned. Within two weeks he was installed as Mee's replacement. His first signing for Arsenal was England centre–forward Malcolm McDonald, whose transfer to Spurs he had been negotiating whilst still in charge at White Hart Lane.

Applicants to take over from Neill were disappointingly few. Perhaps the situation at Manchester United where Matt Busby's successors had been unable to escape the great

Ralph Coates in action against his old club, Burnley, at Turf Moor in March 1976. Pratt and Duncan gave Spurs a 2-1 win.

man's shadow put them off. The board decided to appoint from within giving the job to first-team coach Keith Burkinshaw. A relative unknown, Burkinshaw had been at White Hart Lane for only 12 months after leaving Newcastle United. His only managerial experience had been in the lower divisions with Workington and Scunthorpe United but he had the players behind him and, like Nicholson, was a Yorkshireman.

Not that the similarity ended there. He worked hard, took the game seriously, was more interested in coaching players than becoming a media personality and believed in the same attacking football that Nicholson had always tried to play. His first 'signing' was perhaps his most illuminating and important. He persuaded Bill Nicholson to give up his scouting job with West Ham and return to White Hart Lane as a consultant. If nothing else it showed that Burkinshaw was not afraid of Nicholson's shadow but it also showed he was sensible enough to accept he needed people of experience around him. Sadly though backroom experience was of little help, it was needed on the pitch.

From the start of 1976-77 Spurs were in trouble. With Martin Chivers having left for Switzerland and John Duncan, top scorer for the past two seasons, out injured, the forward line was ineffective. Ian Moores was signed to pep up the attack but proved a disappointment. The defence was simply unable to cope with the extra pressure but when Burkinshaw tried to

strengthen it with the signing of John Gorman, injuries deprived him first of Pat Jennings and then Gorman himself.

Nothing Burkinshaw could do had any effect, losing in the FA Cup to struggling Second Division Cardiff City and in the League Cup to Third Division Wrexham simply emphasising that Spurs were no longer good enough for the top flight. Bottom of the First Division the last match of the season produced unprecedented scenes of loyalty from fans to players and manager alike. The same loyalty was shown by the board to Burkinshaw, there never being any suggestion he would be sacked.

In many ways relegation came as a relief, it had been on the cards for three years. At least Second Division football would give Burkinshaw time to rebuild, time to develop the talents of Glenn Hoddle, Barry Daines and Neil McNab in a less demanding arena than the First Division but still in a pressure situation where every game would be a Cup Final as opponents set out to beat one of the biggest clubs in the country.

Before the new season started Burkinshaw demonstrated his faith in the young players under his control, selling Pat Jennings to Arsenal for a bargain £45,000. It was to prove a decision he would live to regret and he later admitted that had he been blessed with the gift of foresight he would not have let Jennings go.

From the outset of the Second Division campaign it was obvious there were four

Spurs at the start of the 1978-79 season. Back row (left to right): Jones, Villa, Lee, Lacy, Moores, Hoddle, Armstrong. Middle row: Pat Welton (assistant manager), Holmes, Duncan, Kendall, Daines, McAllister, Naylor, Keith Burkinshaw (manager). Front row: Ardíles, Taylor, Gorman, Perryman, Pratt, Stead, McNab.

outstanding teams, Spurs, Bolton Wanderers, Brighton and Hove Albion and Southampton, but only three could go up. By the end of March it looked as if Spurs would be one but three defeats, including one at Brighton, sowed the seeds of doubt. Steve Perryman's crucial goal beat Hull City in the last home game of the season, leaving Spurs with a visit to The Dell and one point needed to send them up on goal-difference at Brighton's expense. Bolton were up, if Spurs and Brighton won Southampton would stay down so it is not surprising both teams concentrated on keeping a clean sheet.

They did. Spurs were back where they belonged and, much to the disappointment of many pundits, they had done it playing football the Tottenham way with Hoddle and McNab fully justifying Burkinshaw's faith in them.

As Spurs' supporters spent the summer contemplating how the team that had climbed out of the Second Division would fare back in the First, Argentina were winning the World Cup in front of their own fans. In a team of all the talents

they had two outstanding individuals, striker Mario Kempes and midfielder Osvaldo Ardíles. Kempes scored the goals and got the headlines but it was Ardíles who pulled the strings, linking defence to attack, making the openings, gliding through the midfield with consummate ease and exhibiting the flair and panache that had been so desperately missing from English football since the 1960s. When Burkinshaw got word that Ardíles was available for transfer – and wanted to play in England – he lost no time in jetting out to Buenos Aires.

Football in Argentina was in a parlous state, even the biggest clubs so deep in debt they were prepared to sell their prize assets for fees that by European standards were bargains. It took Burkinshaw no time to persuade Ardíles to agree terms for a £350,000 transfer but there was one problem. Ardíles was not keen on uprooting his family and coming to England by himself so would Spurs also sign his great friend and international teammate Ricardo Villa? Not much had been seen of Villa in the World Cup, only two

Osvaldo Ardíles bursts through the Liverpool defence at White Hart Lane in March 1980. Spurs won 2-0 with goals from Pratt and Hoddle (penalty).

substitute appearances, but Burkinshaw remembered the big, bearded midfielder.

The subject of Argentina's record domestic transfer and reckoned by many every bit as good as Ardíles, the asking price was only £25,000 more than for Ardíles and too good a chance to miss. The whole deal, completed in only three days and almost complete secrecy, was best summed up by the *Daily Express* headline – 'Spurs Scoop The World'.

The signing of the two Argentines fired the public's imagination and made Spurs a massive draw wherever they played but two players, no matter how good, do not make a team and for two years Spurs could do no better than midtable in the League and the last eight of the FA Cup. Villa struggled to make his mark but despite fears he would find the English game too physical, Ardíles fitted in as if he had known little else.

Alongside Glenn Hoddle he gave Spurs the most exciting midfield in the country but the defence was suspect and the forward line too weak to take advantage of the chances Hoddle and Ardíles created.

Outstanding individuals need the right players around them and it took Burkinshaw time to gather those players together. With youngsters Chris Hughton and Paul Miller introduced and the experienced Steve Perryman switched to full-back the defence began to look stronger, but up front Spurs still lacked a top class goalscorer – in 1979–80 Hoddle was the only player to reach double figures.

In May 1980 Spurs signed Aberdeen's Steve Archibald, a long-time target, for £800,000 and three months later paid £650,000 for Garth Crooks, Stoke City's England Under-21 international. Both were quick, darting players, no slouches in the air but happiest with the ball on the ground. Their speed off the mark and close control were the exact qualities needed to finish off the intricate approach play of Hoddle and Ardíles.

With Archibald and Crooks striking up the perfect partnership from day one Spurs looked to have the makings of a trophy-winning team but the turning point came when two bargain signings from non–League football were given their chance. Graham Roberts was called up in December 1980 and immediately settled in at the centre of defence. Winger Tony Galvin, who had begun to make a claim for a regular place until injury put him out for eight months, returned as a substitute in a hectic but drab goalless draw against Queen's Park Rangers at Loftus Road in the third round of the FA Cup.

With Villa injured and Ardíles absent playing for Argentina in the Gold Cup tournament in Uruguay, Galvin retained his place for the replay and scored once as Spurs went comfortably through 3–1, the other goals coming from Hoddle and Crooks. By the time of the fourth-round meeting with Hull City, Ardíles had returned but it was only when his stand–in, Garry Brooke, replaced him that Spurs at last managed to break down the stubborn defence of the team bottom of the Third Division. Seven minutes were left when Brooke scored with a terrific long-range shot and in the last minute he helped set up Archibald for Spurs' second.

Spurs were drawn at home again in the next round and goals from Ardíles, Archibald and Hughton rounded off a miserable week for a young Coventry City side who only days earlier had been knocked out of the League Cup by West Ham United. In the two previous seasons Spurs' luck had deserted them at the quarter-final stage when they had been drawn to meet Manchester United and then Liverpool.

This time the luck was with them as they were paired with the weakest team left in the competition, Exeter City. If it looked easy on paper it was anything but that on the field. The Third Division club defended in depth and looked like taking Spurs back to their St James' Park ground, scene of victories over Leicester City and Newcastle United, until the last quarter of the game saw Roberts and Miller go up and show the forwards how to score.

Spurs got off to the perfect start in the semi–final against Wolverhampton Wanderers at Hillsborough, Archibald sliding home Galvin's cross in the fourth minute, but six minutes later

Wolves were level as Andy Gray and Wayne Clarke set up Kenny Hibbitt. Spurs controlled the first half and it was nothing less than they deserved when Hoddle curled home a free–kick from the edge of the box five minutes before the break.

The first half had provided a fascinating contrast in styles: Spurs seeking to open up the Wolves' defence with slick interpassing; the Midlanders trying to bludgeon a way through with high balls aimed at Gray and Clarke.

Although Wolves exerted more pressure after the interval Spurs looked to be through to their sixth FA Cup Final when, with only 20 seconds left, Hoddle slid the ball away from Hibbitt on the edge of Spurs' box. Television proved Hoddle had made a clean tackle – and even if he had caught Hibbitt it was outside the area – but referee Clive Thomas, ever controversial, decided Hibbitt's dramatic fall into the penalty area merited a penalty. Willie Carr converted to send the game into extra–time, 30 minutes that were never going to produce a winner as Spurs continued to complain at Thomas' decision and Wolves were just grateful to have a second chance.

Spurs had sat back in the second half and allowed Wolves to go at them; they were not to make the same mistake in the Highbury replay. On top for practically the full 90 minutes, they took an 11th-minute lead when Crooks headed home Hoddle's delightfully chipped up cross. A minute from half-time Crooks grabbed the second, latching on to a precise defence–splitting pass from Hoddle to race clear of Wolves' defence and beat Paul Bradshaw. The final nail in Wolves' coffin was hammered home early in the second half when Villa picked up the ball just inside Wolves' half, cut inside and unleashed an unstoppable shot from 30 yards.

The build up to the 100th FA Cup Final focussed on the first appearance at Wembley of the two Argentinians, particularly Ardíles' well known desire to grace the Final of the world's greatest Cup competition – the players even made a record called *Ossie's Dream* – and how they and Hoddle would turn on the style and give Manchester City the runaround. The media can always talk a good game but their expectations are not always met, and so it proved.

Overall Spurs may have possessed the more gifted players but City had players who were prepared to compensate for their lack of talent with hard work. Hutchison, MacKenzie, Power and Gow imposed themselves in midfield from the start, stifling Spurs' artistry and pushing them

Ricky Villa and Ossie Ardíles took centre stage at Wembley when Spurs met Manchester City in the FA Cup Final in 1981

back all the time. Gow, in particular, made it his job to clamp down on Ardíles and with Villa having one of those anonymous days to which he was too often prone, Crooks and Archibald received little service. City deservedly took the lead with a Hutchison header on the half-hour and could have won the game 30 minutes later when MacKenzie hit the post.

Villa trudged off to be replaced by Brooke and at last Spurs began to get into the game but they had to wait until ten minutes from the end of normal time for that famous old 'Cup–winners' luck' to smile on them. A free–kick on the edge of the box was tapped by Ardíles to Perryman, who set the ball up for Hoddle to strike. His curling shot looked to be going wide until Hutchison – who, of course, had scored for City – broke from the defensive wall to deflect the ball past Joe

Corrigan. Extra–time could not produce a winner and for the first time a Wembley replay was needed five days later.

If the first match was disappointing the replay produced one of the most dramatic Finals ever seen at the famous old stadium and the perfect example of the ups and downs of football. Villa's performance hardly merited a place in the replay but Burkinshaw felt he could not play so badly again and his faith was well and truly rewarded. Only seven minutes had elapsed when Steve Archibald's shot was parried by Corrigan and the ball fell straight to Villa. As he blasted it home the memories of a tearful exit from the first game could be seen to melt away.

Three minutes later City were level with a goal that would normally live long in the memory. Hutchison nodded the ball down to Steve

Ricky Villa celebrates his fantastic goal against Manchester City in the 1981 FA Cup Final replay.

MacKenzie on the edge of Spurs' box and his right-foot volley sped past Aleksic. In the first game Hoddle, Ardíles and Villa had allowed City to dominate in midfield but they showed they had learned their lesson, matched Gow and his men for commitment and kept Spurs so on top it was against the run of play that City took the lead in the 52nd minute.

There looked little danger when Miller and Hughton converged on Dave Bennett as he chased a hopeful ball into Spurs' box but a sudden burst of speed from the City forward took him between the defenders, the three of them tumbled to the ground and when they looked up referee Keith Hackett was pointing to the penalty spot. Milija Aleksic went the right way but Kevin Reeves shot was perfectly placed.

Spurs might have buckled but just raised their game to greater heights and 20 minutes later were level when a corner was only half cleared to Hoddle. A delicate chip over the outrushing defenders was brought down in a flash by Archibald but before he could get in a shot, Crooks had poked the ball past Corrigan.

The winner came five minutes later, and what a winner it was. Villa took the ball from Tony Galvin and set off on a mazy dribble that mesmerised City's defence as he weaved his way past one defender after another, drew Corrigan, allowed the 'keeper to commit himself and then slipped the ball home. The greatest goal seen at Wembley, said many. Certainly a fitting goal to win the Centenary Cup Final.

In the 99 years of their history, Spurs had

Spurs with the FA Cup, won yet again 'when the year ends in one'.

Steve Archibald puts Spurs ahead in the 1982 Milk Cup Final against Liverpool.

earned a reputation as a Cup side – ten major Cup wins against three League titles, and an assault on three Cups did much to enhance that reputation in a centenary season which began and ended at Wembley.

It started with a 2–2 draw against Aston Villa in the FA Charity Shield curtain-raiser and after two more visits finished with an FA Cup replay. The first of those games was notable for the debut of former Liverpool 'keeper Ray Clemence only a fortnight or so after his 33rd birthday – Burkinshaw had clearly learnt from his mistake with Pat Jennings that age is no bar where 'keepers are concerned.

The Cup exploits began in fine style with a 6–1 aggregate defeat of Ajax in the European Cup-winners' Cup. Dundalk proved remarkably stubborn before going down 2–1 in the next round and it took a Glenn Hoddle goal six minutes from time to see off Eintracht Frankfurt, who had retrieved a 2–0 deficit from the White Hart Lane leg in only 14 minutes, to put Spurs through to a semi–final with Barcelona.

A feast of football was expected but the first leg was one of the most violent matches witnessed at White Hart Lane. The Spaniards had little interest in playing football, their only objective to return home without conceding a goal and if that meant kicking Spurs off the pitch, so be it. A weak referee did little to help and it was not until an hour had elapsed that he sent off Estella for a

vicious foul on Tony Galvin. If Spurs thought the advantage was with them they knew better two minutes later when Clemence took his eye off the ball, allowing a speculative 30-yard shot from Barcelona's captain, Olmo, to squirm through his hands.

Much as Spurs laid siege to their opponent's goal they had to wait until three minutes from the end for Graham Roberts to grab an equaliser. In the second leg Barcelona adopted much the same attitude, content to rely on the away goal to see them through to the Final which had already been booked for their own Nou Camp Stadium. As it was a goal from Allan Simonsen in the first minute of the second half gave them victory.

In the League Cup, Spurs set out on the road to Wembley with the toughest possible draw – Manchester United in the two–legged second round. A Steve Archibald goal gave Spurs victory in the first game and Mike Hazard got the only goal to silence Old Trafford in the return. Wrexham, Fulham and Nottingham Forest were overcome at White Hart Lane and another Hazard goal proved decisive in the semi–final second leg against West Bromwich Albion after a tough first game at The Hawthorns.

The competition had been renamed the Milk Cup by the time Spurs met Liverpool in the Final and for the first time Spurs tasted defeat in a domestic Cup Final, although they got to within three minutes of maintaining their unparalleled

Glenn Hoddle's extra-time goal in the 1982 FA Cup Final, which ended 1-1. Hoddle scored the only goal of the replay when his penalty defeated QPR to keep Spurs' grip on the trophy they had won 12 months earlier.

record. They held out for 76 minutes against sustained pressure from the Anfield machine after Steve Archibald's early goal but when Ronnie Whelan got an equaliser it was all over. Spurs were exhausted, and looked it, Liverpool buoyant. Whelan added a second 20 minutes into extra-time and Ian Rush completed the scoring in the dying seconds.

Spurs lost the Milk Cup Final in March, went out of the Cup-winners' Cup in April but come May were back at Wembley for another FA Cup Final. A Garth Crooks goal was enough to beat Arsenal in the third round and he repeated the feat against Leeds United in the fourth, both games being at White Hart Lane. In the next round it was Mark Falco who got the only goal to see off Aston Villa and send Spurs through to a sixth-round tie at Stamford Bridge a week before the Wembley meeting with Liverpool.

Chelsea had beaten Liverpool in the fifth round and even before the match the winners were installed as Cup favourites. The game lived up to all expectations with Chelsea having the early advantage, Spurs getting on top but then conceding a goal a minute before half-time. In the second half Spurs turned on the style, sweeping down on the Chelsea goal with one attack after another. Steve Archibald equalised and then two exquisite moves tore the Chelsea defence apart to provide openings for Glenn Hoddle and Micky Hazard. Chelsea pulled one back but Spurs were rarely in danger.

Queen's Park Rangers and West Bromwich Albion met in a Highbury semi-final while Spurs were drawn against Second Division Leicester City at Villa Park. An unremarkable match saw Spurs comfortable winners with Ian Wilson calmly lobbing the ball over Mark Wallington's head when under no pressure for a bizarre own-goal to add to Garth Crooks' opener.

Of equal importance to Spurs though were the events of the previous day. Argentinian troops had landed on the Falklands Islands, sparking off war in the South Atlantic. Ossie Ardíles was due to return home after the match to help his country prepare for their defence of the World Cup, but Argentina's manager, César Menotti, had already indicated he would release Ardíles if Spurs reached Wembley. The actions of the military junta in Buenos Aires made that impossible. Ricky Villa was not part of Menotti's plans and at first filled Ardíles' place, but when it came to the big day Burkinshaw decided he could not expose the hero of only 12 months earlier to what was bound to be intense pressure and the Argentinian was forced to watch from the touch-lines.

The 1982 FA Cup Final against Queens' Park Rangers was a dull affair. Clearly tired after an arduous season, players carrying injuries and deprived of two stars who might have provided that extra little spark, Spurs had the upper hand throughout but could not find a way past Peter Hucker until the 11th minute of extra-time,

Glenn Hoddle's 20-yard shot taking a slight deflection off Tony Currie.

Four minutes from the final whistle, and looking forward to their lap of honour, Spurs were jolted back to reality when Bob Hazell flicked on Simon Stainrod's long throw for Terry Fenwick to score an improbable equaliser.

A replay was the last thing Spurs wanted, but if a season that had promised so much was not to end empty-handed, it had to be faced. It was settled in the seventh minute when Graham Roberts' surging run into the heart of the Rangers' area was stopped only by Tony Currie's foul. Hoddle slotted the penalty past Hucker with ease. Hopes of a repeat of the 1981 replay faded as Rangers took control and pushed Spurs back, but they could not find a way past Clemence and had to be content with almost as much applause from

Spurs' fans on their lap of honour as the winners themselves received.

While Spurs had been fighting their Cup battles, the League campaign had not been ignored. They were always near the top, usually with games in hand and theoretically, at least, still capable of taking the title, but injuries and the heavy burden of games took their toll. In the seven weeks between the FA Cup semi-final and Final they were forced to play 14 games, one-third of the League season, of which only five were won.

Inexperienced young reserves had to be thrown in at the deep end, players forced to turn out when injured and in need of rest. Fourth place was no disgrace and at least ensured that even if the FA Cup had slipped from their grasp, a place in Europe had again been secured.

More Cups and More Controversy

OR two years Keith Burkinshaw's team had delivered that elusive combination – entertainment and success – with a team built around the flair and skill of two outstanding midfield players, Glenn Hoddle and Ossie Ardíles. The most gifted player of his generation, Hoddle could control a game with inch perfect long passes, intricate one–twos and powerful shooting. Alongside him Ardíles was always available, probing for openings and keen to get in where most damage could be inflicted. They worked perfectly together but were not so dependant on each other that the absence of one could not be compensated for.

When they were both absent, though, Spurs suffered and so it proved in 1982–83. Ardíles decided it would not be wise to return to England after the Falklands War and went on a year's loan to Paris St-Germain. He returned before the 12 months were up but broke a shin in only his fourth game back. With Hoddle injured for much of the time Spurs had a poor season, going out of the European Cup–winners' Cup in the second round, FA Cup in round five and Milk Cup to struggling Second Division Burnley. It was only a run of nine victories in the last dozen games that secured fourth place and UEFA Cup qualification.

Action from the 1982 FA Charity Shield game against Liverpool when Ian Rush's first-half goal gained a victory for the Reds

Gary O'Reilly is challenged by 17-year-old West Ham United debutant Tony Cottee at Upton Park on New Year's Day 1983. Spurs went down 3-0 and Cottee marked his League baptism with a goal.

If Spurs were not stunning the football world on the pitch, then events off it were certainly dramatic. For years the club had been run by the Wale family, one of the largest shareholders. They did not hold a majority of shares but with the 4,892 issued spread amongst 600 shareholders, many of them untraced, held effective control. As a private limited company any transfer of shares could go ahead only with the approval of the board, so ensuring that a takeover bid could not even get off the ground. For almost 50 years the position of the directors had been unassailable but things were about to change.

Football itself was going through a period of rapid change. No longer able to survive on the patronage of wealthy individuals who treated it as a hobby a new breed of successful young businessmen were moving in determined to revitalise the country's number-one spectator sport.

At White Hart Lane the decision to rebuild the West Stand had split the board and resulted in Sidney Wale resigning as chairman. His doubts were to prove well–founded with the cost going well over budget, Burkinshaw short of funds to secure new players and Spurs facing the kind of financial problems that had so nearly seen Chelsea go to the wall.

The registration of any share purchase might be vetoed but the board could not stop shares, and with them crucial voting rights, being sold. Monte Carlo-based millionaire property developer Irving Scholar, a Spurs fanatic concerned at the way the club was going, saw his opportunity and quietly built up a big shareholding. When he had persuaded Sidney Wale to sell his shares and secured the support of another property developer, Paul Bobroff, Scholar made his move. It was December 1982. The board had been outmanoeuvred. It could either resign and let Scholar take over or fight a bitter battle with no chance of winning. The honourable course was chosen.

The new regime soon discovered all was not well at what was supposed to be one of the wealthiest clubs in the League, one of the so-

Goalkeeper Ray Clemence joined Spurs from Liverpool in August 1981 for £300,000 and through most of the decade was Tottenham's first-choice, taking his tally of appearances for them to 330 and his career total to well over 1,000. Only the presence of Peter Shilton restricted him to 61 England caps.

called 'Big Five'. The West Stand had proved a bigger drain on resources than anyone, even Sidney Wale, could have imagined. With debts over £5 million there was no money for new signings, an injection of cash was needed, and a big injection at that, but Scholar and Bobroff were not possessed of limitless resources. The answer was found in, of all places, the Stock Market. Tottenham Hotspur plc was floated on the Stock Exchange, the first football club to do so. The flotation, in October 1983, was a veritable success. It was oversubscribed three and a half-times and £3.8 million was raised. The club was back on a firm financial footing but no one was to know the heavy price that was to be paid in years to come.

Back on the football field Spurs started the 1983–84 season as one of the favourites for the League title but early performances were disappointing and they were soon out of the title race. They fared no better in the Milk Cup or FA Cup but there was always the UEFA Cup and it provided a fitting finale to Keith Burkinshaw's reign. Burkinshaw was a manager from the old school, believing it was his job to sign new players, negotiate contracts, run the club in all respects. The new board had other ideas, Scholar in particular favouring the European style where players were secured by the directors and the manager's job was confined to coaching and picking the team. A clash was inevitable and in April 1984 the story got out that at the end of the season Burkinshaw would be leaving.

Spurs' first opponents in a competition they had not graced for ten years were the Irish part-timers, Drogheda United and they were seen off 14–0 over the two legs. The second round pitted Spurs against Ajax, the new master, Glenn Hoddle, against the old master, Johann Cruyff, and the young pretender, Ruud Gullit. Hoddle won the first leg contest with what was probably his greatest 90-minute performance in a Spurs' shirt. At the heart of every move, he had a hand in three of the four goals Spurs scored in the first 45 minutes. Ajax pulled two back in the last 15 minutes but another outstanding team performance in the second leg saw Spurs through on a 6–2 aggregate.

They returned from Munich a goal down to Bayern, equalised early in the second half at White Hart Lane but had to wait until three minutes from the end for Mark Falco to grab the vital second. A 2–0 home victory and 2–2 draw in Vienna put out FK Austria and gave Spurs a semi-final against Hajduk Split.

Mark Falco scored a vital early goal in Yugoslavia but despite controlling the game for long periods Spurs allowed Hajduk back in. They visited London one up but Micky Hazard's sixth-minute goal proved enough to secure a Final against Anderlecht, the Cup holders, who had overturned Nottingham Forest's 2–0 first leg lead in their own compact stadium and went into the first leg of the Final as favourites to take an advantage into the second leg.

Inspired by Graham Roberts and Paul Miller, Spurs rode out the Belgians' early onslaught and gradually but surely got on top. Their confidence received a massive boost just before the hour when Miller rose head and shoulders above Anderlecht's defence to thunder home a header from Micky Hazard's corner. Anderlecht's proud ten-year unbeaten home record in European competition looked to have been broken but with only five minutes left a scramble in Spurs' goalmouth ended with Morton Olsen forcing the ball home to secure a draw.

The only disappointing note for Spurs was a booking for Steve Perryman. His second of the competition it meant that he was automatically suspended for the return leg. Spurs were already without long-term injury victims Hoddle and Clemence and Burkinshaw decided Ardíles, out for two months, was not fit enough to start the second leg. On one of those European nights for which White Hart Lane had become famous the Belgians, as they had to, took the game to Spurs and fully justified their reputation as one of the best teams in Europe.

Both teams had their chances but Anderlecht had the better of the play and deservedly took the lead after 60 minutes through Alex Czerniatinski. For 15 minutes it looked as if Spurs were going to lose their record of never having lost a European game at White Hart Lane but it all changed when Ardíles was called from the bench to replace first-leg hero, Miller. He inspired Spurs to a level of sustained pressure that looked sure to produce a goal and the little man seemed certain to provide it himself when he broke through only to prod the ball against the bar. As Ardíles bemoaned his luck Hazard returned the ball to the centre and Graham Roberts emerged from nowhere to guide it past Munaron.

Extra-time could not separate the teams so the destiny of the trophy went to penalty kicks. Roberts scored first, Tony Parks saved from Olsen and the next six kicks were all converted. Danny Thomas went forward to take Spurs' last kick and win the Cup, only to see Munaron save. The last

Graham Roberts celebrates his goal for Spurs against Anderlecht in the 1984 UEFA Cup Final.

of the first ten penalties was taken by the Icelandic international, Gudjohnsen. Parks flung himself to his right to push the ball away and carve his name permanently into Spurs' history. It was a truly dramatic end to Burkinshaw's reign, if not an exhibition of the free–flowing football that

had made him second only to Bill Nicholson as Spurs' most successful manager.

The search for a successor saw many of the biggest names in football, both at home and abroad, mentioned, but whether they were put off by Burkinshaw's disenchantment with the new

Mark Falco scored 90 goals in 236 first-team games for Spurs, his best period coming in the mid-1980s. Injury held him back earlier in his career.

Winger Tony Galvin, an automatic choice and unsung hero of the Spurs team after the 1981 FA Cup Final. He made 273 senior appearances before moving to Sheffield Wednesday in August 1987.

hierarchy or just unable to accept the challenge, it was one of the lesser lights that got the job. Bought to the club by Terry Neill as youth team coach in 1975 and latterly Burkinshaw's assistant, Peter Shreeve was popular with the players, many

of whom he had known since their days in the juniors. Promoting from within also ensured that wholesale disruption was avoided.

A 4-1 win at Everton got Shreeve's reign got off to the best possible start and for a long time a

When Steve Perryman left White Hart Lane in 1986 he could look back on a remarkable career that spanned 17 years and an astonishing 855 appearances in Spurs' first team, winning more honours than any other player in the club's history. Strangely, he gained only one England cap.

serious challenge for the League title was at last mounted. Early exits from the Milk Cup and FA Cup lessened the burden and left Spurs fighting on two fronts, the League and the defence of the UEFA Cup. Comfortable victories over SC Braga, Brugge and Bohemians of Prague before Christmas saw Spurs through to the fourth round and Real Madrid, not the power they had once been but still the most magical name in European football. With almost three months between the visit to Prague and the first meeting with Real, Spurs concentrated on their two-horse race with Everton for the League title and entered the new year top of the table, ahead on goal-difference.

By the time of the the first meeting with Real in early March, Everton were back in front, but only two points ahead and Spurs had ten of their remaining 15 games at home. The two games with the Spaniards, though, effectively bought Spurs' season to an end. In the first leg an own-goal from, of all people, Steve Perryman saw the end of Spurs' unbeaten home record in Europe. In the second leg Perryman was sent off as Spurs fought gamely, but vainly, to retrieve the deficit.

Between the two games an in–form Manchester United won at White Hart Lane although the loss of midfielder Gary Stevens with a serious knee injury was probably felt more than the loss of three points. Spurs bounced back with their first victory at Anfield in 73 years only four days later and a returning Ardíles inspired Spurs to a 5–1 win over Southampton, but 16 points were dropped in the next seven games, including three at home to Everton. The loss of key players – Hazard, Stevens, Chris Hughton and John Chiedozie – proved crucial. The championship trophy made the short journey from Anfield to Goodison, Spurs having to settle for third place.

Glenn Hoddle, scored 110 goals in 491 senior games for Tottenham, signing as a full-time professional in 1975 and moving to AS Monaco in 1987. He was, quite simply, one of the most gifted footballers of his generation.

Chris Waddle in action against Nottingham Forest's Gary Fleming at White Hart Lane in November 1986, when Brian Clough's team triumphed 3-2.

It was enough to qualify for another shot at the UEFA Cup but the tragic events of Heysel dictated otherwise.

Shreeve's first season in charge had promised much but, despite signing Paul Allen and Chris Waddle, his second was a disappointment, early exits from the two Cup competitions being matched by a drop to tenth in the League. It was not good enough for a board as anxious for glory as the fans. Shreeve was sacked and replaced by the Luton Town manager, David Pleat.

Pleat had a reputation for producing good, attractive football on a limited budget. At Spurs he had the financial resources to back his undoubted managerial skills and he made full use of them, signing Richard Gough, Nico Claesen, Mitchell Thomas and Steve Hodge. A heavy outlay, true, but it looked money well spent as Spurs sustained a serious assault on the three domestic honours. In the Littlewoods Cup, Barnsley, Birmingham City, Cambridge United and West Ham United were disposed off before a titanic semi–final battle with Arsenal. Clive Allen,

relishing his role as lone striker in front of a five-man midfield, gave Spurs a one-goal victory in the first leg at Highbury and within 15 minutes of the second leg starting Allen had doubled Spurs' lead.

Goals from Viv Anderson and Niall Quinn levelled the aggregate scores and with extra–time proving indecisive, Pleat won the toss to give Spurs home advantage for the replay. Again Allen gave Spurs the lead but Ian Allinson equalised with eight minutes to go and in injury time David Rocastle grabbed the winner. In five hours of football Spurs had been behind for less than a minute, but it was enough to take Arsenal through to a Final against Liverpool.

In the League, Spurs were always around the top but again suffered from their own Cup success. Often three or four games in hand of the leaders, Liverpool and Everton, the sheer backlog of fixtures proved too much and again third place had to suffice.

The FA Cup provided the last hope of some reward from a season that had been so rich in

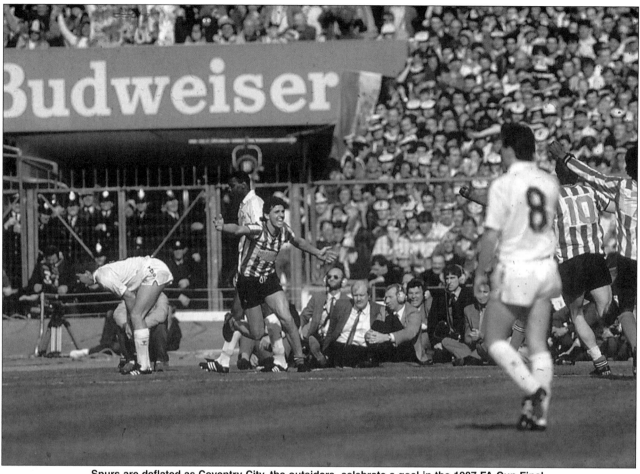

Spurs are deflated as Coventry City, the outsiders, celebrate a goal in the 1987 FA Cup Final.

promise. Scunthorpe United, Crystal Palace, Newcastle United, Wimbledon and Watford were all beaten on the road to Wembley. Only Coventry City, making their first appearance in a major Final, stood between Spurs and their eighth FA Cup win. Spurs were hot favourites and justified the bookies' view within two minutes when Clive Allen nodded home Chris Waddle's near post cross for his 49th goal of the season.

Coventry had even less to lose now and played with a freedom Spurs lacked. Dave Bennett equalised in the ninth minute and even when Gary Mabbutt forced home a Hoddle free–kick five minutes before the break, Coventry never gave up hope, never stopped running at Spurs' defence, Bennett in particular a real thorn in Spurs' side.

Just after the hour, Keith Houchen's diving header from Bennett's cross restored parity and as the game ebbed and flowed from one end to the other either team could have secured the winner. As it was when the winner came it was one of those moments every footballer dreads. Lloyd McGrath found space on the right to cross low towards the near post. Mabbutt stuck out a leg to block the cross but the ball struck his thigh,

ballooned over Ray Clemence and came to rest in the far corner of the net. Even Spurs' supporters could not begrudge Coventry their victory but it was a sad way to decide one of the most open and entertaining Finals for years.

The Final marked Glenn Hoddle's last appearance for Spurs. He had decided to take up the challenge of proving himself on the continent and was soon to sign for Monaco. It was bound to take time to recover from the loss of Spurs number-one star but matters were not helped when Richard Gough was allowed to return to Scotland because his wife was homesick.

The loss of two cornerstones of the team was bad enough, but in October 1987 David Pleat also left. His departure had nothing to do with results, seventh place in the table was no disgrace, but rather his off-field activities. Allegations about his private life had first surfaced in the summer. He seemed to have ridden out the storm but when further stories began to appear he had no option but to resign.

Irving Scholar wasted no time in searching for a replacement. Within days he had flown out to Florida to see Terry Venables and persuaded the former Barcelona manager to join Spurs.

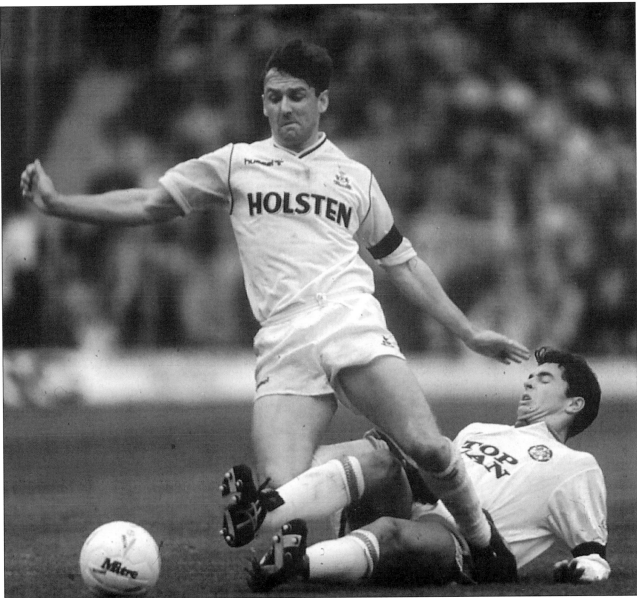

Paul Allen is tackled by Gary Speed of Leeds United during Spurs' 2-0 victory at Elland Road in September 1990. Tottenham went ten games undefeated from the start of the season.

Venables was a more than popular choice. A former Spurs player, he had led Crystal Palace's 'Team of the Eighties' from Third Division to First and taken Queen's Park Rangers to the FA Cup Final and Second Division title before guiding Barcelona to the Spanish League title and European Cup Final.

An innovative coach, hotly tipped as a future England manager, Venables was unable to join Spurs immediately which did nothing to help a dispirited team. Despite his signing Terry Fenwick, Bobby Mimms and Paul Walsh, results were abysmal, the low point coming with a fourth-round FA Cup exit at Third Division Port Vale. Relegation was never a serious threat but there were times when Spurs got too close to the danger zone for comfort.

Further big money sorties into the transfer market were made in the summer of 1988 to sign Paul Gascoigne and Paul Stewart, but the season began in farcical style with the first match against Coventry City called off due to doubts about the safety of the partially rebuilt East Stand. A two-point deduction was the penalty imposed by the Football League, not much by itself, but as only seven points had been collected from the first six games enough to leave Spurs bottom of the table. An FA appeal hearing later substituted a £15,000 fine for the lost points but the damage had been done.

It was only after another miserable FA Cup exit to lower division opposition, this time Bradford City, that Spurs started to display any sort of form, climbing to sixth place. Gascoigne had settled in from the outset, showing the exhilarating skills that had persuaded Spurs to fork out £2 million

Spurs' Gary Lineker at Highbury in September 1990 when the teams drew 0-0.

for his signature. With Stewart finding his form after a poor start and Waddle consistently showing the style that made him one of the country's most exciting players, Venables seemed to be getting together the team he wanted.

The growing promise was reinforced with the summer signing of England's premier striker, Gary Lineker, from Barcelona. The prospect of Lineker linking up with Gascoigne and Waddle was mouth–watering but it was not to be, before the new season even started Waddle had gone to Olympique Marseille for £4.25 million. Selling such a valuable member of the team was, perhaps, a sign all was not well with the finances. If so it was not appreciated. It took time to compensate for the loss of Waddle, a poor start followed by another third round exit from the FA Cup, but Lineker proved his time in Spain had only made him a better player and another late run gave Spurs a final League placing of third.

A big splash in the transfer market had become almost customary for Spurs every summer but there was no major signing in 1990. The *Sunday Times* revealed why after only four games of the new season. Spurs, one of the biggest clubs in the country, quoted on the Stock Exchange, a club who spent millions on players, were broke. Negotiations had started with media magnate Robert Maxwell for him to take a large stake in the public company; one of Scholar's companies had even borrowed money from one of Maxwell's and lent it to Spurs so the final payment to Barcelona on the transfer of Lineker and Nayim could be made.

Part of the price Spurs had to pay for the Stock Market flotation was to diversify. A simple football club would not be attractive to investors, it had to be part of a more broad–based leisure group. In theory it sounded fine, profits from other ventures such as sportswear and computer systems would be ploughed into the football club. In practice, though, exactly the opposite happened. It was the success of the football club that subsided the losses made in other areas.

At first all the headlines had little effect on results but as rumour and speculation gave way to fact performances dipped. The club was desperate for cash. £20 million in debt, money had to be found. If it could not be raised players would have to be sold. Gascoigne, star of the summer's World Cup was worth £5 million plus. Lineker, over a million. The club might be saved, but at what cost?

By Christmas Spurs were out of the running for the League title. A good run in the FA Cup was

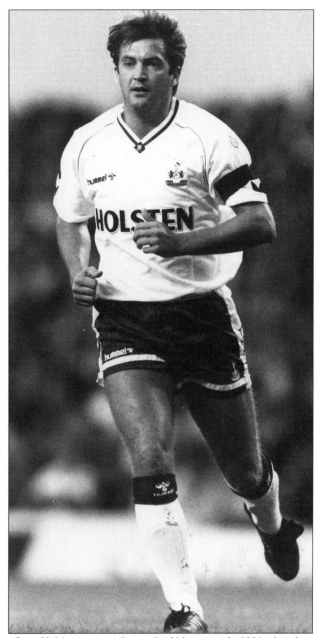

Gary Mabbutt was at the peak of his career in 1991 when he was recalled by England's Graham Taylor after a six year absence for the match against Turkey.

essential, not for the glory but the money. The competition had not been kind to Venables, only once in three years had Spurs got past the third round, and now there were stories he was trying to put together a consortium to take over the club – hardly the best preparation. Paul Stewart's goal at rain–lashed Bloomfield Road gave Spurs a third-round win over Blackpool but now Gascoigne was injured and needed a hernia operation. He scored twice to help eliminate Oxford United and another pair put out Portsmouth, but the injury was getting worse and he could not be risked in anything but the most important game.

After scoring in the sixth-round defeat of Notts County, Gascoigne had his operation and it was

Paul Gascoigne celebrates his spectacular goal which gave Spurs the lead over Arsenal in the 1991 FA Cup semi-final at Wembley. Vinny Samways gives chase.

Arsenal goalkeeper David Seaman is beaten by Gary Lineker for his second and Spurs' third goal in the 1991 FA Cup semi-final.

Lineker celebrates his first goal, helped by Paul Allen.

then a question of whether he would be fit for the semi–final. It was the first semi–final to be held at Wembley, for Spurs had been paired with Arsenal and even the biggest stadium in the country could not accommodate one-fifth of the people who wanted to witness the game.

Gascoigne lined up against Arsenal. It was an enormous gamble by Venables for what was arguably Spurs' most important match ever. Arsenal were well clear of Liverpool in the race for the League title and favourites to become the first club to do the 'double' twice. Spurs could not afford a passenger, but any doubts Gascoigne was not up to it were dispelled after only five minutes. Only he would have had the audacity to even consider beating David Seaman with a 30-yard free–kick. Only he would have the power to do it. It was a sensational start and five minutes later it got even better when Gascoigne linked with Paul Allen to create a goal for Lineker. Alan Smith pulled one back for Arsenal on the stroke of half–time to set up a second-half siege of Erik

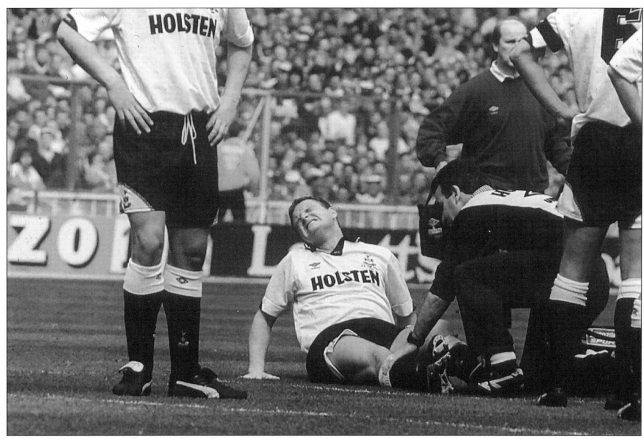

Paul Gascoigne lies injured after his reckless challenge in the opening minutes of the 1991 FA Cup Final against Nottingham Forest.

Thorstvedt's goal but the big Norwegian would not be beaten again and when Lineker broke away to score his second the dream was still alive.

To turn the dream into reality Spurs had to beat Brian Clough's Nottingham Forest. It was the first time as player or manager Clough had got to the FA Cup Final and public sentiment was on his side. But Gascoigne was fit, the year did end in '1' and Spurs' desperate need to win was enough to make them favourites. Right up to the day of the Final rumours persisted about one rescue package or another. At the forefront was Venables, still trying to put together a consortium to take over the club even in the midst of preparations for the biggest day in the domestic football calendar. About the only thing for sure was that come what may, rescue or not, the Final was to be Gascoigne's last appearance in a Spurs' shirt. A move to Lazio was signed, sealed and all but delivered.

The FA Cup Final is a special day for players and fans alike. At least for a few hours Spurs' problems could be forgotten – or could they? From the moment the players emerged from the tunnel it was clear Gascoigne was hyped up. Unfair as it may be to his teammates, one has to say that Gascoigne had almost single-handedly taken Spurs to Wembley. It was to be his last

game for the club, on a worldwide stage, and he was determined to make his mark. That he did, but not in the way he or Spurs would have wanted. In the first minute he felled Forest's Garry Parker with a boot high up the chest; 15 minutes later he lunged in on full-back Gary Charles on the edge of Spurs penalty area with a shameful hack across the thighs. Stuart Pearce stepped up to drill the free-kick past Thorstvedt but if that was not bad enough worse was to follow. Gascoigne collapsed.

As he was stretchered off, not only did Spurs' hopes of winning the game seem to go with him but also the club's financial salvation. If Gascoigne had taken centre stage in the run to Wembley his teammates now had to do it all without him. Gary Lineker netted in the 23rd minute only, to see his effort disallowed, wrongly, for offside. Nine minutes later he looked set to make amends after being brought down by Mark Crossley, but then saw the Forest 'keeper save his penalty. Were the gods conspiring to stop Spurs lifting the Cup for a record eighth time? Ten minutes into the second half, Paul Allen and Nayim combined to set up Paul Stewart on the edge of the Forest box. The striker converted to midfielder hit a perfect shot out of Crossley's reach. Spurs took control now but it was not until

Forest goalkeeper Mark Crossley saves Gary Lineker's penalty at Wembley.

Des Walker, Forest's England defender, heads into his own net and Spurs have again 'won the Cup when the year ends in one.'

the fourth minute of extra-time that the winner arrived. Nayim's corner was flicked on by Stewart and as Gary Mabbutt moved in at the far post to get the finishing touch, Forest's Des Walker beat him to it – and headed into his own net.

The celebrations did not last long. The Cup may have been won but attention soon returned to Spurs' financial problems. Gascoigne had

Spurs players celebrate yet another FA Cup Final triumph.

suffered serious cruciate ligament damage and there was no way his £8.5 million transfer to Lazio could proceed. The Italians still wanted him, but not at the same price and not until he had proved his fitness.

Robert Maxwell continued to express interest but faced fierce opposition from supporters only too aware of his past track record with Oxford United and Derby County. Venables was the fans' choice and when he teamed up with Amstrad electronics magnate Alan Sugar, a deal at last materialised. The partnership was described as 'The Dream Ticket', the East End boy who had risen to the top of football and the East End boy who had made it to the top in business. Sugar became chairman, his brief to sort out the money problems, Venables, chief executive, with responsibility for the day to day running of the company.

Venables new position would not allow enough time to handle team affairs so Peter Shreeve returned as first-team coach on a one year contract. Shreeve faced an almost impossible job. He knew that even if Gascoigne was ever fit

Paul Gascoigne enjoyed a short, controversial but distinguished career with Spurs and his move to Lazio in Italy for a record £5.5 million was essential to enable manager Terry Venables to build a new team.

Spurs' new strike partnership celebrate Gordon Durie's opener away to Forest in August 1991 and went on to win 3-1.

enough to play his presence would only be short–lived before his move to Lazio and the money problems could not be sorted out overnight so there would be little available to strengthen the team. Enough was found to fund the transfer of Gordon Durie from Chelsea but early season promise soon disappeared.

The loss of the FA Cup at the first hurdle was followed by a semi–final exit from the Littlewoods Cup and a third-round defeat by Feyenoord in the European Cup–winners' Cup. When Spurs found themselves on the fringe of the relegation fight, Shreeve discarded the passing style of football in favour of the long–ball game so alien to Tottenham supporters, but at least it ensured Spurs retained a place in the top flight for the start of the FA Premiership.

Above: Spurs' short-lived management team of Terry Venables and Peter Shreeve, pictured in the close season of 1991.

Peter Shreeve, Doug Livermore, Ray Clemence and kitman Roy Reyland at the start of the 1991-92 season. Within a year Clemence and Livermore were promoted to first-team duties and Shreeve's one year contract was just that!

Spurs on the defensive against Sparkasse Stockerau in the first round of the European Cup-winners' Cup in August 1991. Spurs won 1-0 in Vienna with a goal from Gordon Durie and repeated that scoreline in the second leg at White Hart Lane.

At the end of the season Shreeve's contract was not renewed. Sugar and Venables had done enough to turn the finances around and Venables resumed control of team matters with Doug Livermore and Ray Clemence first-team coaches.

With Gascoigne's move to Italy at last going through and Gary Lineker departing for Japan, Venables set about building a new team, signing Darren Anderton, Teddy

Gary Lineker beats Nottingham Forest's Mark Crossley from the penalty spot in the Rumbelows Cup semi-final first leg at the City Ground in February 1992. Lineker also scored in the home leg but Spurs lost 2-1.

Paul Stewart rises high above the Feyenoord defence but heads wide during the European Cup-winners' Cup quarter-final first leg in Holland in March 1992. The game ended in a 1-0 win for the Dutch club and Tottenham could not pull back that slender deficit at White Hart Lane.

Sheringham and Neil Ruddock, one of the first players he had discarded when taking over from David Pleat. Another FA Cup semi-final at Wembley was the closest Spurs got to honours, Arsenal taking revenge for their defeat two years earlier, but in the Premiership consistency remained the problem. Eighth place was a definite improvement, though, and hopes were high that good times were around the corner. Those hopes were shattered on the eve of the FA Cup Final when Venables was sacked.

It had taken Venables every penny he had, and many he borrowed, to buy control of Spurs, and he was unable to take up a rights issue. Sugar had no such problems, effectively gaining control of the club. The exact circumstances of Venables' departure remain the subject of litigation but the effect was to once more throw the club into turmoil. Again Spurs problems covered the front pages as, amid allegation and counter-allegation, Venables was at first reinstated thanks to a High Court injunction, but when that was not renewed, out in the cold.

Sugar moved quickly to appoint Ossie Ardíles as manager but even that did not go smoothly with West Bromwich Albion accusing Spurs of poaching, an offence for which they were to be fined £25,000. The former Spurs favourite showed not only great courage but also his genuine affection for the club in taking on the job. Player unrest, the continuing bitter feud between Venables and Sugar and an FA investigation into the club's affairs made it a frightening task.

A reasonable start was made but when Teddy Sheringham was injured at Old Trafford in October 1993, Ardíles was unable to replace him and results suffered. It was only victory at Oldham in the last but one match of the season that took Spurs clear of a relegation spot. Meanwhile, the club's name continued to attract attention for all the wrong reasons. Defeated in the courts, Venables sold his shares and gave up the battle to return but amid media allegations about his business dealings decided to pursue a claim for unfair dismissal.

New Spurs manager Ossie Ardíles during his side's win over Newcastle United at White Hart Lane in August 1993.

Tottenham's Darren Caskey goes flying from a challenge by Liverpool's Nigel Clough at White Hart Lane in December 1993.

A Most Memorable Season

FOR Tottenham Hotspur these were unhappy days and even the close season brought no respite. Scholar and Venables were gone but the FA charged Spurs with making illegal payments to players during their time in charge. Spurs co-operated fully with the authorities, making their job easy by providing the evidence themselves and not contesting the charges. Openness and honesty were rewarded with a £600,000 fine, a 12-point deduction for the 1994-95 season and a ban from the FA Cup. It was a vicious penalty bearing little relation to the charges. With four clubs to go down at the end of the season the loss of 12 points made Spurs certainties for the drop. Immediate relegation would have been preferable to the slow lingering death the FA seemed to prefer.

On appeal the 12-point penalty deduction was reduced to six but only at the expense of a £900,000 increase in the fine. At least Spurs had a chance of staying in the Premiership but nothing was done about the FA Cup ban. While the club paid the penalty for the misdemeanours of the previous management, the 'guilty' escaped and the 'innocent'; the fans, of course, paid the heaviest penalty with exclusion from a competition that has always been special to Spurs and their supporters.

The penalties imposed by football's governing body hurt. £1.5 million could be better used than swelling the FA's coffers depleted by England's failure to qualify for the summer's World Cup finals. Sugar's response was to make available the best part of £10 million so Ardíles could sign

White Hart Lane, home of Tottenham Hotspur for 95 years, pictured on a sunny day at the start of the 1994-95 season. Tottenham began the campaign under a cloud with points docked, an FA Cup ban and a massive fine.

Teddy Sheringham congratulates goalscorer Jürgen Klinsmann in the match against Ipswich Town in August 1994.

three World Cup stars, Romania's Ilie Dumitrescu and Gica Popescu and Germany's Jürgen Klinsmann. It was a another coup for Spurs, particularly the signing of Klinsmann, arguably the world's most complete all-round striker, and erased any doubts about Sugar's commitment to the club.

The arrival of three world-class players immediately lifted the gloom that had settled over White Hart Lane and early results seemed to justify the new found optimism – but it was not to last. Ardíles believed in playing 'the beautiful game', passing football, all-out attack, outscoring the opposition. It is an admirable philosophy and

one that certainly provides the entertainment for which fans crave but there is more to football than simply overwhelming opponents with intricate passing movements. In modern football a strong defence is essential but Ardíles concentrated on attack at the expense of defence.

Results turned against him and when bottom-of-the-First Division Notts County dumped Tottenham out of the Coca-Cola Cup he was sacked. There were 11 clubs below Spurs in the Premiership but the Coca-Cola Cup had, at that stage, provided Tottenham's only real hope of picking up a trophy and the ignominy of defeat left Sugar with little alternative. Steve Perryman,

New Tottenham Hotspur manager Gerry Francis, who took over with the club in trouble but soon improved matters on the pitch.

Gica Popescu is happy and so he should be; he has just scored against Arsenal in January 1995.

Ardíles' assistant, was given the manager's job on a caretaker basis but had control for only one game before Gerry Francis took over.

A former England captain, Francis had developed his managerial talents at Bristol Rovers and Queen's Park Rangers, smaller clubs where, with money in short supply, it was his organisational skills and tactical acumen that brought success. He had left Loftus Road after rumours that the Rangers' board was going to appoint former hero Rodney Marsh to a managerial position and Spurs had to move quickly to secure his services. At White Hart Lane he might have expected money to be available but Sugar made it clear there was no more cash in the kitty, Francis would have to make do with the players he inherited.

With a few tactical changes he did more than that. Francis appreciated the array of attacking talent Ardíles had assembled but knew that no matter how good the team might be going forward, they had to learn to defend first. David Howells, a steadying influence who had been strangely out of favour under Ardíles, was recalled in midfield. It meant sacrificing the exciting talents of Dumitrescu but every player had a job to do and if that meant foresaking their attacking instincts, so be it. With the defence tightened performances soon improved, but it was not just on the pitch that events took a turn for the better.

Sugar had pressured the FA into setting up a three-man arbitration panel of leading QCs to review the disciplinary action taken. They

Spurs began the 1994-95 season barred from the FA Cup. But common sense prevailed and at the first hurdle they defeated non-League Altrincham. Here, Darren Anderton tangles with Altrincham's Darren Heeson.

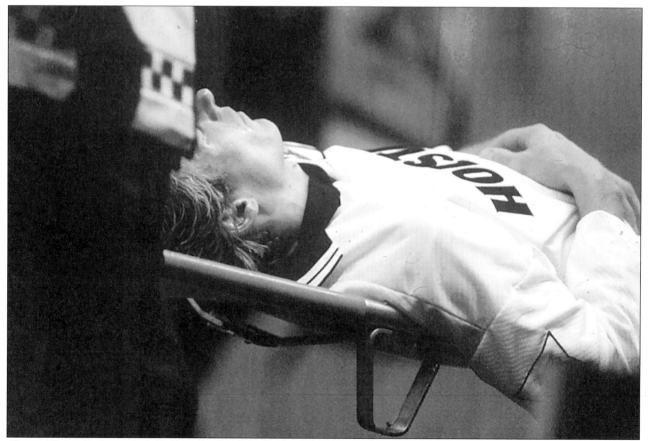

Jürgen Klinsmann is carried off after a fearful clattering involving Aston Villa goalkeeper Mark Bosnich in January 1995. Happily, Klinsmann was not badly injured.

Spurs' goalkeeper Ian Walker cannot bear to watch when Klinsmann took the spot-kick in the FA Cup semi-final .

decided that the authorities had exceeded their powers in deducting six points and banning Spurs from the FA Cup. The points deduction was cancelled and Spurs were readmitted to the Cup. Any chance of challenging for the Premiership title had evaporated before Francis' appointment but being back on level terms with their rivals gave Spurs the perfect lift as the big clubs embarked on the road to Wembley.

For a while it looked as if Spurs might go all the way on that long road. Altrincham were beaten in the third round, Sunderland in the fourth. They looked to be out when Southampton took a 2-0 lead in a fifth-round replay at The Dell before an

Jürgen Klinsmann is congratulated by Teddy Sheringham after his successful penalty against Everton in the FA Cup semi-final.

incredible hat-trick from substitute Ronny Rosenthal turned the game to set up a 6-2 success and a sixth-round clash at Anfield. Another outstanding performance was crowned by a last-minute winner from Klinsmann but in the Elland Road semi-final Spurs were never in the game as a totally committed Everton belied their lowly League position with a 4-1 victory.

The change in fortunes under Francis was apparent not only in the FA Cup but also in the League. A steady climb up the table saw a UEFA Cup spot a realistic possibility but a late surge by Leeds ended any hopes of a season that had begun so miserably for Spurs ending in a return to Europe.

Seventh place was better than many had predicted and Spurs were not only playing the type of football their fans demand, football with flair and panache, attacking and entertaining, but they now had the discipline and organisation that gives hope the future may be as successful and glorious as the past has been. Even the disappointment of Klinsmann's departure for pastures new could not deny that.

Gary Mabbutt gets above Everton's Paul Rideout in the semi-final. At the start of the season Spurs weren't even in the FA Cup. Once they had been reinstated many people felt that their name was already on the trophy. In the end they fell just short of their target.

Where Spurs Finished

1908-09
DIVISION 2

	P	W	D	L	F	A	W	D	L	F	A	Pts
Bolton W	38	14	3	2	37	8	10	1	8	22	20	52
Tottenham Hotspur	**38**	**12**	**5**	**2**	**42**	**12**	**8**	**6**	**5**	**25**	**20**	**51**
West Bromwich A	38	13	5	1	35	9	6	8	5	21	18	51
Hull C	38	14	2	3	44	15	5	4	10	19	24	44
Derby Co	38	13	5	1	38	11	3	6	10	17	30	43
Oldham Ath	38	14	4	1	39	9	3	2	14	16	34	40
Wolves	38	10	6	3	32	12	4	5	10	24	36	39
Glossop	38	11	5	3	35	17	4	3	12	22	36	38
Gainsborough T	38	12	3	4	30	20	3	5	11	19	50	38
Fulham	38	8	4	7	39	26	5	7	7	19	22	37
Birmingham	38	10	6	3	35	21	4	3	12	23	40	37
Leeds C	38	12	3	4	35	19	2	4	13	8	34	35
Grimsby T	39	9	5	5	23	14	5	2	12	18	40	35
Burnley	38	8	4	7	33	28	5	3	11	18	30	33
Clapton Orient	38	7	7	5	25	19	5	2	12	12	30	33
Bradford	38	9	2	8	30	25	4	4	11	21	34	32
Barnsley	38	11	3	5	36	19	0	7	12	12	38	32
Stockport Co	38	11	2	6	25	19	3	1	15	14	32	31
Chesterfield	38	10	3	6	30	28	1	5	13	7	39	30
Blackpool	38	9	6	4	30	22	0	5	14	16	46	29

1909-10
DIVISION 1

	P	W	D	L	F	A	W	D	L	F	A	Pts
Aston Villa	38	17	2	0	62	19	6	5	8	22	23	53
Liverpool	38	13	3	3	47	23	8	3	8	31	34	48
Blackburn R	38	13	6	0	47	17	5	3	11	26	38	45
Newcastle U	38	11	3	5	33	22	8	4	7	37	34	45
Manchester U	38	14	2	3	41	20	5	5	9	28	41	45
Sheffield U	38	10	5	4	42	19	6	5	8	20	22	42
Bradford C	38	12	3	4	38	17	5	5	9	26	30	42
Sunderland	38	12	3	4	40	18	6	2	11	26	33	41
Notts Co	38	10	5	4	41	26	5	5	9	26	33	40
Everton	38	8	6	5	30	28	8	2	9	21	28	40
Sheffield W	38	11	4	4	38	28	4	5	10	22	35	39
Preston NE	38	14	2	3	36	13	1	3	15	16	45	35
Bury	38	8	3	8	35	30	4	6	9	27	36	33
Nottingham F	38	4	7	8	19	34	7	4	8	35	38	33
Tottenham Hotspur	**38**	**10**	**6**	**3**	**35**	**23**	**1**	**4**	**14**	**18**	**46**	**32**
Bristol C	38	9	5	5	28	18	3	3	13	17	42	32
Middlesbrough	38	8	4	7	34	36	3	5	11	22	37	31
W Arsenal	38	6	5	8	17	19	5	4	10	20	48	31
Chelsea	38	10	4	5	32	24	1	3	15	15	46	29
Bolton W	38	7	2	10	31	34	2	4	13	13	37	24

1910-11
DIVISION 1

	P	W	D	L	F	A	W	D	L	F	A	Pts
Manchester U	38	14	4	1	47	18	8	4	7	25	22	52
Aston Villa	38	15	3	1	50	18	7	4	8	19	23	51
Sunderland	38	10	6	3	44	22	5	9	5	23	26	45
Everton	38	12	3	4	34	17	7	4	8	16	19	45
Bradford C	38	13	1	5	33	16	7	4	8	18	26	45
Sheffield W	38	10	5	4	24	15	7	3	9	23	33	42
Oldham Ath	38	13	4	2	30	12	3	5	11	14	29	41
Newcastle U	38	8	7	4	37	18	7	3	9	24	25	40
Sheffield U	38	8	3	8	27	21	7	5	7	22	22	38
W Arsenal	38	9	6	4	24	14	4	6	9	17	35	38
Notts Co	38	9	6	4	21	16	5	4	10	16	29	38
Blackburn R	38	12	2	5	40	14	1	9	9	22	40	37
Liverpool	38	11	3	5	38	19	4	4	11	15	34	37
Preston NE	38	8	5	6	25	19	4	6	9	15	30	35
Tottenham Hotspur	**38**	**10**	**5**	**4**	**40**	**23**	**3**	**1**	**15**	**12**	**40**	**32**
Middlesbrough	38	9	5	5	31	21	2	5	12	18	42	32
Manchester C	38	7	5	7	26	26	2	8	9	17	32	31
Bury	38	8	9	2	27	18	1	2	16	16	53	29
Bristol C	38	8	4	7	23	21	3	1	15	20	45	27
Nottingham F	38	5	4	10	28	31	4	3	12	27	44	25

1911-12
DIVISION 1

	P	W	D	L	F	A	W	D	L	F	A	Pts
Blackburn R	38	13	6	0	35	10	7	3	9	25	33	49
Everton	38	13	5	1	29	12	7	1	11	17	30	46
Newcastle U	38	10	4	5	37	25	8	4	7	27	25	44
Bolton W	38	14	2	3	35	15	6	1	12	19	28	43
Sheffield W	38	11	3	5	44	17	5	6	8	25	32	41
Aston Villa	38	12	2	5	48	22	5	5	9	28	41	41
Middlesbrough	38	11	6	2	35	17	5	2	12	21	28	40
Sunderland	38	10	6	3	37	14	4	5	10	21	37	39
West Bromwich A	38	10	6	3	23	15	5	3	11	20	32	39
W Arsenal	38	12	3	4	38	19	3	5	11	17	40	38
Bradford C	38	12	3	4	31	15	3	5	11	15	35	38
Tottenham Hotspur	**38**	**10**	**4**	**5**	**35**	**20**	**4**	**5**	**10**	**18**	**33**	**37**
Manchester U	38	9	5	5	29	19	4	6	9	16	41	37
Sheffield U	38	10	4	5	47	29	3	6	10	16	27	36
Manchester C	38	10	5	4	39	20	3	4	12	17	38	35
Notts Co	38	9	4	6	26	20	5	3	11	20	43	35
Liverpool	38	8	4	7	27	23	4	6	9	22	32	34
Oldham Ath	38	10	3	6	32	19	2	7	10	14	35	34
Preston NE	38	8	4	7	26	25	5	3	11	14	32	33
Bury	38	5	8	5	23	25	0	4	15	9	34	21

1912-13
DIVISION 1

	P	W	D	L	F	A	W	D	L	F	A	Pts
Sunderland	38	14	2	3	47	17	11	2	6	39	26	54
Aston Villa	38	13	4	2	57	21	6	8	5	29	31	50
Sheffield W	38	12	4	3	44	23	9	3	7	31	32	49
Manchester U	38	13	3	3	41	14	6	5	8	28	29	46
Blackburn R	38	10	5	4	54	21	6	8	5	25	22	45
Manchester C	38	12	3	4	34	15	6	5	8	19	22	44
Derby Co	38	10	2	7	40	29	7	6	6	29	37	42
Bolton W	28	10	6	3	36	20	6	4	9	26	43	42
Oldham Ath	38	11	7	1	33	12	3	7	9	17	43	42
West Bromwich A	38	8	7	4	30	20	5	5	9	27	30	38
Everton	38	8	2	9	28	31	7	5	7	20	23	37
Liverpool	38	12	2	5	40	24	4	3	12	21	47	37
Bradford C	38	8	4	7	33	22	2	6	11	17	38	35
Newcastle U	38	8	5	6	30	23	5	3	11	17	24	34
Sheffield U	38	10	5	4	36	24	4	1	14	20	46	34
Middlesbrough	38	6	9	4	29	22	5	1	13	26	47	32
Tottenham Hotspur	**38**	**9**	**3**	**7**	**28**	**25**	**3**	**3**	**13**	**17**	**47**	**30**
Chelsea	38	7	2	10	29	40	4	4	11	22	33	28
Notts Co	38	6	4	9	19	20	1	5	13	9	36	23
W Arsenal	38	1	8	10	11	31	2	4	13	15	43	18

1913-14
DIVISION 1

	P	W	D	L	F	A	W	D	L	F	A	Pts
Blackburn R	38	14	4	1	51	15	6	7	6	27	27	51
Aston Villa	38	11	3	5	36	21	8	3	8	29	29	44
Middlesbrough	38	14	2	3	55	20	5	3	11	22	40	43
Oldham Ath	38	11	5	3	34	16	6	4	9	21	29	43
West Bromwich A	38	11	7	1	30	16	4	6	9	16	26	43
Bolton W	38	13	4	2	31	14	3	6	10	24	38	42
Sunderland	38	11	3	5	32	17	6	3	10	31	35	40
Chelsea	38	12	3	4	28	18	4	4	11	18	37	39
Bradford C	38	8	5	6	23	17	4	8	7	17	23	38
Sheffield U	38	11	4	4	36	19	5	1	13	27	41	37
Newcastle U	38	9	6	4	27	18	4	5	10	12	30	37
Burnley	38	10	4	5	43	20	2	8	9	18	33	36
Manchester C	38	9	3	7	28	23	5	5	9	23	30	36
Manchester U	38	8	4	7	27	23	7	2	10	25	39	36
Everton	38	8	7	4	32	18	4	4	11	14	37	35
Liverpool	38	11	4	4	27	25	6	3	10	19	37	35
Tottenham Hotspur	**38**	**9**	**6**	**4**	**30**	**19**	**3**	**4**	**12**	**20**	**43**	**34**
Sheffield W	38	8	4	7	34	34	5	4	10	19	36	34
Preston NE	38	9	4	6	39	31	3	2	14	13	38	30
Derby Co	38	6	5	8	34	32	2	6	11	21	39	27

1914-15
DIVISION 1

	P	W	D	L	F	A	W	D	L	F	A	Pts
Everton	38	8	5	6	44	29	11	3	5	32	18	46
Oldham Ath	38	11	5	3	46	25	6	6	7	24	31	45
Blackburn R	38	11	4	4	51	27	7	3	9	32	34	43
Burnley	38	12	1	6	38	18	6	6	7	23	29	43
Manchester C	38	9	7	3	29	15	6	6	7	20	24	43
Sheffield U	38	11	5	3	28	13	4	8	7	21	28	43
Sheffield W	38	10	7	2	43	23	5	6	8	18	31	43
Sunderland	38	11	3	5	46	30	7	2	10	35	42	41
Bradford	38	11	4	4	40	20	6	3	10	29	45	41
West Bromwich A	38	11	5	3	31	9	4	5	10	18	34	40
Bradford C	38	11	7	1	40	18	2	7	10	15	31	40
Middlesbrough	38	10	6	3	42	24	3	6	10	20	50	38
Liverpool	38	11	5	3	45	34	3	4	12	20	41	37
Aston Villa	38	10	5	4	39	32	3	6	10	23	40	37
Newcastle U	38	8	4	7	29	23	3	6	10	17	25	32
Notts C	38	8	7	4	28	18	1	6	12	13	39	31
Bolton W	38	8	5	6	35	27	3	3	13	33	57	30
Manchester U	38	8	6	5	27	19	1	6	12	19	43	30
Chelsea	38	8	6	5	32	25	0	7	12	19	40	29
Tottenham Hotspur	**38**	**7**	**7**	**5**	**30**	**29**	**1**	**5**	**13**	**27**	**61**	**28**

1919-20
DIVISION 2

	P	W	D	L	F	A	W	D	L	F	A	Pts
Tottenham Hotspur	**42**	**19**	**2**	**0**	**60**	**11**	**13**	**4**	**4**	**42**	**21**	**70**
Huddersfield T	42	16	4	1	58	13	12	4	5	39	25	64
Birmingham	42	14	3	4	54	16	10	5	6	31	18	56
Blackpool	42	13	4	4	40	18	8	6	7	25	29	52
Bury	42	14	4	3	35	15	6	4	11	25	29	48
Fulham	42	11	6	4	36	18	8	3	10	25	32	47
West Ham U	42	14	3	4	34	14	5	6	10	13	26	47
Bristol C	42	9	9	3	30	18	4	8	9	16	25	43
South Shields	42	13	5	3	47	18	2	7	12	11	30	42
Stoke	42	13	3	5	37	15	5	3	13	23	39	42
Hull C	42	13	4	4	53	23	5	2	14	25	49	42
Barnsley	42	9	5	7	41	28	6	5	10	20	27	40
Port Vale*	42	11	3	7	35	27	5	5	11	24	35	40
Leicester C	42	8	6	7	26	29	7	4	10	15	32	40
Clapton Orient	42	14	3	4	34	17	2	3	16	17	42	38
Stockport Co	42	11	4	6	34	24	3	5	13	18	37	37
Rotherham Co	42	10	4	7	32	27	3	4	14	19	56	34
Nottingham F	42	9	4	8	23	22	2	5	14	20	51	31
Wolves	42	8	4	9	41	32	2	6	13	14	48	30
Coventry C	42	7	7	7	20	26	2	4	15	15	47	29
Lincoln C	42	8	6	7	27	30	1	3	17	17	71	27
Grimsby T	42	8	4	9	23	24	2	1	18	11	51	25

*Port Vale replaced Leeds C

1920-21
DIVISION 1

	P	W	D	L	F	A	W	D	L	F	A	Pts
Burnley	42	17	3	1	56	16	6	10	5	23	20	59
Manchester C	42	19	2	0	50	13	5	4	12	20	37	54
Bolton W	42	15	6	0	53	17	4	8	9	24	36	52
Liverpool	42	11	7	3	41	17	7	8	6	22	18	51
Newcastle U	42	14	3	4	43	18	6	7	8	23	27	50
Tottenham Hotspur	**42**	**15**	**2**	**4**	**46**	**16**	**4**	**7**	**10**	**24**	**32**	**47**
Everton	42	9	8	4	40	26	8	5	8	26	29	47
Middlesbrough	42	10	6	5	29	21	7	6	8	24	32	46
Arsenal	42	9	8	4	31	25	6	6	9	28	38	44
Aston Villa	42	11	4	6	39	21	7	3	11	24	49	43
Blackburn R	42	7	9	5	36	27	6	6	9	21	32	41
Sunderland	42	11	4	6	34	19	3	9	9	23	41	41
Manchester U	42	9	4	8	34	23	6	6	9	30	42	40
West Bromwich A	42	8	7	6	31	23	5	7	9	23	35	40
Bradford C	42	7	9	5	38	28	5	6	10	23	35	39
Preston NE	42	10	4	7	38	25	5	5	11	23	40	39
Huddersfield T	42	11	4	6	26	16	4	5	12	16	33	39
Chelsea	42	9	7	5	35	24	4	6	11	13	34	39
Oldham Ath	42	6	9	6	23	26	3	6	12	26	60	33
Sheffield U	42	5	11	5	22	19	1	7	13	20	49	30
Derby Co	42	3	12	6	21	23	2	4	15	11	35	26
Bradford	42	6	5	10	29	35	2	3	16	14	41	24

1921-22
DIVISION 1

	P	W	D	L	F	A	W	D	L	F	A	Pts
Liverpool	42	15	4	2	43	15	7	9	5	20	21	57
Tottenham Hotspur	**42**	**15**	**3**	**3**	**43**	**17**	**6**	**6**	**9**	**22**	**22**	**51**
Burnley	42	16	3	2	49	18	6	2	13	23	36	49
Cardiff C	42	13	2	6	40	26	6	8	7	21	27	48
Aston Villa	42	16	3	2	50	19	6	0	15	24	36	47
Bolton W	42	12	4	5	40	24	8	3	10	28	35	47
Newcastle U	42	11	5	5	36	19	7	5	9	23	26	46
Middlesbrough	42	12	6	3	46	19	4	8	9	33	50	46
Chelsea	42	9	6	6	17	16	8	6	7	23	27	46
Manchester C	42	13	7	1	44	21	5	2	14	21	49	45
Sheffield U	42	11	3	7	32	17	4	7	10	27	37	40
Sunderland	42	13	4	4	46	23	3	4	14	14	39	40
West Bromwich A	42	8	6	7	26	23	7	4	10	25	40	40
Huddersfield T	42	12	3	6	33	14	3	6	12	20	40	39
Blackburn R	42	7	6	8	35	31	6	6	9	19	26	38
Preston NE	42	12	7	2	33	20	1	5	15	9	45	38
Arsenal	42	10	6	5	27	19	5	1	15	20	37	37
Birmingham	42	9	2	10	25	29	6	5	10	23	31	37
Oldham Ath	42	8	7	6	21	15	5	4	12	17	35	37
Everton	42	10	7	4	42	22	2	5	14	15	33	36
Bradford C	42	8	5	8	28	30	3	5	13	20	42	32
Manchester U	42	7	7	7	25	26	1	5	15	16	47	28

1922-23
DIVISION 1

	P	W	D	L	F	A	W	D	L	F	A	Pts
Liverpool	42	17	3	1	50	13	9	5	7	20	18	60
Sunderland	42	15	5	1	50	25	7	5	9	22	29	54
Huddersfield	42	14	2	5	35	15	7	9	5	25	17	53
Newcastle U	42	13	6	2	31	11	5	6	10	14	26	48
Everton	42	14	4	3	41	20	6	3	12	22	39	47
Aston Villa	42	15	3	3	42	11	3	7	11	22	40	46
West Bromwich A	42	12	7	2	38	10	5	4	12	20	39	45
Manchester C	42	14	6	1	38	16	3	5	13	12	33	45
Cardiff C	42	15	2	4	51	18	3	5	13	22	41	43
Sheffield U	42	11	7	3	41	20	5	3	13	27	44	42
Arsenal	42	13	4	4	38	16	3	6	12	23	46	42
Tottenham Hotspur	**42**	**11**	**3**	**7**	**34**	**22**	**6**	**4**	**11**	**16**	**28**	**41**
Bolton W	42	11	8	2	36	17	3	4	14	14	41	40
Blackburn R	42	12	7	2	32	19	2	5	14	15	43	40
Burnley	42	12	3	6	39	24	4	3	14	19	35	38
Preston NE	42	12	3	6	41	26	1	8	12	19	38	37
Birmingham	42	10	4	7	25	19	3	7	11	16	38	37
Middlesbrough	42	11	4	6	41	25	2	6	13	16	38	36
Chelsea	42	5	13	3	29	20	4	5	12	16	33	36
Nottingham F	42	12	2	7	25	23	1	6	14	16	47	34
Stoke	42	7	9	5	28	19	3	1	17	19	48	30
Oldham Ath	42	9	6	6	21	20	1	4	16	14	45	30

1923-24
DIVISION 1

	P	W	D	L	F	A	W	D	L	F	A	Pts
Huddersfield T	42	15	5	1	35	9	8	6	7	25	24	57
Cardiff C	42	14	5	2	35	13	8	6	7	26	21	57
Sunderland	42	12	7	2	38	20	10	2	9	33	34	53
Bolton W	42	13	6	2	45	13	5	8	8	23	21	50
Sheffield U	42	12	5	4	39	16	7	7	7	30	33	50
Aston Villa	42	10	10	1	33	11	8	3	10	19	35	49
Everton	42	13	7	1	43	18	5	6	10	19	35	49
Blackburn R	42	14	5	2	40	13	3	6	12	14	37	45
Newcastle U	42	13	5	3	40	21	4	5	12	20	33	44
Notts Co	42	9	7	5	21	15	5	7	9	23	34	42
Manchester C	42	11	7	3	34	24	4	5	12	20	47	42
Liverpool	42	11	5	5	35	20	4	6	11	14	28	41
West Ham U	42	10	6	5	26	17	3	9	9	14	26	41
Birmingham	42	10	4	7	25	19	3	9	9	16	30	39
Tottenham Hotspur	**42**	**9**	**6**	**6**	**30**	**22**	**3**	**8**	**10**	**20**	**34**	**38**
West Bromwich A	42	10	6	5	43	30	2	8	11	8	32	38
Burnley	42	10	5	6	39	27	2	7	12	16	33	36
Preston NE	42	8	4	9	34	27	4	6	11	18	40	34
Arsenal	42	8	5	8	25	24	4	4	13	15	39	33
Nottingham F	42	7	9	5	19	15	3	3	15	23	49	32
Chelsea	42	7	9	5	23	21	2	5	14	8	32	32
Middlesbrough	42	6	4	11	23	23	1	4	16	14	37	22

1924-25
DIVISION 1

	P	W	D	L	F	A	W	D	L	F	A	Pts
Huddersfield T	42	10	8	3	31	10	11	8	2	38	18	58
West Bromwich A	42	13	6	2	40	17	10	4	7	18	17	56
Bolton W	42	18	2	1	61	13	4	9	8	15	21	55
Liverpool	42	13	5	3	43	20	7	5	9	20	35	50
Bury	42	13	4	4	35	20	4	11	6	19	31	49
Newcastle U	42	11	6	4	43	18	5	10	6	18	24	48
Sunderland	42	13	6	2	39	14	6	4	11	25	37	48
Birmingham	42	10	8	3	27	17	7	4	10	22	36	46
Notts Co	42	11	6	4	29	12	5	7	9	13	19	45
Manchester C	42	11	7	3	44	29	6	2	13	32	39	43
Cardiff C	42	11	5	5	35	19	5	6	10	21	32	43
Tottenham Hotspur	**42**	**9**	**8**	**4**	**32**	**16**	**6**	**4**	**11**	**20**	**27**	**42**
West Ham U	42	12	7	2	37	12	3	5	13	25	48	42
Sheffield U	42	10	5	6	34	25	3	8	10	21	38	39
Aston Villa	42	10	7	4	34	25	3	6	12	24	46	39
Blackburn R	42	7	6	8	31	26	4	7	10	22	40	35
Everton	42	11	4	6	25	20	1	7	13	15	40	35
Leeds U	42	9	8	4	29	17	2	4	15	17	42	34
Burnley	42	7	8	6	28	31	4	4	13	18	44	34
Arsenal	42	12	3	6	33	17	2	2	17	13	41	33
Preston NE	42	8	2	11	29	35	2	4	15	8	39	26
Nottingham F	42	5	6	10	17	23	1	6	14	12	42	24

1925-26
DIVISION 1

	P	W	D	L	F	A	W	D	L	F	A	Pts
Huddersfield T	42	14	6	1	50	17	9	5	7	42	43	57
Arsenal	42	16	2	3	57	19	6	6	9	30	44	52
Sunderland	42	17	2	2	67	30	4	4	13	29	50	48
Bury	42	12	4	5	55	34	8	3	10	30	43	47
Sheffield U	42	15	3	3	72	29	4	5	12	30	53	46
Aston Villa	42	12	7	2	56	25	4	5	12	30	51	44
Liverpool	42	9	8	4	43	27	5	8	8	27	36	44
Bolton W	42	11	6	4	46	31	6	4	11	29	45	44
Manchester U	42	12	4	5	40	26	7	2	12	26	47	44
Newcastle U	42	13	3	5	59	33	3	7	11	25	42	42
Everton	42	9	9	3	42	26	3	9	9	30	44	42
Blackburn R	42	11	6	4	59	33	4	5	12	32	47	41
West Bromwich A	42	13	5	3	59	29	3	3	15	20	49	40
Birmingham	42	14	2	5	35	25	2	6	13	31	56	40
Tottenham Hotspur	**42**	**11**	**4**	**6**	**45**	**36**	**4**	**5**	**12**	**21**	**43**	**39**
Cardiff C	42	8	5	8	30	25	8	2	11	31	51	39
Leicester C	42	11	3	7	42	32	3	7	11	28	48	38
West Ham U	42	14	2	5	45	27	1	5	15	18	49	37
Leeds U	42	11	5	5	38	28	3	1	15	26	48	36
Burnley	42	7	7	7	43	35	6	3	12	42	73	36
Manchester C	42	8	7	6	48	42	4	4	13	41	58	35
Notts Co	42	11	4	6	37	26	2	3	16	17	48	33

1926-27
DIVISION 1

	P	W	D	L	F	A	W	D	L	F	A	Pts
Newcastle U	42	19	1	1	64	20	6	5	10	32	38	56
Huddersfield T	42	13	6	2	41	19	4	11	6	35	41	51
Sunderland	42	15	3	3	70	28	6	4	11	28	42	49
Bolton W	42	15	5	1	54	19	4	5	12	30	43	48
Burnley	42	15	2	4	55	30	4	5	12	36	50	47
West Ham U	42	9	6	6	50	36	10	2	9	36	34	46
Leicester C	42	13	4	4	58	33	4	8	9	27	37	46
Sheffield U	42	12	6	3	46	33	5	4	12	28	53	44
Liverpool	42	13	4	4	47	27	5	3	13	22	34	43
Aston Villa	42	11	4	6	51	34	7	3	11	30	49	43
Arsenal	42	12	5	4	47	30	5	4	12	30	56	43
Derby Co	42	14	4	3	60	28	3	3	15	26	45	41
Tottenham Hotspur	**42**	**11**	**4**	**6**	**48**	**33**	**5**	**5**	**11**	**28**	**45**	**41**
Cardiff C	42	12	3	6	31	17	4	6	11	24	48	41
Manchester U	42	8	4	9	29	19	4	6	11	23	45	40
Sheffield W	42	15	3	3	49	29	0	6	15	26	63	39
Birmingham	42	13	3	5	36	17	4	1	16	28	56	38
Blackburn R	42	9	5	7	40	40	6	3	12	37	56	38
Bury	42	8	5	8	43	38	4	7	10	25	39	36
Everton	42	10	6	5	35	30	2	4	15	29	60	34
Leeds U	42	9	7	5	43	31	2	1	18	26	57	30
West Bromwich A	42	10	4	7	47	33	1	4	16	18	53	30

1927-28
DIVISION 1

	P	W	D	L	F	A	W	D	L	F	A	Pts
Everton	42	11	8	2	60	28	9	5	7	42	38	53
Huddersfield T	42	15	1	5	57	31	7	6	8	34	37	51
Leicester C	42	14	5	2	66	25	4	7	10	30	47	48
Derby Co	42	12	4	5	59	30	5	6	10	37	53	44
Bury	42	13	1	7	53	35	7	3	11	27	45	44
Cardiff C	42	12	7	2	44	27	5	3	13	26	53	44
Bolton W	42	12	5	4	47	26	4	6	11	34	40	43
Aston Villa	42	13	3	5	52	30	4	6	11	26	43	43
Newcastle U	42	9	7	5	49	41	6	6	9	30	40	43
Arsenal	42	10	6	5	49	33	3	9	9	33	53	41
Birmingham	42	10	7	4	36	25	3	8	10	34	50	41
Blackburn R	42	13	5	3	41	22	3	4	14	25	56	41
Sheffield U	42	12	4	5	56	42	3	6	12	23	44	40
Sheffield W	42	9	6	6	45	29	4	7	10	36	49	39
Sunderland	42	9	5	7	37	29	6	4	11	37	47	39
Liverpool	42	10	6	5	54	36	3	7	11	30	51	39
West Ham U	42	9	7	5	48	34	5	4	12	33	54	39
Manchester U	42	12	6	3	51	27	4	1	16	21	53	39
Burnley	42	12	5	4	55	31	4	2	15	27	67	39
Portsmouth	42	13	4	4	40	23	3	3	15	26	67	39
Tottenham Hotspur	**42**	**12**	**3**	**6**	**47**	**34**	**3**	**5**	**13**	**27**	**52**	**38**
Middlesbrough	42	7	9	5	46	35	4	6	11	35	53	37

1928-29
DIVISION 2

	P	W	D	L	F	A	W	D	L	F	A	Pts
Middlesbrough	42	14	4	3	54	22	8	7	6	38	35	55
Grimsby T	42	16	2	3	49	24	8	3	10	33	37	53
Bradford	42	18	2	1	62	22	4	2	15	26	48	48
Southampton	42	12	6	3	48	22	5	8	8	26	38	48
Notts Co	42	13	4	4	51	24	6	5	10	27	41	47
Stoke C	42	12	7	2	46	16	5	5	11	28	35	46
West Bromwich A	42	13	4	4	50	25	6	4	11	30	54	46
Blackpool	42	13	4	4	49	18	6	3	12	43	58	45
Chelsea	42	10	6	5	40	30	7	4	10	24	35	44
Tottenham Hotspur	**42**	**16**	**3**	**2**	**50**	**26**	**1**	**6**	**14**	**25**	**55**	**43**
Nottingham F	42	8	6	7	34	33	7	6	8	37	37	42
Hull C	42	8	8	5	38	24	5	6	10	20	39	40
Preston NE	42	12	6	3	58	27	3	3	15	20	52	39
Millwall	42	10	4	7	43	35	6	3	12	28	51	39
Reading	42	12	3	6	48	30	3	6	12	15	56	39
Barnsley	42	12	4	5	51	28	4	2	15	18	38	38
Wolves	42	9	6	6	41	31	6	1	14	36	50	37
Oldham Ath	42	15	2	4	37	24	1	3	17	17	51	37
Swansea T	42	12	3	6	46	26	1	7	13	16	49	36
Bristol C	42	11	6	4	37	25	2	4	15	21	47	36
Port Vale	42	14	1	6	53	25	1	3	17	18	61	34
Clapton Orient	42	10	4	7	29	25	2	4	15	16	47	32

1929-30
DIVISION 2

	P	W	D	L	F	A	W	D	L	F	A	Pts
Blackpool	42	17	1	3	63	22	10	3	8	35	45	58
Chelsea	42	17	3	1	49	14	5	8	8	25	32	55
Oldham Ath	42	14	5	2	60	21	7	6	8	30	30	53
Bradford	42	14	5	2	65	28	5	7	9	26	42	50
Bury	42	14	2	5	45	27	8	3	10	33	40	49
West Bromwich A	42	16	1	4	73	31	5	4	12	32	42	47
Southampton	42	14	6	1	46	22	3	5	13	31	54	45
Cardiff C	42	14	4	3	41	16	4	4	13	20	43	44
Wolves	42	14	3	4	53	24	2	6	13	24	55	41
Nottingham F	42	9	6	6	36	28	4	9	8	19	41	41
Stoke C	42	12	4	5	41	20	4	4	13	33	52	40
Tottenham Hotspur	**42**	**11**	**8**	**2**	**43**	**24**	**4**	**1**	**16**	**16**	**37**	**39**
Charlton Ath	42	10	6	5	39	23	4	5	12	20	40	39
Millwall	42	10	7	4	36	26	2	8	11	21	47	39
Swansea T	42	11	5	5	42	23	3	4	14	15	38	37
Preston NE	42	7	7	7	42	36	6	4	11	23	44	37
Barnsley	42	12	7	2	39	22	2	1	18	17	49	36
Bradford C	42	7	7	7	33	30	5	5	11	27	47	36
Reading	42	10	7	4	31	20	2	4	15	23	47	35
Bristol C	42	11	4	6	36	30	2	5	14	25	53	35
Hull C	42	11	3	7	30	24	3	4	14	21	54	35
Notts Co	42	8	7	6	33	26	1	8	12	21	44	33

High jinks following a corner at White Hart Lane in September 1929, when Tottenham drew 2-2 with Bury and went on to finish the season 12th in Division Two under new manager Percy Smith.

1930-31
DIVISION 2

	P	W	D	L	F	A	W	D	L	F	A	Pts
Everton	42	18	1	2	76	31	10	4	7	45	35	61
West Bromwich A	42	14	3	4	40	16	8	7	6	43	33	54
Tottenham Hotspur	**42**	**15**	**5**	**1**	**64**	**20**	**7**	**2**	**12**	**24**	**35**	**51**
Wolves	42	15	2	4	56	25	6	3	12	28	42	47
Port Vale	42	15	3	3	39	16	6	2	13	28	45	47
Bradford	42	15	4	2	71	24	3	6	12	26	42	46
Preston NE	42	12	5	4	55	31	5	6	10	28	33	45
Burnley	42	13	5	3	55	30	4	6	11	26	47	45
Southampton	42	13	4	4	46	22	6	2	13	28	40	44
Bradford C	42	12	5	4	39	26	5	5	11	22	37	44
Stoke C	42	11	6	4	34	17	6	4	11	30	54	44
Oldham Ath	42	13	5	3	45	28	3	5	13	16	44	42
Bury	42	14	3	4	44	20	5	0	16	31	62	41
Millwall	42	12	4	5	47	25	4	3	14	24	55	39
Charlton Ath	42	11	4	6	35	33	4	5	12	24	53	39
Bristol C	42	11	5	5	29	23	4	3	14	25	59	38
Nottingham F	42	12	6	3	54	35	2	3	16	26	50	37
Plymouth Ath	42	10	3	8	47	33	4	5	12	29	51	36
Barnsley	42	13	3	5	42	23	0	6	15	17	56	35
Swansea T	42	11	5	5	40	29	1	5	15	11	45	34
Reading	42	11	2	8	47	33	1	4	16	25	63	30
Cardiff C	42	7	6	8	32	31	1	3	17	15	56	25

1931-32
DIVISION 2

	P	W	D	L	F	A	W	D	L	F	A	Pts
Wolves	42	17	3	1	71	11	7	5	9	44	38	56
Leeds U	42	12	5	4	36	22	10	5	6	42	32	54
Stoke C	42	14	6	1	47	19	5	8	8	22	29	52
Plymouth Ath	42	14	4	3	69	29	6	5	10	31	37	49
Bury	42	13	4	4	44	21	8	3	10	26	37	49
Bradford	42	17	2	2	44	18	4	5	12	28	45	49
Bradford C	42	10	7	4	53	26	6	6	9	27	35	45
Tottenham Hotspur	**42**	**11**	**6**	**4**	**58**	**37**	**5**	**5**	**11**	**29**	**41**	**43**
Millwall	42	13	3	5	43	21	4	6	11	18	40	43
Charlton Ath	42	11	5	5	38	28	6	4	11	23	38	43
Nottingham F	42	13	4	4	49	27	3	6	12	28	45	42
Manchester U	42	12	3	6	44	31	5	5	11	27	41	42
Preston NE	42	11	6	4	37	25	5	4	12	38	52	42
Southampton	42	10	5	6	39	30	7	2	12	27	47	41
Swansea T	42	12	4	5	45	22	4	3	14	28	53	39
Notts Co	42	10	4	7	43	30	3	8	10	32	45	38
Chesterfield	42	11	3	7	43	33	2	7	11	21	53	37
Oldham Ath	42	10	4	7	41	34	3	6	12	21	50	36
Burnley	42	7	8	6	36	36	6	1	14	23	51	35
Port Vale	42	8	4	9	30	33	5	3	13	28	56	33
Barnsley	42	8	7	6	35	30	4	2	15	20	61	33
Bristol C	42	4	7	10	22	37	2	4	15	17	41	23

1932-33
DIVISION 2

	P	W	D	L	F	A	W	D	L	F	A	Pts
Stoke C	42	13	3	5	40	15	12	3	6	38	24	56
Tottenham Hotspur	**42**	**14**	**7**	**0**	**58**	**19**	**6**	**8**	**7**	**38**	**32**	**55**
Fulham	42	12	5	4	46	31	8	5	8	32	34	50
Bury	42	13	7	1	55	23	7	2	12	29	36	49
Nottingham F	42	9	8	4	37	28	8	7	6	30	31	49
Manchester U	42	11	5	5	40	24	4	8	9	31	44	43
Millwall	42	11	7	3	40	20	5	4	12	19	37	43
Bradford	42	13	4	4	51	27	4	4	13	26	44	42
Preston NE	42	12	2	7	53	36	4	8	9	21	34	42
Swansea T	42	17	0	4	36	12	2	4	15	14	42	42
Bradford C	42	10	6	5	43	24	4	7	10	22	37	41
Southampton	42	15	3	3	48	22	3	2	16	18	44	41
Grimsby T	42	8	10	3	49	34	6	3	12	30	50	41
Plymouth Ath	42	13	4	4	45	22	3	5	13	18	45	41
Notts Co	42	10	4	7	41	31	5	6	10	26	47	40
Oldham Ath	42	10	4	7	38	31	5	4	12	29	49	38
Port Vale	42	12	3	6	49	27	2	7	12	17	52	38
Lincoln C	42	11	6	4	46	28	1	7	13	26	59	37
Burnley	42	8	9	4	35	20	3	5	13	32	59	36
West Ham U	42	12	6	3	56	31	1	3	17	19	62	35
Chesterfield	42	10	5	6	36	25	2	5	14	25	59	34
Charlton Ath	42	9	3	9	35	35	3	4	14	25	56	31

1933-34
DIVISION 1

	P	W	D	L	F	A	W	D	L	F	A	Pts
Arsenal	42	15	4	2	45	19	10	5	6	30	28	59
Huddersfield T	42	16	3	2	53	19	7	7	7	37	42	56
Tottenham Hotspur	**42**	**14**	**3**	**4**	**51**	**24**	**7**	**4**	**10**	**28**	**32**	**49**
Derby Co	42	11	8	2	45	22	6	3	12	23	32	45
Manchester C	42	14	4	3	50	29	3	7	11	15	43	45
Sunderland	42	14	6	1	57	17	2	6	13	24	39	44
West Bromwich A	42	12	4	5	49	28	5	6	10	29	42	44
Blackburn R	42	16	5	0	57	21	2	2	17	17	60	43
Leeds U	42	13	5	3	52	21	4	3	14	23	45	42
Portsmouth	42	11	5	5	31	21	4	7	10	21	34	42
Sheffield W	42	9	5	7	33	24	7	4	10	29	43	41
Stoke C	42	11	5	5	33	19	4	6	11	25	52	41
Aston Villa	42	10	5	6	45	34	4	7	10	33	41	40
Everton	42	9	7	5	38	27	3	9	9	24	36	40
Wolves	42	13	4	4	50	28	1	8	12	24	58	40
Middlesbrough	42	13	3	5	51	27	3	4	14	17	53	39
Leicester C	42	10	6	5	36	26	4	5	12	23	48	39
Liverpool	42	10	6	5	52	37	4	4	13	27	50	38
Chelsea	42	12	3	6	44	24	2	5	14	23	45	36
Birmingham	42	8	6	7	29	20	4	6	11	25	36	36
Newcastle U	42	6	11	4	42	29	4	3	14	26	48	34
Sheffield U	42	11	5	5	40	25	1	2	18	18	76	31

1934-35
DIVISION 1

	P	W	D	L	F	A	W	D	L	F	A	Pts
Arsenal	42	15	4	2	74	17	8	8	5	41	29	58
Sunderland	42	13	4	4	57	24	6	12	3	33	27	54
Sheffield W	42	14	7	0	42	17	4	6	11	28	47	49
Manchester C	42	13	5	3	53	25	7	3	11	29	42	48
Grimsby T	42	13	6	2	49	25	4	5	12	29	35	45
Derby Co	42	10	4	7	44	28	8	5	8	37	38	45
Liverpool	42	13	4	4	53	26	6	3	12	32	59	45
Everton	42	14	5	2	64	32	2	7	12	25	56	44
West Bromwich A	42	10	8	3	55	33	7	2	12	28	50	44
Stoke C	42	12	5	4	46	20	6	1	14	25	50	42
Preston NE	42	11	5	5	33	22	4	7	10	29	45	42
Chelsea	42	11	5	5	49	32	5	4	12	24	50	41
Aston Villa	42	11	6	4	50	36	3	7	11	24	52	41
Portsmouth	42	10	5	6	41	24	5	5	11	30	48	40
Blackburn R	42	12	5	4	42	23	2	6	13	24	55	39
Huddersfield T	42	11	5	5	52	27	3	5	13	24	44	38
Wolves	42	13	3	5	65	38	2	5	14	23	56	38
Leeds U	42	10	6	5	48	35	3	6	12	27	57	38
Birmingham	42	10	3	8	36	36	3	7	11	27	45	36
Middlesbrough	42	8	9	4	38	29	2	5	14	32	61	34
Leicester C	42	9	4	8	39	30	3	5	13	22	56	33
Tottenham Hotspur	**42**	**8**	**8**	**5**	**34**	**31**	**2**	**2**	**17**	**20**	**62**	**30**

1935-36
DIVISION 2

	P	W	D	L	F	A	W	D	L	F	A	Pts
Manchester U	42	16	3	2	55	16	6	9	6	30	27	56
Charlton Ath	42	15	6	0	53	17	7	5	9	32	41	55
Sheffield U	42	15	4	2	51	15	5	8	8	28	35	52
West Ham U	42	15	3	3	51	23	9	3	9	39	45	52
Tottenham Hotspur	**42**	**12**	**6**	**3**	**60**	**25**	**6**	**7**	**8**	**31**	**30**	**49**
Leicester C	42	14	5	2	53	19	5	5	11	26	38	48
Plymouth	42	15	2	4	50	20	5	6	10	21	37	48
Newcastle U	42	13	5	3	56	27	7	1	13	32	52	46
Fulham	42	11	6	4	58	24	4	8	9	18	28	44
Blackpool	42	14	3	4	64	34	4	4	13	29	38	43
Norwich C	42	14	2	5	47	24	3	7	11	25	41	43
Bradford C	42	12	7	2	32	18	3	6	12	23	47	43
Swansea T	42	11	3	7	42	26	4	6	11	25	50	39
Bury	42	10	6	5	41	27	3	6	12	25	57	38
Burnley	42	9	8	4	35	21	3	6	12	15	43	38
Bradford	42	13	6	2	43	26	1	3	17	19	58	37
Southampton	42	11	4	7	32	24	3	6	12	15	41	37
Doncaster R	42	10	7	4	28	17	4	2	15	23	54	37
Nottingham F	42	8	8	5	43	22	4	3	14	26	54	35
Barnsley	42	9	8	4	40	32	3	5	13	14	48	33
Port Vale	42	10	5	6	34	39	2	3	16	22	76	32
Hull C	42	4	7	10	33	45	1	3	17	14	66	20

1936-37
DIVISION 2

	P	W	D	L	F	A	W	D	L	F	A	Pts
Leicester C	42	14	4	3	56	26	10	4	7	33	31	56
Blackpool	42	13	4	4	49	19	11	3	7	39	34	55
Bury	42	13	4	4	46	26	9	4	8	28	29	52
Newcastle U	42	11	3	7	45	23	11	2	8	35	33	49
Plymouth Ath	42	11	6	4	42	22	7	7	7	29	31	49
West Ham U	42	14	5	2	47	18	5	6	10	26	37	49
Sheffield U	42	16	4	1	48	14	2	6	13	18	40	46
Coventry C	42	11	5	5	35	19	6	6	9	31	35	45
Aston Villa	42	10	6	5	47	30	6	6	9	35	40	44
Tottenham Hotspur	**42**	**13**	**3**	**5**	**57**	**26**	**4**	**6**	**11**	**31**	**40**	**43**
Fulham	42	11	5	5	43	24	4	8	9	28	37	43
Blackburn R	42	11	3	7	49	32	5	7	9	21	30	42
Burnley	42	11	5	5	37	20	5	5	11	20	41	42
Barnsley	42	11	6	4	30	23	5	3	13	20	41	41
Chesterfield	42	12	3	6	54	34	4	5	12	30	55	40
Swansea T	42	14	2	5	40	16	1	5	15	10	49	37
Norwich C	42	8	6	7	38	29	6	2	13	25	42	36
Nottingham F	42	10	6	5	42	30	2	4	15	26	60	34
Southampton	42	10	8	3	38	25	1	4	16	15	52	34
Bradford	42	10	4	7	33	33	2	5	14	19	55	33
Bradford C	42	8	8	5	36	31	1	4	16	18	63	30
Doncaster R	42	6	6	9	18	29	1	4	16	12	55	24

1937-38
DIVISION 2

	P	W	D	L	F	A	W	D	L	F	A	Pts
Aston Villa	42	17	2	2	50	12	8	5	8	23	23	57
Manchester U	42	15	3	3	50	18	7	6	8	32	32	53
Sheffield U	42	15	4	2	46	19	7	5	9	27	37	53
Coventry C	42	12	5	4	31	15	8	7	6	35	30	52
Tottenham Hotspur	**42**	**14**	**3**	**4**	**46**	**16**	**5**	**3**	**13**	**30**	**38**	**44**
Burnley	42	15	4	2	35	11	2	6	13	19	43	44
Bradford	42	13	4	4	51	22	4	5	12	18	34	43
Fulham	42	10	7	4	44	23	6	4	11	17	34	43
West Ham U	42	13	5	3	34	16	1	9	11	19	36	42
Bury	42	12	3	6	43	26	6	2	13	20	34	41
Chesterfield	42	12	2	7	39	24	4	7	10	24	39	41
Luton T	42	10	6	5	53	36	5	4	12	36	50	40
Plymouth Ath	42	10	7	4	40	30	4	5	12	17	35	40
Norwich C	42	11	5	5	35	28	3	6	12	21	47	39
Southampton	42	12	6	3	42	26	3	3	15	13	51	39
Blackburn R	42	13	6	2	51	30	1	4	16	20	50	38
Sheffield W	42	10	5	6	27	21	4	5	12	22	35	38
Swansea T	42	12	6	3	31	21	1	6	14	14	52	38
Newcastle U	42	12	4	5	38	18	2	4	15	13	40	36
Nottingham F	42	12	3	6	29	21	2	5	14	18	39	36
Barnsley	42	7	11	3	30	20	4	3	14	20	44	36
Stockport Co	42	8	6	7	24	24	3	3	15	19	46	31

1938-39
DIVISION 2

	P	W	D	L	F	A	W	D	L	F	A	Pts
Blackburn R	42	17	1	3	59	23	8	4	9	35	37	55
Sheffield U	42	9	9	3	35	15	11	5	5	34	26	54
Sheffield W	42	14	4	3	47	18	7	7	7	41	41	53
Coventry C	42	13	4	4	35	13	8	4	9	27	32	50
Manchester C	42	13	3	5	56	35	8	4	9	40	37	49
Chesterfield	42	16	1	4	54	20	4	8	9	15	32	49
Luton T	42	13	4	4	47	27	9	1	11	35	39	49
Tottenham Hotspur	**42**	**13**	**6**	**2**	**48**	**27**	**6**	**3**	**12**	**19**	**35**	**47**
Newcastle U	42	13	3	5	44	21	5	7	9	17	27	46
West Bromwich A	42	15	3	3	54	22	3	6	12	35	50	45
West Ham U	42	10	5	6	36	21	7	5	9	34	31	44
Fulham	42	12	5	4	35	20	5	5	11	26	35	44
Millwall	42	12	6	3	44	18	2	8	11	20	35	42
Burnley	42	13	5	3	32	20	2	6	13	18	36	39
Plymouth Ath	42	9	7	5	24	13	6	1	14	25	42	38
Bury	42	9	5	7	48	36	3	8	10	17	38	37
Bradford	42	8	6	7	33	35	4	5	12	28	47	35
Southampton	42	9	6	6	35	34	4	3	14	21	48	35
Swansea T	42	8	6	7	33	30	3	6	12	17	53	34
Nottingham F	42	8	6	7	33	29	2	5	14	16	53	31
Norwich C	42	10	5	6	39	29	3	0	18	11	62	31
Tranmere R	42	6	4	11	26	38	0	1	20	13	61	17

1939-40
DIVISION 2

	P	W	D	L	F	A	W	D	L	F	A	Pts
Luton T	3	1	0	0	3	0	1	1	0	4	1	5
Birmingham	3	2	0	0	4	0	0	1	0	1	1	5
Coventry C	3	1	1	0	7	5	0	1	0	1	1	4
Plymouth Ath	3	0	0	1	1	3	2	0	0	3	0	4
West Ham U	3	1	0	1	2	3	1	0	0	3	1	4
Leicester C	3	1	0	0	4	3	1	0	1	2	2	4
Tottenham Hotspur	**3**	**0**	**1**	**0**	**1**	**1**	**1**	**1**	**0**	**5**	**4**	**4**
Nottingham F	3	2	0	0	4	1	0	0	1	1	4	4
Millwall	3	1	0	1	3	2	0	1	0	2	2	3
Newport Co	3	1	1	0	4	2	0	0	1	1	2	3
Manchester C	3	1	1	0	3	1	0	0	1	3	4	3
West Bromwich A	3	0	0	1	3	4	1	1	0	5	4	3
Bury	3	1	0	0	3	1	0	1	1	1	4	3
Newcastle U	3	1	0	0	8	1	0	0	2	0	5	2
Chesterfield	2	1	0	0	2	0	0	0	1	0	2	2
Barnsley	3	1	0	0	4	1	0	0	2	3	7	2
Southampton	3	1	0	1	4	3	0	0	1	1	3	2
Sheffield W	3	1	0	1	3	2	0	0	1	0	3	2
Swansea T	3	0	0	1	1	2	1	0	1	4	9	2
Fulham	3	0	1	0	1	1	0	0	2	2	5	1
Burnley	2	0	1	0	1	1	0	0	1	0	2	1
Bradford	3	0	1	1	2	5	0	0	1	0	2	1

1946-47
DIVISION 2

	P	W	D	L	F	A	W	D	L	F	A	Pts
Manchester C	42	17	3	1	49	14	9	7	5	29	21	62
Burnley	42	11	8	2	30	14	11	6	4	35	15	58
Birmingham C	42	17	2	2	51	11	8	3	10	23	22	55
Chesterfield	42	12	6	3	37	17	6	8	7	21	27	50
Newcastle U	42	11	4	6	60	32	8	6	7	35	30	48
Tottenham Hotspur	**42**	**11**	**8**	**2**	**35**	**21**	**6**	**6**	**9**	**30**	**32**	**48**
West Bromwich A	42	12	4	5	53	37	8	4	9	35	38	48
Coventry C	42	12	8	1	40	17	4	5	12	26	42	45
Leicester C	42	11	4	6	42	25	7	3	11	27	39	43
Barnsley	42	13	2	6	48	29	4	6	11	36	57	42
Nottingham F	42	13	5	3	47	20	2	5	14	22	54	40
West Ham U	42	12	4	5	46	31	4	4	13	24	45	40
Luton T	42	13	4	4	50	29	3	3	15	21	44	39
Southampton	42	11	5	5	45	24	4	4	13	24	52	39
Fulham	42	12	4	5	40	25	3	5	13	23	49	39
Bradford	42	7	6	8	29	28	7	5	9	36	49	39
Bury	42	11	6	4	62	34	1	6	14	18	44	36
Millwall	42	7	7	7	30	30	7	1	13	26	49	36
Plymouth Ath	42	11	3	7	45	34	3	2	16	34	62	33
Sheffield W	42	10	5	6	39	28	2	3	16	28	60	32
Swansea T	42	9	1	11	36	40	2	6	13	19	43	29
Newport C	42	9	1	11	41	52	1	2	18	20	81	23

1947-48
DIVISION 2

	P	W	D	L	F	A	W	D	L	F	A	Pts
Birmingham C	42	12	7	2	34	13	10	8	3	21	11	59
Newcastle U	42	18	1	2	46	13	6	7	8	26	28	56
Southampton	42	15	3	3	53	23	6	7	8	18	30	52
Sheffield W	42	13	6	2	39	21	7	5	9	27	32	51
Cardiff C	42	12	6	3	36	8	6	5	10	25	40	47
West Ham U	42	10	7	4	29	19	6	7	8	26	34	46
West Bromwich A	42	11	4	6	37	29	7	5	9	26	29	45
Tottenham Hotspur	**42**	**10**	**6**	**5**	**36**	**24**	**5**	**8**	**8**	**20**	**19**	**44**
Leicester C	42	10	5	6	36	29	6	6	9	24	29	43
Coventry C	42	10	5	6	33	16	4	8	9	26	36	41
Fulham	42	6	9	6	24	19	9	1	11	23	27	40
Barnsley	42	10	5	6	31	22	5	5	11	31	42	40
Luton T	42	8	5	8	37	25	6	4	11	25	34	40
Bradford	42	11	3	7	45	30	5	5	11	23	42	40
Brentford	42	10	6	5	31	26	3	8	10	13	35	40
Chesterfield	42	8	4	9	32	26	8	3	10	22	29	39
Plymouth Ath	42	8	9	4	27	22	1	11	9	13	36	38
Leeds U	42	12	5	4	44	20	2	3	16	18	52	36
Nottingham F	42	10	5	6	32	23	2	6	13	22	37	35
Bury	42	6	8	7	27	28	3	8	10	31	40	34
Doncaster R	42	7	8	6	23	20	2	3	16	17	46	29
Millwall	42	7	7	7	27	28	2	4	15	17	46	29

1948-49
DIVISION 2

	P	W	D	L	F	A	W	D	L	F	A	Pts
Fulham	42	16	4	1	52	14	8	5	8	25	23	57
West Bromwich A	42	16	3	2	47	16	8	5	8	22	23	56
Southampton	42	16	4	1	48	10	7	5	9	21	26	55
Cardiff C	42	14	4	3	45	21	5	9	7	17	26	51
Tottenham Hotspur	**42**	**14**	**4**	**3**	**50**	**18**	**3**	**12**	**6**	**22**	**26**	**50**
Chesterfield	42	9	7	5	24	18	6	10	5	27	27	47
West Ham U	42	13	5	3	38	23	5	5	11	18	35	46
Sheffield W	42	12	6	3	36	17	3	7	11	27	39	43
Barnsley	42	10	7	4	40	18	4	5	12	22	43	40
Luton T	42	11	6	4	32	16	3	6	12	23	41	40
Grimsby T	42	10	5	6	44	28	5	5	11	28	48	40
Bury	42	12	5	4	41	23	5	1	15	26	53	40
QPR	42	11	4	6	31	26	3	7	11	13	36	39
Blackburn R	42	12	5	4	41	23	3	3	15	12	40	38
Leeds U	42	11	6	4	36	21	1	7	13	19	42	37
Coventry C	42	12	3	6	35	20	3	4	14	20	44	37
Bradford	42	8	8	5	37	26	5	3	13	28	52	37
Brentford	42	7	10	4	8	21	4	4	13	14	32	36
Leicester C	42	6	10	5	41	38	4	6	11	21	41	36
Plymouth Ath	42	11	4	6	33	25	1	8	12	16	39	36
Nottingham F	42	9	6	6	22	14	5	1	15	28	40	35
Lincoln C	42	6	7	8	31	35	2	5	14	22	56	28

1949-50
DIVISION 2

	P	W	D	L	F	A	W	D	L	F	A	Pts
Tottenham Hotspur	**42**	**15**	**3**	**3**	**51**	**15**	**12**	**4**	**5**	**30**	**20**	**61**
Sheffield W	42	12	7	2	46	23	6	9	6	21	25	52
Sheffield U	42	9	10	2	36	19	10	4	7	32	30	52
Southampton	42	13	4	4	44	25	6	10	5	20	23	52
Leeds U	42	11	8	2	33	16	6	5	10	21	29	47
Preston NE	42	12	5	4	37	21	6	4	11	23	28	45
Hull C	42	11	8	2	39	25	6	3	12	25	47	45
Swansea T	42	11	3	7	34	18	6	6	9	19	31	43
Brentford	42	11	5	5	21	12	4	8	9	23	37	43
Cardiff C	42	13	3	5	28	14	3	7	11	13	30	42
Grimsby T	42	13	5	3	53	25	3	3	15	21	48	40
Coventry C	42	8	6	7	32	24	5	7	9	23	31	39
Barnsley	42	11	6	4	45	28	2	7	12	19	39	39
Chesterfield	42	12	3	6	28	16	3	6	12	15	31	39
Leicester C	42	8	9	3	30	25	4	6	11	25	40	39
Blackburn R	42	10	5	6	30	15	4	5	12	25	45	38
Luton T	42	8	9	4	28	22	2	9	10	13	29	38
Bury	42	10	8	3	37	19	4	1	16	23	46	37
West Ham U	42	8	7	6	30	25	4	5	12	23	36	36
QPR	42	6	5	10	21	30	5	7	9	19	27	34
Plymouth Ath	42	6	6	9	19	24	2	10	9	25	41	32
Bradford	42	7	6	8	34	34	3	5	13	17	43	31

1950-51
DIVISION 1

	P	W	D	L	F	A	W	D	L	F	A	Pts
Tottenham Hotspur	**42**	**17**	**2**	**2**	**54**	**21**	**8**	**8**	**5**	**28**	**23**	**60**
Manchester U	42	14	4	3	42	16	10	4	7	32	24	56
Blackpool	42	12	6	3	43	19	8	4	9	36	34	50
Newcastle U	42	10	6	5	36	22	8	7	6	26	31	49
Arsenal	42	11	5	5	47	28	8	4	9	26	28	47
Middlesbrough	42	12	7	2	51	25	6	4	11	25	40	47
Portsmouth	42	8	1	3	39	30	8	5	8	32	38	47
Bolton W	42	11	2	8	31	20	8	5	8	33	41	45
Liverpool	42	11	5	5	28	25	5	6	10	25	34	43
Burnley	42	9	7	5	27	16	5	7	9	21	27	42
Derby Co	42	10	5	6	53	33	6	3	12	28	42	40
Sunderland	42	8	9	4	30	21	4	7	10	33	52	40
Stoke C	42	10	5	6	28	19	3	9	9	22	40	40
Wolves	42	9	3	9	44	30	6	5	10	30	31	38
Aston Villa	42	9	6	6	39	29	3	7	11	27	39	37
West Bromwich A	42	7	4	10	30	27	6	7	8	23	34	37
Charlton Ath	42	9	4	8	35	31	5	5	11	28	49	37
Fulham	42	8	5	8	35	37	5	6	10	17	31	37
Huddersfield T	42	8	4	9	40	40	7	2	12	24	52	36
Chelsea	42	9	4	8	31	25	4	4	14	22	40	32
Sheffield W	42	9	6	6	43	32	3	2	16	21	51	32
Everton	42	7	5	9	26	35	5	3	13	22	51	32

1951-52
DIVISION 1

	P	W	D	L	F	A	W	D	L	F	A	Pts
Manchester U	42	15	3	3	55	21	8	8	5	40	31	57
Tottenham Hotspur	**42**	**16**	**1**	**4**	**45**	**20**	**6**	**8**	**7**	**31**	**31**	**53**
Arsenal	42	13	7	1	54	30	8	4	9	26	31	53
Portsmouth	42	13	3	5	42	25	7	5	9	26	33	48
Bolton W	42	11	7	3	35	26	8	3	10	30	35	48
Aston Villa	42	13	3	5	49	28	6	6	9	30	42	47
Preston NE	42	10	5	6	39	22	7	7	7	35	32	46
Newcastle U	42	12	4	5	62	28	6	5	10	36	45	45
Blackpool	42	12	5	4	40	27	6	4	11	24	37	45
Charlton Ath	42	12	5	4	41	24	5	5	11	27	39	44
Liverpool	42	6	11	4	31	25	6	8	7	26	36	43
Sunderland	42	8	6	7	41	28	7	6	8	29	33	42
West Bromwich A	42	8	9	4	38	29	6	4	11	36	48	41
Burnley	42	9	6	6	32	19	6	4	11	24	44	40
Manchester C	42	7	5	9	29	28	6	8	7	29	33	39
Wolves	42	8	6	7	40	33	4	8	9	33	40	38
Derby Co	42	10	4	7	43	37	5	3	13	20	43	37
Middlesbrough	42	12	4	5	37	25	3	2	16	27	63	36
Chelsea	42	10	3	8	31	29	4	5	12	21	43	36
Stoke C	42	8	6	7	34	32	4	1	16	15	56	31
Huddersfield T	42	9	3	9	32	35	1	5	15	17	47	28
Fulham	42	5	7	9	38	31	3	4	14	20	46	27

1952-53
DIVISION 1

	P	W	D	L	F	A	W	D	L	F	A	Pts
Arsenal	42	15	3	3	60	30	6	9	6	37	34	54
Preston NE	42	15	3	3	46	25	6	9	6	39	35	54
Wolves	42	13	5	3	54	27	6	8	7	32	36	51
West Bromwich A	42	13	3	5	35	19	8	5	8	31	41	50
Charlton Ath	42	12	8	1	47	22	7	3	11	30	41	49
Burnley	42	11	6	4	36	20	7	6	8	31	32	48
Blackpool	42	13	5	3	45	22	6	4	11	26	48	47
Manchester U	42	11	5	5	35	30	7	5	9	34	42	46
Sunderland	42	11	9	1	42	27	4	4	13	26	55	43
Tottenham Hotspur	**42**	**11**	**6**	**4**	**55**	**37**	**4**	**5**	**12**	**23**	**32**	**41**
Aston Villa	42	9	7	5	36	23	5	6	10	27	38	41
Cardiff C	42	7	8	6	32	17	7	4	10	22	29	40
Middlesbrough	42	12	5	4	46	27	2	6	13	24	50	39
Bolton W	42	9	4	8	39	35	6	5	10	22	34	39
Portsmouth	42	10	6	5	44	34	4	4	13	30	49	38
Newcastle U	42	9	5	7	34	33	5	4	12	25	37	37
Liverpool	42	10	6	5	36	28	4	2	15	25	54	36
Sheffield W	42	8	6	7	35	32	4	5	12	27	40	35
Chelsea	42	10	4	7	35	24	2	7	12	21	42	35
Manchester C	42	12	2	7	45	28	2	5	14	27	59	35
Stoke C	42	10	4	7	35	26	2	6	13	18	40	34
Derby Co	42	9	6	6	41	29	2	4	15	18	45	32

1953-54
DIVISION 1

	P	W	D	L	F	A	W	D	L	F	A	Pts
Wolves	42	16	1	4	61	25	9	6	6	35	31	57
West Bromwich A	42	13	5	3	51	24	9	4	8	35	39	53
Huddersfield T	42	13	6	2	45	24	7	5	9	33	37	51
Manchester U	52	11	6	4	41	27	7	6	8	32	31	48
Bolton W	42	14	6	1	45	20	4	6	11	30	40	48
Blackpool	42	13	6	2	43	19	6	4	11	37	50	48
Burnley	42	16	2	3	51	23	5	2	14	27	44	46
Chelsea	42	12	3	6	45	26	4	9	8	29	42	44
Charlton Ath	42	14	4	3	51	26	5	2	14	24	51	44
Cardiff C	42	12	4	5	32	27	6	4	11	19	44	44
Preston NE	42	12	2	7	43	24	7	3	11	44	34	43
Arsenal	42	8	8	5	42	37	7	5	9	33	36	43
Aston Villa	42	12	5	4	50	28	4	4	13	20	40	41
Portsmouth	42	13	5	3	43	27	1	6	14	38	58	39
Newcastle U	42	9	2	10	43	40	5	8	8	29	37	38
Tottenham Hotspur	**42**	**11**	**3**	**7**	**38**	**33**	**5**	**2**	**14**	**27**	**43**	**37**
Manchester C	42	10	4	7	35	31	4	5	12	27	46	37
Sunderland	42	11	4	6	50	37	3	4	14	31	52	36
Sheffield W	42	12	4	5	43	30	3	2	16	27	61	36
Sheffield U	42	9	5	7	43	38	2	6	13	26	52	33
Middlesbrough	42	6	6	9	29	35	4	4	13	31	56	30
Liverpool	42	7	8	6	49	38	2	2	17	19	59	28

Ted Ditchburn and Alf Ramsey in an undignified scramble in the Liverpool goalmouth at Anfield in January 1954. The game ended 2-2 as Spurs struggled in the lower reaches of the First Division.

1954-55
DIVISION 1

	P	W	D	L	F	A	W	D	L	F	A	Pts
Chelsea	42	11	5	5	43	29	8	7	5	38	28	52
Wolves	42	13	5	3	58	30	6	5	10	31	40	48
Portsmouth	42	13	5	3	44	21	5	7	9	30	41	48
Sunderland	42	8	1	2	39	27	7	7	7	25	27	48
Manchester U	42	12	4	5	44	30	8	3	10	40	44	47
Aston Villa	42	11	3	7	38	31	9	4	8	34	42	47
Manchester C	42	11	5	5	45	36	7	5	9	31	33	46
Newcastle U	42	12	5	4	53	27	5	4	12	36	50	43
Arsenal	42	12	3	6	44	25	5	6	10	25	38	43
Burnley	42	11	3	7	29	19	6	6	9	22	29	43
Everton	42	9	6	6	32	24	7	4	10	30	44	42
Huddersfield T	42	10	4	7	28	23	4	9	8	35	45	41
Sheffield U	42	10	3	8	41	34	7	4	10	29	52	41
Preston NE	42	8	5	8	47	33	8	3	10	36	31	40
Charlton Ath	42	8	6	7	43	34	7	4	10	33	41	40
Tottenham Hotspur	**42**	**9**	**4**	**8**	**42**	**35**	**7**	**4**	**10**	**30**	**38**	**40**
West Bromwich A	42	11	5	5	44	33	5	3	13	32	63	40
Bolton W	42	11	6	4	45	29	2	7	12	17	40	39
Blackpool	42	8	6	7	33	26	6	4	11	27	38	38
Cardiff C	42	9	4	8	41	38	4	7	10	21	38	37
Leicester C	42	9	6	6	43	32	3	5	13	31	54	35
Sheffield W	42	7	7	7	42	38	1	3	17	21	62	26

1955-56
DIVISION 1

	P	W	D	L	F	A	W	D	L	F	A	Pts
Manchester U	42	18	3	0	51	20	7	7	7	32	31	60
Blackpool	42	13	4	4	56	27	7	5	9	30	35	49
Wolves	42	15	2	4	51	27	5	7	9	38	38	49
Manchester C	42	11	5	5	40	27	7	5	9	42	42	46
Arsenal	42	13	4	4	38	22	5	6	10	22	39	46
Birmingham C	42	12	4	5	51	26	6	5	10	24	31	45
Burnley	42	11	3	7	37	20	7	5	9	27	34	44
Bolton W	42	13	3	5	50	24	5	4	12	21	34	43
Sunderland	42	10	8	3	44	36	7	1	13	36	59	43
Luton T	42	12	4	5	44	27	5	4	12	22	37	42
Newcastle U	42	12	4	5	49	24	5	4	13	36	46	41
Portsmouth	42	9	8	4	46	38	7	1	13	32	47	41
West Bromwich A	42	13	3	5	37	25	5	2	14	21	45	41
Charlton Ath	42	13	2	6	47	26	4	4	13	28	55	40
Everton	42	11	5	5	37	29	4	5	12	18	40	40
Chelsea	42	10	4	7	32	26	4	7	10	32	51	39
Cardiff C	42	11	4	6	36	32	4	5	12	19	37	39
Tottenham Hotspur	**42**	**9**	**4**	**8**	**37**	**33**	**6**	**3**	**12**	**24**	**38**	**37**
Preston NE	42	6	5	10	32	36	8	3	10	41	36	36
Aston Villa	42	9	6	6	32	29	2	7	12	20	40	35
Huddersfield T	42	9	4	8	32	30	5	3	13	22	53	35
Sheffield U	42	8	6	7	31	35	4	3	14	32	42	33

1956-57
DIVISION 1

	P	W	D	L	F	A	W	D	L	F	A	Pts
Manchester U	42	14	4	3	55	25	14	4	3	48	29	64
Tottenham Hotspur	**42**	**15**	**4**	**2**	**70**	**24**	**7**	**8**	**6**	**34**	**32**	**56**
Preston NE	42	15	4	2	50	19	8	6	7	34	37	56
Blackpool	42	14	3	4	55	26	8	6	7	38	39	53
Arsenal	42	12	5	4	45	21	9	3	9	40	48	50
Wolves	42	17	2	2	70	29	3	6	12	24	41	48
Burnley	42	14	5	2	41	21	4	5	12	15	29	46
Leeds U	42	10	8	3	42	18	5	6	10	30	45	44
Bolton W	42	13	6	2	42	23	3	6	12	23	42	44
Aston Villa	42	10	8	3	45	25	4	7	10	20	30	43
West Bromwich A	42	8	8	5	31	25	6	6	9	28	36	42
Birmingham C*	42	12	5	4	52	25	3	4	14	17	44	39
Chelsea*	42	7	8	6	43	36	6	5	10	30	37	39
Sheffield W	42	14	3	4	55	29	2	3	16	27	59	38
Everton	42	10	5	6	34	28	4	5	12	27	51	38
Luton T	42	10	4	7	32	26	4	3	14	26	50	37
Newcastle U	42	10	5	6	43	31	4	3	14	24	56	36
Manchester C	42	10	2	9	48	42	3	7	11	30	46	35
Portsmouth	42	8	6	7	37	35	2	7	12	25	57	33
Sunderland	42	9	5	7	40	30	3	3	15	27	58	32
Cardiff C	42	7	6	8	35	34	3	3	15	18	54	29
Charlton Ath	42	7	3	11	31	44	2	1	18	31	76	22

*Birmingham C & Chelsea finished in equal 12th position.

1957-58
DIVISION 1

	P	W	D	L	F	A	W	D	L	F	A	Pts
Wolves	42	17	3	1	60	21	11	5	5	43	26	64
Preston NE	42	18	2	1	63	14	8	5	8	37	37	59
Tottenham Hotspur	**42**	**13**	**4**	**4**	**58**	**33**	**8**	**5**	**8**	**35**	**44**	**51**
West Bromwich A	42	14	4	3	59	29	4	10	7	33	41	50
Manchester C	42	14	4	3	58	33	8	1	12	46	67	49
Burnley	42	16	2	3	52	21	5	3	13	28	53	47
Blackpool	42	11	2	8	47	35	8	4	9	33	32	44
Luton T	42	13	3	5	45	22	6	3	12	24	41	44
Manchester U	42	10	4	7	45	31	6	7	8	40	44	43
Nottingham F	42	10	4	7	41	27	6	6	9	28	36	42
Chelsea	42	10	5	6	47	34	5	7	9	36	45	42
Arsenal	42	10	4	7	48	39	6	3	12	25	46	39
Birmingham C	42	8	6	7	43	37	6	5	10	33	52	39
Aston Villa	42	12	4	5	46	26	4	3	14	27	60	39
Bolton W	42	9	5	7	38	35	5	5	11	27	52	38
Everton	42	5	9	7	34	35	8	2	11	31	40	37
Leeds U	42	10	6	5	33	23	4	3	14	18	40	37
Leicester C	42	11	4	6	59	41	3	1	17	32	71	33
Newcastle U	42	6	4	11	38	42	6	4	11	35	39	32
Portsmouth	42	10	6	5	45	34	2	2	17	28	54	32
Sunderland	42	7	7	7	32	33	3	5	13	22	64	32
Sheffield W	42	12	2	7	45	40	0	5	10	24	52	31

1958-59
DIVISION 1

	P	W	D	L	F	A	W	D	L	F	A	Pts
Wolves	42	15	3	3	68	19	13	2	6	42	30	61
Manchester U	42	14	4	3	58	27	10	3	7	45	39	55
Arsenal	42	14	3	4	53	29	7	5	9	35	39	50
Bolton W	42	14	3	4	56	30	6	7	8	23	36	50
West Bromwich A	42	8	7	6	41	33	10	6	5	47	35	49
West Ham U	42	15	3	3	59	29	6	3	12	26	41	48
Burnley	42	11	4	6	41	29	8	6	7	40	41	48
Blackpool	42	12	7	2	39	13	6	4	11	27	36	47
Birmingham C	42	14	1	6	54	35	6	5	10	30	33	46
Blackburn R	42	12	4	6	48	28	5	7	9	28	42	44
Newcastle U	42	11	3	7	40	29	6	4	11	40	51	41
Preston NE	42	9	3	9	40	39	8	4	9	30	38	41
Nottingham F	42	9	4	8	37	32	8	2	11	34	42	40
Chelsea	42	13	2	6	52	37	5	2	14	25	61	40
Leeds U	42	8	7	6	28	27	7	2	12	29	47	39
Everton	42	11	3	7	39	38	6	1	14	32	49	38
Luton T	42	11	6	4	50	26	1	7	13	18	45	37
Tottenham Hotspur	**42**	**10**	**3**	**8**	**56**	**42**	**3**	**7**	**11**	**29**	**53**	**36**
Leicester C	42	7	6	8	34	36	4	4	13	33	62	32
Manchester C	42	8	7	6	40	32	3	2	16	24	63	31
Aston Villa	42	8	5	8	31	33	3	3	15	27	54	30
Portsmouth	42	5	4	12	38	47	1	5	15	26	65	21

1959-60
DIVISION 1

	P	W	D	L	F	A	W	D	L	F	A	Pts
Burnley	42	15	2	4	52	28	9	5	7	33	33	55
Wolves	42	15	3	3	63	28	9	3	9	43	39	54
Tottenham Hotspur	**42**	**10**	**6**	**5**	**43**	**24**	**11**	**5**	**5**	**43**	**26**	**53**
West Bromwich A	42	12	4	5	48	25	7	7	7	35	32	49
Sheffield W	42	12	7	2	48	20	7	4	10	32	39	49
Bolton W	42	12	5	4	37	27	8	3	10	22	24	48
Manchester U	42	13	3	5	53	30	6	4	11	49	50	45
Newcastle U	42	10	5	6	42	32	8	3	10	40	46	44
Preston NE	42	10	6	5	43	34	6	6	9	36	42	44
Fulham	42	12	4	5	42	28	5	6	10	31	52	44
Blackpool	42	9	6	6	32	32	6	4	11	27	39	40
Leicester C	42	8	6	7	38	32	5	7	9	28	43	39
Arsenal	42	9	5	7	39	38	6	4	11	29	42	39
West Ham U	42	12	3	6	47	33	4	3	14	28	58	38
Everton	42	13	3	5	50	20	0	8	13	23	58	37
Manchester C	42	11	2	8	47	34	6	1	14	31	50	37
Blackburn	42	12	3	6	38	29	4	2	15	22	41	37
Chelsea	42	7	5	9	44	50	7	4	10	32	41	37
Birmingham C	42	9	5	7	37	36	4	5	12	26	44	36
Nottingham F	42	8	6	7	30	28	5	3	13	20	46	35
Leeds U	42	7	5	9	37	46	5	5	11	28	46	34
Luton T	42	6	5	10	25	29	3	7	11	25	44	30

Action around the Tottenham goal at Ewood Park in August 1958. There was plenty of action, too, as Spurs were hammered 5-0 by Blackburn Rovers.

1960-61 DIVISION 1

	P	W	D	L	F	A	W	D	L	F	A	Pts
Tottenham Hotspur	42	15	3	3	65	28	16	1	4	50	27	66
Sheffield W	42	15	4	2	45	17	8	8	5	33	30	58
Wolves	42	17	2	2	61	32	8	5	8	42	43	57
Burnley	42	11	4	6	58	40	11	3	7	44	37	51
Everton	42	13	4	4	47	23	9	2	10	40	46	50
Leicester C	42	12	4	5	54	31	6	5	10	33	39	45
Manchester U	42	14	5	2	58	20	4	4	13	30	56	45
Blackburn R	42	12	3	6	48	34	3	10	8	29	42	43
Aston Villa	42	13	3	5	48	28	4	6	11	30	49	43
West Bromwich A	42	10	3	8	43	32	8	2	11	24	39	41
Arsenal	42	12	3	6	44	35	3	8	10	33	50	41
Chelsea	42	10	5	6	61	48	5	2	14	37	52	37
Manchester C	42	10	5	6	41	30	3	6	12	38	60	37
Nottingham F	42	8	7	6	34	33	6	2	13	28	45	37
Cardiff C	42	11	5	5	34	26	2	6	13	26	59	37
West Ham U	42	12	4	5	53	31	1	6	14	24	57	36
Fulham	42	8	8	5	39	39	6	0	15	33	56	36
Bolton W	42	9	5	7	38	29	3	6	12	20	44	35
Birmingham C	42	10	4	7	35	31	4	2	15	27	53	34
Blackpool	42	9	3	9	44	34	3	6	12	24	39	33
Newcastle U	42	7	7	7	51	49	4	3	14	35	60	32
Preston NE	42	7	6	8	28	25	3	4	14	15	46	30

1961-62 DIVISION 1

	P	W	D	L	F	A	W	D	L	F	A	Pts
Ipswich T	42	17	2	2	58	28	7	6	8	35	39	56
Burnley	42	14	4	3	57	26	7	7	7	44	41	53
Tottenham Hotspur	42	14	4	3	59	34	7	6	8	29	35	52
Everton	42	17	2	2	64	21	3	9	9	24	33	51
Sheffield U	42	13	5	3	37	23	6	4	11	24	46	47
Sheffield W	42	14	4	3	47	23	6	2	13	25	35	46
Aston Villa	24	13	5	3	45	20	5	3	13	20	36	44
West Ham U	42	11	6	4	49	37	6	4	11	27	45	44
West Bromwich A	42	10	7	4	50	23	5	6	10	33	44	43
Arsenal	42	9	6	6	39	31	7	5	9	32	41	43
Bolton W	42	11	7	3	35	22	5	3	13	28	44	42
Manchester C	42	11	3	7	36	38	6	4	11	32	43	41
Blackpool	42	10	4	7	41	30	5	7	9	29	45	41
Leicester C	42	12	7	2	38	27	5	4	12	34	44	40
Manchester U	42	10	3	8	44	31	5	6	10	28	44	39
Blackburn R	42	10	6	5	33	22	4	5	12	17	36	39
Birmingham C	42	9	6	6	37	35	5	4	12	28	46	38
Wolves	42	8	7	6	38	34	5	3	13	35	52	36
Nottingham F	42	12	4	5	39	23	1	6	14	24	56	36
Fulham	42	8	3	10	38	34	5	4	12	28	40	33
Cardiff C	42	6	9	6	30	33	3	5	13	20	48	32
Chelsea	42	7	7	7	34	29	2	3	16	29	65	28

1962-63 DIVISION 1

	P	W	D	L	F	A	W	D	L	F	A	Pts
Everton	42	14	7	0	48	17	11	4	6	36	25	61
Tottenham Hotspur	42	14	6	1	72	28	9	3	9	39	34	55
Burnley	42	14	4	3	41	17	8	6	7	37	40	54
Leicester C	42	14	6	1	53	23	6	6	9	26	30	52
Wolves	42	11	4	6	51	25	9	4	8	42	40	50
Sheffield W	42	10	5	6	38	26	9	5	7	39	37	48
Arsenal	42	11	4	6	44	33	7	6	8	42	44	46
Liverpool	42	13	3	5	45	22	4	7	10	26	37	44
Nottingham F	42	12	4	5	39	28	5	6	10	28	41	44
Sheffield U	42	11	7	3	33	20	5	5	11	25	40	44
Blackburn R	42	11	4	6	55	34	4	8	9	24	37	42
West Ham U	42	8	6	7	39	34	6	6	9	34	35	40
Blackpool	42	8	7	6	34	27	5	7	9	24	37	40
West Bromwich A	42	11	1	9	40	37	5	6	10	31	42	39
Aston Villa	42	12	2	7	38	23	3	6	12	24	45	38
Fulham	42	8	6	7	28	30	6	4	11	22	41	38
Ipswich T	42	5	8	8	34	39	7	3	11	25	39	35
Bolton W	42	13	3	5	35	18	2	2	17	20	57	35
Manchester U	42	6	6	9	36	38	6	4	11	31	43	34
Birmingham C	42	6	8	7	40	40	4	5	12	23	50	33
Manchester C	42	7	5	9	30	45	3	6	12	28	57	31
Leyton Orient	42	4	5	12	22	37	2	4	15	15	44	21

1963-64 DIVISION 1

	P	W	D	L	F	A	W	D	L	F	A	Pts
Liverpool	42	16	0	5	60	18	10	5	6	32	27	57
Manchester U	42	15	3	3	54	19	8	4	9	36	43	53
Everton	42	14	4	3	53	26	7	6	8	31	38	52
Tottenham Hotspur	42	13	3	5	54	31	9	4	8	43	50	51
Chelsea	42	12	3	6	36	24	8	7	6	36	32	50
Sheffield W	42	15	3	3	50	24	4	8	9	34	43	49
Blackburn R	42	10	4	7	44	28	8	6	7	45	37	46
Arsenal	42	10	7	4	56	37	7	4	10	34	45	45
Burnley	42	14	3	4	46	23	3	7	11	25	41	44
West Bromwich A	42	9	6	6	43	35	7	5	9	27	26	43
Leicester C	42	9	4	8	33	27	7	7	7	28	31	43
Sheffield U	42	10	6	5	35	22	6	5	10	26	42	43
Nottingham F	42	9	5	7	34	24	7	4	10	30	44	41
West Ham U	42	8	7	6	45	38	6	5	10	24	36	40
Fulham	42	11	8	2	45	23	2	5	14	13	42	39
Wolves	42	6	9	6	36	34	6	6	9	34	46	39
Stoke C	42	9	6	6	49	33	5	4	12	28	45	38
Blackpool	42	8	6	7	26	29	5	3	13	26	44	35
Aston Villa	42	8	6	7	35	29	3	6	12	27	42	34
Birmingham C	42	7	7	7	33	32	4	0	17	21	60	29
Bolton W	42	6	5	10	39	35	4	3	14	18	45	28
Ipswich T	42	9	3	9	38	45	0	4	17	18	76	25

1964-65 DIVISION 1

	P	W	D	L	F	A	W	D	L	F	A	Pts
Manchester U	42	16	4	1	52	13	10	5	6	37	26	61
Leeds U	42	16	3	2	53	23	10	6	5	30	29	61
Chelsea	42	15	2	4	48	19	9	6	6	41	35	56
Everton	42	9	10	2	37	22	8	5	8	32	38	49
Nottingham F	42	10	7	4	45	33	7	6	8	26	34	47
Tottenham Hotspur	42	18	3	0	65	20	1	4	16	22	51	45
Liverpool	42	12	5	4	42	33	5	5	11	25	40	44
Sheffield W	42	13	5	3	37	15	3	6	12	20	40	43
West Ham U	42	14	2	5	48	25	5	2	14	34	46	42
Blackburn R	42	12	2	7	46	33	4	8	9	37	46	42
Stoke C	42	11	4	6	40	27	5	6	10	27	39	42
Burnley	42	9	9	3	39	26	7	1	13	31	44	42
Arsenal	42	11	5	5	41	31	6	2	13	27	44	41
West Bromwich A	42	10	5	6	45	25	3	8	10	25	40	39
Sunderland	42	12	6	3	45	26	2	3	16	19	48	37
Aston Villa	42	14	1	6	36	24	2	4	15	21	58	37
Blackpool	42	9	7	5	41	28	3	4	14	26	50	35
Leicester C	42	9	6	6	43	36	2	7	12	26	49	35
Sheffield U	42	7	5	9	30	29	5	6	10	20	35	35
Fulham	42	10	5	6	44	32	1	7	13	16	46	34
Wolves	42	8	2	11	33	36	5	2	14	26	53	30
Birmingham C	42	6	8	7	36	40	2	3	16	28	56	27

1965-66 DIVISION 1

	P	W	D	L	F	A	W	D	L	F	A	Pts
Liverpool	42	17	2	2	52	15	9	7	5	27	19	61
Leeds U	42	14	4	3	49	15	9	5	7	30	23	55
Burnley	42	15	3	3	45	20	9	4	8	34	27	55
Manchester U	42	12	8	1	50	20	6	7	8	34	39	51
Chelsea	42	11	6	4	30	21	11	3	7	35	32	51
West Bromwich A	42	11	6	4	58	34	8	6	7	33	35	50
Leicester C	42	12	4	5	40	28	9	3	9	40	37	49
Tottenham Hotspur	42	11	6	4	55	37	5	6	10	20	29	44
Sheffield U	42	11	6	4	37	25	5	5	11	19	34	43
Stoke C	42	12	6	3	42	22	3	6	12	23	42	42
Everton	42	12	6	3	39	19	3	5	13	17	43	41
West Ham U	42	12	5	4	46	33	3	4	14	24	50	39
Blackpool	42	9	5	7	36	29	5	4	12	19	36	37
Arsenal	42	8	8	5	36	31	4	5	12	26	44	37
Newcastle U	42	10	5	6	26	20	4	4	13	24	43	37
Aston Villa	42	10	3	8	39	34	5	3	13	30	46	36
Sheffield W	42	11	6	4	35	18	3	2	16	21	48	36
Nottingham F	42	11	3	7	31	26	3	5	13	25	46	36
Sunderland	42	13	2	6	36	28	1	6	14	15	44	36
Fulham	42	9	3	9	36	38	5	2	13	13	48	35
Northampton T	42	8	6	7	31	32	2	7	12	24	60	33
Blackburn R	42	6	1	14	30	36	2	3	16	27	52	20

Spurs goalkeeper Bill Brown watches a shot go just over his bar at Deepdale in February 1960, when Tottenham drew 1-1 with Preston North End.

1966-67
DIVISION 1

	P	W	D	L	F	A	W	D	L	F	A	Pts
Manchester U	42	17	4	0	51	13	7	8	6	33	32	60
Nottingham F	42	16	4	1	41	13	7	6	8	23	28	56
Tottenham Hotspur	**42**	**15**	**3**	**3**	**44**	**21**	**9**	**5**	**7**	**27**	**27**	**56**
Leeds U	42	15	4	2	41	17	7	7	7	21	25	55
Liverpool	42	12	7	2	36	17	7	6	8	28	30	51
Everton	42	11	4	6	39	22	8	6	7	26	24	48
Arsenal	42	11	6	4	32	20	5	8	8	26	27	46
Leicester C	42	12	4	5	47	28	6	4	11	31	43	44
Chelsea	42	7	9	5	33	29	8	5	8	34	33	44
Sheffield U	42	11	5	5	34	22	5	5	11	18	37	42
Sheffield W	42	9	7	5	39	19	5	6	10	17	28	41
Stoke C	42	11	5	5	40	21	6	2	13	23	37	41
West Bromwich A	42	11	1	9	40	28	5	6	10	37	45	39
Burnley	42	11	4	6	43	28	4	5	12	23	48	39
Manchester C	42	8	9	4	27	25	4	6	11	16	27	39
West Ham U	42	8	6	7	40	31	6	2	13	40	53	36
Sunderland	42	12	3	6	39	26	2	5	14	19	46	36
Fulham	42	8	7	6	49	34	3	5	13	22	49	34
Southampton	42	10	3	8	49	41	4	3	14	25	51	34
Newcastle U	42	9	5	7	24	27	3	4	14	15	54	33
Aston Villa	42	7	5	9	30	33	4	2	15	24	52	29
Blackpool	42	1	5	15	18	36	5	4	12	23	40	21

1967-68
DIVISION 1

	P	W	D	L	F	A	W	D	L	F	A	Pts
Manchester C	42	17	2	2	52	16	9	4	8	34	27	58
Manchester U	42	15	2	4	49	21	9	6	6	40	34	56
Liverpool	42	17	2	2	51	17	5	9	7	20	23	55
Leeds U	42	17	3	1	49	14	5	6	10	22	27	53
Everton	42	18	1	2	43	13	5	5	11	24	27	52
Chelsea	42	11	7	3	34	25	7	5	9	28	43	48
Tottenham Hotspur	**42**	**11**	**7**	**3**	**44**	**20**	**8**	**2**	**11**	**26**	**39**	**47**
West Bromwich A	42	12	4	5	45	25	5	8	8	30	37	46
Arsenal	42	12	6	3	37	23	5	4	12	23	33	44
Newcastle U	42	12	7	2	38	20	1	8	12	16	47	41
Nottingham F	42	11	6	4	34	22	3	5	13	18	42	39
West Ham U	42	8	5	8	43	30	6	5	10	30	39	38
Leicester C	42	7	7	7	37	34	6	5	10	27	35	38
Burnley	42	12	7	2	38	16	2	3	16	26	55	38
Sunderland	42	8	7	6	28	25	5	4	12	23	33	37
Southampton	42	9	8	4	37	31	4	3	14	29	52	37
Wolves	42	10	4	7	45	36	4	4	13	21	39	36
Stoke C	42	10	3	8	30	29	4	4	13	20	44	35
Sheffield W	42	6	10	5	32	24	5	2	14	19	39	34
Coventry C	42	8	5	8	32	32	1	10	10	19	39	33
Sheffield U	42	7	4	10	25	31	4	6	11	24	39	32
Fulham	42	6	4	11	27	41	4	3	14	29	57	27

1968-69
DIVISION 1

	P	W	D	L	F	A	W	D	L	F	A	Pts
Leeds U	42	18	3	0	41	9	9	10	2	25	17	67
Liverpool	42	16	4	1	36	10	9	7	5	27	14	61
Everton	42	14	5	2	43	10	7	10	4	34	26	57
Arsenal	42	12	6	3	31	12	10	6	5	25	15	56
Chelsea	42	11	7	3	40	24	9	3	9	33	29	50
Tottenham Hotspur	**42**	**10**	**8**	**3**	**39**	**22**	**4**	**9**	**8**	**22**	**29**	**45**
Southampton	42	13	5	3	41	21	3	8	10	16	27	45
West Ham U	42	10	8	3	47	22	3	10	8	19	28	44
Newcastle U	42	12	7	2	40	20	3	7	11	21	35	44
West Bromwich A	42	11	7	3	43	26	5	4	12	21	41	43
Manchester U	42	13	5	3	38	18	2	7	12	19	35	42
Ipswich T	42	10	4	7	32	26	5	7	9	27	34	41
Manchester C	42	13	6	2	49	20	2	4	15	15	35	40
Burnley	42	11	6	4	36	25	4	3	14	19	57	39
Sheffield W	42	7	9	5	27	26	3	7	11	14	28	36
Wolves	42	7	10	4	26	22	3	5	13	15	36	35
Sunderland	42	10	6	5	28	18	1	6	14	15	49	34
Nottingham F	42	6	6	9	17	22	4	7	10	28	35	33
Stoke C	42	9	7	5	24	24	0	8	13	16	39	33
Coventry C	42	8	6	7	32	22	2	5	14	14	42	31
Leicester C	42	8	8	5	27	24	1	4	16	12	44	30
QPR	42	4	7	10	20	33	0	3	18	19	62	18

1969-70
DIVISION 1

	P	W	D	L	F	A	W	D	L	F	A	Pts
Everton	42	17	3	1	46	19	12	5	4	26	15	66
Leeds U	42	15	4	2	50	19	6	11	4	34	30	57
Chelsea	42	13	7	1	36	18	8	6	7	34	32	55
Derby Co	42	15	3	3	45	14	7	6	8	19	23	53
Liverpool	42	10	7	4	34	20	10	4	7	31	22	51
Coventry C	42	9	6	6	35	28	10	5	6	23	20	49
Newcastle U	42	14	2	5	42	16	3	11	7	15	19	47
Manchester U	42	8	9	4	37	27	6	8	7	29	34	45
Stoke C	42	10	7	4	31	23	5	8	8	25	29	45
Manchester C	42	8	6	7	25	22	8	5	8	30	26	43
Tottenham Hotspur	**42**	**11**	**2**	**8**	**27**	**21**	**6**	**7**	**8**	**27**	**34**	**43**
Arsenal	42	7	10	4	29	23	5	8	8	22	26	42
Wolves	42	8	8	5	30	23	4	8	9	25	34	40
Burnley	42	7	7	7	33	29	5	8	8	23	32	39
Nottingham F	42	8	9	4	28	28	2	9	10	22	43	38
West Bromwich A	42	10	6	5	39	25	4	3	14	19	41	37
West Ham U	42	8	8	5	28	21	4	4	13	23	39	36
Ipswich T	42	9	5	7	23	20	1	6	14	17	43	31
Southampton	42	3	12	6	24	27	3	5	13	22	40	29
Crystal Palace	42	5	6	10	20	36	1	9	11	14	32	27
Sunderland	42	4	11	6	17	24	2	3	16	13	44	26
Sheffield W	42	6	5	10	23	27	2	4	15	17	44	25

1970-71
DIVISION 1

	P	W	D	L	F	A	W	D	L	F	A	Pts
Arsenal	42	18	3	0	41	6	11	4	6	30	23	65
Leeds U	42	16	2	3	40	12	11	8	2	32	18	64
Tottenham Hotspur	**42**	**11**	**5**	**5**	**33**	**19**	**8**	**9**	**4**	**21**	**14**	**52**
Wolves	42	13	3	5	33	22	9	5	7	31	32	52
Liverpool	42	11	10	0	30	10	6	7	8	12	14	51
Chelsea	42	12	6	3	34	21	6	9	6	18	21	51
Southampton	42	12	5	4	35	15	5	7	9	21	29	46
Manchester U	42	9	6	6	29	24	7	5	9	36	42	43
Derby Co	42	9	5	7	32	26	7	5	9	24	28	42
Coventry C	42	12	4	5	24	12	4	6	11	13	26	42
Manchester C	42	7	9	5	30	22	5	8	8	17	20	41
Newcastle U	42	9	9	3	27	16	5	4	12	17	30	41
Stoke C	42	10	7	4	28	11	2	6	13	16	37	37
Everton	42	10	7	4	32	16	2	6	13	22	44	37
Huddersfield T	42	7	8	6	19	16	4	6	11	21	33	36
Nottingham F	42	9	4	8	29	26	5	4	12	13	35	36
West Bromwich A	42	9	8	4	34	25	1	7	13	24	50	35
Crystal Palace	42	9	5	7	24	24	3	6	12	15	33	35
Ipswich T	42	9	4	8	28	22	3	6	12	14	26	34
West Ham U	42	6	8	7	28	30	4	6	11	19	30	34
Burnley	42	4	8	9	20	31	3	5	13	9	32	27
Blackpool	42	3	9	9	22	31	1	6	14	12	35	23

1971-72
DIVISION 1

	P	W	D	L	F	A	W	D	L	F	A	Pts
Derby Co	42	16	4	1	43	10	8	6	7	26	23	58
Leeds U	42	17	4	0	54	10	7	5	9	19	21	57
Liverpool	42	17	3	1	48	16	7	6	8	16	14	57
Manchester C	42	16	3	2	48	15	7	8	6	29	30	57
Arsenal	42	15	2	4	36	13	7	6	8	22	27	52
Tottenham Hotspur	**42**	**16**	**3**	**2**	**45**	**13**	**3**	**10**	**8**	**18**	**29**	**51**
Chelsea	42	12	7	2	41	20	6	5	10	17	29	48
Manchester U	42	13	2	6	39	26	6	8	7	30	35	48
Wolves	42	10	7	4	35	23	8	4	9	30	34	47
Sheffield U	42	10	8	3	39	26	7	4	10	22	34	46
Newcastle U	42	10	6	5	30	18	5	5	11	19	34	41
Leicester C	42	9	6	6	18	11	4	7	10	23	35	39
Ipswich T	42	7	8	6	19	19	4	8	9	20	34	38
West Ham U	42	10	6	5	31	19	2	6	13	16	32	36
Everton	42	8	9	4	28	17	1	9	11	9	31	36
West Bromwich A	42	6	7	8	22	23	6	4	11	20	31	35
Stoke C	42	6	10	5	26	25	4	5	12	13	31	35
Coventry C	42	7	10	4	27	23	2	5	14	17	44	33
Southampton	42	8	5	8	31	28	4	2	15	21	52	31
Crystal Palace	42	8	4	9	26	31	4	5	12	13	34	29
Nottingham F	42	6	4	11	25	29	2	5	14	22	52	25
Huddersfield T	42	4	7	10	12	22	2	6	13	15	37	25

Alan Gilzean puts the Burnley defence under pressure at Turf Moor in September 1966. The sides drew 2-2.

1972-73
DIVISION 1

	P	W	D	L	F	A	W	D	L	F	A	Pts
Liverpool	42	17	3	1	45	19	8	7	6	27	23	60
Arsenal	42	14	5	2	31	14	9	6	6	26	29	57
Leeds U	42	15	4	2	45	13	6	7	8	26	32	53
Ipswich T	42	10	7	4	34	20	7	7	7	21	25	48
Wolves	42	13	3	5	43	23	5	8	8	23	31	47
West Ham U	42	12	5	4	45	25	5	7	9	22	28	46
Derby Co	42	15	3	3	43	18	4	5	12	13	36	46
Tottenham Hotspur	**42**	**10**	**5**	**6**	**33**	**23**	**6**	**8**	**7**	**25**	**25**	**45**
Newcastle U	42	12	6	3	35	19	4	7	10	25	32	45
Birmingham C	42	11	7	3	39	22	4	5	12	14	32	42
Manchester C	42	12	4	5	36	20	3	7	11	21	40	41
Chelsea	42	9	6	6	30	22	4	8	9	19	29	40
Southampton	42	8	11	2	26	17	3	7	11	21	35	40
Sheffield U	42	11	4	6	28	18	4	6	11	23	41	40
Stoke C	42	11	8	2	38	17	3	2	16	23	39	38
Leicester C	42	7	9	5	23	18	3	8	10	17	28	37
Everton	42	9	5	7	27	21	4	6	11	14	28	37
Manchester U	42	9	7	5	24	19	3	6	12	20	41	37
Coventry C	42	9	5	7	27	24	4	4	13	13	31	35
Norwich C	42	7	9	5	22	19	4	1	16	14	44	32
Crystal Palace	42	7	7	7	25	21	2	5	14	16	37	30
West Bromwich A	42	8	7	6	25	24	1	3	17	13	38	28

1973-74
DIVISION 1

	P	W	D	L	F	A	W	D	L	F	A	Pts
Leeds U	42	12	8	1	38	18	12	6	3	28	13	62
Liverpool	42	18	2	1	34	11	4	11	6	18	20	57
Derby Co	42	13	7	1	40	16	4	7	10	12	26	48
Ipswich T	42	10	7	4	38	21	8	4	9	29	37	47
Stoke C	42	13	6	2	39	15	2	10	9	15	27	46
Burnley	42	10	9	2	29	16	6	5	10	27	37	46
Everton	42	12	6	2	29	14	4	5	12	21	34	44
QPR	42	8	10	3	30	17	5	7	9	26	35	43
Leicester C	42	10	7	4	35	17	3	9	9	16	24	42
Arsenal	42	9	7	5	23	16	5	7	9	26	35	42
Tottenham Hotspur	**42**	**9**	**4**	**8**	**26**	**27**	**5**	**10**	**6**	**19**	**23**	**42**
Wolves	42	11	6	4	30	18	2	9	10	19	31	41
Sheffield U	42	7	7	7	25	22	7	5	9	19	27	40
Manchester C	42	7	7	7	25	17	4	5	12	14	29	40
Newcastle U	42	9	6	6	28	21	4	6	11	21	27	38
Coventry C	42	10	5	6	25	18	4	5	12	18	36	38
Chelsea	42	9	4	8	36	29	3	9	9	20	31	37
West Ham U	42	7	7	7	36	32	4	8	9	19	28	37
Birmingham C	42	10	7	4	30	21	2	6	13	22	43	37
Southampton	42	8	10	3	30	20	3	4	14	17	48	36
Manchester U	42	7	7	7	23	20	3	5	13	15	28	32
Norwich C	42	6	9	6	25	27	1	6	14	12	35	29

1974-75
DIVISION 1

	P	W	D	L	F	A	W	D	L	F	A	Pts
Derby Co	42	14	4	3	41	18	7	7	7	26	31	53
Liverpool	42	14	5	2	44	17	6	6	9	16	22	51
Ipswich T	42	17	2	2	47	14	6	3	12	19	30	51
Everton	42	10	9	2	33	19	6	9	6	23	23	50
Stoke C	42	12	7	2	40	18	5	8	8	24	30	49
Sheffield U	42	12	7	2	35	20	6	6	9	23	31	49
Middlesbrough	42	11	7	3	33	14	7	5	9	21	26	48
Manchester C	42	16	3	2	40	15	2	7	12	14	39	46
Leeds U	42	10	8	3	34	20	6	5	10	23	29	45
Burnley	42	11	6	4	40	29	6	5	10	28	38	45
QPR	42	10	4	7	25	17	6	6	9	29	37	42
Wolves	42	12	5	4	43	21	2	6	13	14	33	39
West Ham U	42	10	6	5	38	22	3	7	11	20	37	39
Coventry C	42	8	9	4	31	27	4	6	11	20	35	39
Newcastle U	42	12	4	5	39	23	3	5	13	20	49	39
Arsenal	42	10	6	5	31	16	3	5	13	16	33	37
Birmingham C	42	10	4	7	34	28	4	5	12	19	33	37
Leicester C	42	8	7	6	25	17	4	5	12	21	43	36
Tottenham Hotspur	**42**	**8**	**4**	**9**	**29**	**27**	**5**	**4**	**12**	**23**	**36**	**34**
Luton T	42	8	6	7	27	26	3	5	13	20	39	33
Chelsea	42	4	9	8	22	31	5	6	10	20	41	33
Carlisle U	42	8	2	11	22	21	4	3	14	21	38	29

1975-76
DIVISION 1

	P	W	D	L	F	A	W	D	L	F	A	Pts
Liverpool	42	14	5	2	41	21	9	9	3	25	10	60
QPR	42	17	4	0	42	13	7	7	7	25	20	59
Manchester U	42	16	4	1	40	13	7	6	8	28	29	56
Derby Co	42	15	3	3	45	30	6	8	7	30	28	53
Leeds U	42	13	5	3	37	19	8	6	7	28	27	51
Ipswich T	42	11	6	4	36	23	5	8	8	18	25	46
Leicester C	42	9	9	3	29	24	4	10	7	19	27	45
Manchester C	42	14	5	2	46	18	2	6	13	18	28	43
Tottenham Hotspur	**42**	**6**	**10**	**5**	**33**	**32**	**8**	**5**	**8**	**30**	**31**	**43**
Norwich C	42	10	5	6	33	26	6	5	10	25	32	42
Everton	42	10	7	4	37	24	5	5	11	23	42	42
Stoke C	42	8	5	8	25	24	7	6	8	23	26	41
Middlesbrough	42	9	7	5	23	11	6	3	12	23	34	40
Coventry C	42	6	9	6	22	22	7	5	9	25	35	40
Newcastle U	42	11	4	6	51	26	4	5	12	20	36	39
Aston Villa	42	11	8	2	32	17	0	9	12	19	42	39
Arsenal	42	11	4	6	33	19	2	6	13	14	34	36
West Ham U	42	10	5	6	26	23	3	5	13	22	48	36
Birmingham C	42	11	5	5	36	26	2	2	17	21	49	33
Wolves	42	7	6	8	27	25	3	4	14	24	43	30
Burnley	42	6	6	9	23	26	3	4	14	20	40	28
Sheffield U	42	4	7	10	19	32	2	3	16	14	50	22

1976-77
DIVISION 1

	P	W	D	L	F	A	W	D	L	F	A	Pts
Liverpool	42	18	3	0	47	11	5	8	8	15	22	57
Manchester C	42	15	5	1	38	13	6	9	6	22	21	56
Ipswich T	42	15	4	2	41	11	7	4	10	25	28	52
Aston Villa	42	17	3	1	55	17	5	4	12	21	33	51
Newcastle U	42	14	6	1	40	15	4	7	10	24	34	49
Manchester U	42	12	6	3	41	22	6	5	10	30	40	47
West Bromwich A	42	10	6	5	38	22	6	7	8	24	34	45
Arsenal	42	11	6	4	37	20	5	5	11	27	39	43
Everton	42	9	7	5	35	24	5	7	9	27	40	42
Leeds U	42	8	8	5	28	26	7	4	10	20	25	42
Leicester C	42	8	9	4	30	28	4	9	8	17	32	42
Middlesbrough	42	11	6	4	25	14	3	7	11	15	31	41
Birmingham C	42	10	6	5	38	25	3	6	12	25	36	38
QPR	42	10	7	4	31	21	3	5	13	16	31	38
Derby Co	42	9	9	3	36	18	0	10	11	14	37	37
Norwich C	42	12	4	5	30	23	2	5	14	17	41	37
West Ham U	42	9	6	6	28	23	2	8	11	18	42	36
Bristol C	42	8	7	6	25	19	3	6	12	13	29	35
Coventry C	42	7	9	5	34	26	3	6	12	14	33	35
Sunderland	42	9	5	7	29	16	2	7	12	17	38	34
Stoke C	42	9	8	4	21	16	1	6	14	7	35	34
Tottenham Hotspur	**42**	**9**	**7**	**5**	**26**	**20**	**3**	**2**	**16**	**22**	**52**	**33**

1977-78
DIVISION 2

	P	W	D	L	F	A	W	D	L	F	A	Pts
Bolton W	42	16	4	1	39	14	8	6	7	24	19	58
Southampton	42	15	4	2	44	16	7	9	5	26	23	57
Tottenham Hotspur	**42**	**13**	**7**	**1**	**50**	**19**	**7**	**9**	**5**	**33**	**30**	**56**
Brighton & HA	42	15	5	1	43	21	7	7	7	20	17	56
Blackburn R	42	12	4	5	33	16	4	9	8	23	44	45
Sunderland	42	11	6	4	36	17	3	10	8	31	42	44
Stoke C	42	13	5	3	38	16	3	5	13	15	33	42
Oldham Ath	42	9	10	2	32	20	4	6	11	22	38	42
Crystal Palace	42	9	7	5	31	19	4	8	9	19	27	41
Fulham	42	9	8	4	32	19	5	5	11	17	30	41
Burnley	42	11	6	4	35	20	4	4	13	21	44	40
Sheffield U	42	13	4	4	38	22	3	4	14	24	51	40
Luton T	42	11	4	6	35	20	3	6	12	19	32	38
Orient	42	8	11	2	30	20	2	7	12	13	29	38
Notts Co	42	10	9	2	36	22	1	7	13	18	40	38
Millwall	42	8	8	5	23	20	4	6	11	26	37	38
Charlton Ath	42	11	6	4	38	27	2	6	13	17	41	38
Bristol R	42	10	7	4	40	26	3	5	13	21	51	38
Cardiff C	42	12	6	3	32	23	1	6	14	19	48	38
Blackpool	42	7	8	6	35	25	5	5	11	24	35	37
Mansfield T	42	6	6	9	30	34	4	5	12	19	35	31
Hull C	42	6	6	9	23	25	2	6	13	11	27	28

Steve Perryman bursts through the QPR defence to score in the 1-1 draw at White Hart Lane in April 1979. Derek Richardson is the Rangers goalkeeper.

1978-79
DIVISION 1

	P	W	D	L	F	A	W	D	L	F	A	Pts
Liverpool	42	19	2	0	51	4	11	6	4	34	12	68
Nottingham F	42	11	10	0	34	10	10	8	3	27	16	60
West Bromwich A	42	13	5	3	38	15	11	6	4	34	20	59
Everton	42	12	7	2	32	17	5	10	6	20	23	51
Leeds U	42	11	4	6	41	25	7	10	4	29	27	50
Ipswich T	42	11	4	6	34	21	9	5	7	29	28	49
Arsenal	42	11	8	2	37	18	6	6	9	24	30	48
Aston Villa	42	8	9	4	37	26	7	7	7	22	23	46
Manchester U	42	9	7	5	29	25	6	8	7	31	38	45
Coventry C	42	11	7	3	41	29	3	9	9	17	39	44
Tottenham Hotspur	**42**	**7**	**8**	**6**	**19**	**25**	**6**	**7**	**8**	**29**	**36**	**41**
Middlesbrough	42	10	5	6	33	21	5	5	11	24	29	40
Bristol C	42	11	6	4	34	19	4	4	13	13	32	40
Southampton	42	9	10	2	35	20	3	6	12	12	33	40
Manchester C	42	9	5	7	34	28	4	8	9	24	28	39
Norwich C	42	7	10	4	29	19	0	13	8	22	38	37
Bolton W	42	10	5	6	36	28	2	6	13	18	47	35
Wolves	42	10	4	7	26	26	3	4	14	18	42	34
Derby Co	42	8	5	8	25	25	2	6	13	19	46	31
QPR	42	4	9	8	24	33	2	4	15	21	40	25
Birmingham C	42	5	9	7	24	25	1	1	19	13	39	22
Chelsea	42	3	5	13	23	42	2	5	14	21	50	20

1979-80
DIVISION 1

	P	W	D	L	F	A	W	D	L	F	A	Pts
Liverpool	42	15	6	0	46	8	10	4	7	35	22	60
Manchester U	42	17	3	1	43	8	7	7	7	22	27	58
Ipswich T	42	14	4	3	43	14	8	5	8	25	26	53
Arsenal	42	8	10	3	24	12	10	6	5	28	24	52
Nottingham F	42	16	4	1	44	11	4	4	13	19	32	48
Wolves	42	9	6	6	29	20	10	3	8	29	27	47
Aston Villa	42	11	5	5	29	22	5	9	7	22	28	46
Southampton	42	14	2	5	53	24	4	7	10	12	29	45
Middlesbrough	42	11	7	3	31	14	5	5	11	19	30	44
West Bromwich A	42	9	8	4	37	23	2	11	8	17	27	41
Leeds U	42	10	7	4	30	17	3	7	11	16	33	40
Norwich C	42	10	8	3	38	30	3	6	12	20	36	40
Crystal Palace	42	9	9	3	26	13	3	7	11	15	37	40
Tottenham Hotspur	**42**	**11**	**5**	**5**	**30**	**22**	**4**	**5**	**12**	**22**	**40**	**40**
Coventry C	42	12	2	7	34	24	4	5	12	22	42	39
Brighton & HA	42	8	8	5	25	20	3	7	11	22	37	37
Manchester C	42	8	8	5	28	25	4	5	12	15	41	37
Stoke C	42	9	4	8	27	26	4	6	11	17	32	36
Everton	42	7	7	7	28	25	2	10	9	15	26	35
Bristol C	42	6	6	9	22	30	3	7	11	15	36	31
Derby Co	42	9	4	8	36	29	2	4	15	11	38	30
Bolton W	42	5	11	5	19	21	0	4	17	19	52	25

1980-81
DIVISION 1

	P	W	D	L	F	A	W	D	L	F	A	Pts
Aston Villa	42	16	3	2	40	13	10	5	6	32	27	60
Ipswich T	42	15	4	2	45	14	8	6	7	32	29	56
Arsenal	42	13	8	0	36	17	6	7	8	25	28	53
West Bromwich A	42	15	4	2	40	15	5	8	8	20	27	52
Liverpool	42	13	5	3	38	15	4	12	5	24	27	51
Southampton	42	15	4	2	47	22	5	6	10	29	34	50
Nottingham F	42	15	3	3	44	20	4	9	8	18	24	50
Manchester U	42	9	11	1	30	14	6	7	8	21	22	48
Leeds U	42	10	5	6	19	19	7	5	9	20	28	44
Tottenham Hotspur	**42**	**9**	**9**	**3**	**44**	**31**	**5**	**6**	**10**	**26**	**37**	**43**
Stoke C	42	8	9	4	31	23	4	9	8	20	37	42
Manchester C	42	10	7	4	35	25	4	4	13	21	34	39
Birmingham C	42	11	5	5	32	23	2	7	12	18	38	38
Middlesbrough	42	14	4	3	38	16	2	1	18	15	45	37
Everton	42	8	6	7	35	25	5	4	12	23	33	36
Coventry C	42	9	6	6	31	30	4	4	13	17	38	36
Sunderland	42	10	4	7	32	19	4	3	14	20	34	35
Wolves	42	11	2	8	26	20	2	7	12	17	35	35
Brighton & HA	42	10	3	8	30	26	4	4	13	24	41	35
Norwich C	42	9	7	5	34	25	4	0	17	15	48	33
Leicester C	42	7	5	9	20	23	6	1	14	20	44	32
Crystal Palace	42	6	4	11	32	37	0	3	18	15	46	19

1981-82
DIVISION 1

	P	W	D	L	F	A	W	D	L	F	A	Pts
Liverpool	42	14	3	4	39	14	12	6	3	41	18	87
Ipswich T	42	17	1	3	47	25	9	4	8	28	28	83
Manchester U	42	12	6	3	27	9	10	6	5	32	20	78
Tottenham Hotspur	**42**	**12**	**4**	**5**	**41**	**26**	**8**	**7**	**6**	**26**	**22**	**71**
Arsenal	42	13	5	3	27	15	7	6	8	21	22	71
Swansea C	42	13	3	5	34	16	8	3	10	24	35	69
Southampton	42	15	2	4	49	30	4	7	10	23	37	66
Everton	42	11	7	3	33	21	6	6	9	23	29	64
West Ham U	42	9	10	2	42	29	5	6	10	24	28	58
Manchester C	42	9	7	5	32	23	6	6	9	17	27	58
Aston Villa	42	9	6	6	28	24	6	6	9	27	29	57
Nottingham F	42	7	7	7	19	20	8	5	8	23	28	57
Brighton & HA	42	8	7	6	30	24	5	6	10	13	28	52
Coventry C	42	9	4	8	31	24	4	7	10	25	38	50
Notts Co	42	8	5	8	32	33	5	3	13	29	36	47
Birmingham C	42	8	6	7	29	25	2	8	11	24	36	44
West Bromwich A	42	6	6	9	24	25	5	5	11	22	32	44
Stoke C	42	9	2	10	27	28	3	6	12	17	35	44
Sunderland	42	6	5	10	19	26	5	6	10	19	32	44
Leeds U	42	6	11	4	23	20	4	1	16	16	41	42
Wolves	42	8	5	8	19	20	2	5	14	13	43	40
Middlesbrough	42	5	9	7	20	24	3	6	12	14	28	39

1982-83
DIVISION 1

	P	W	D	L	F	A	W	D	L	F	A	Pts
Liverpool	42	16	4	1	55	16	8	6	7	32	21	82
Watford	42	16	2	3	49	20	6	3	12	25	37	71
Manchester U	42	14	7	0	39	10	5	6	10	17	28	70
Tottenham Hotspur	**42**	**15**	**4**	**2**	**50**	**15**	**5**	**5**	**11**	**35**	**35**	**69**
Nottingham F	42	12	5	4	34	18	8	4	9	28	32	69
Aston Villa	42	17	2	2	47	15	3	14	15	35	68
Everton	42	13	6	2	43	19	5	4	12	23	29	64
West Ham U	42	13	3	5	41	23	7	1	13	27	39	64
Ipswich T	42	11	3	7	39	23	4	10	7	25	27	58
Arsenal	42	11	6	4	36	19	5	4	12	22	37	58
West Bromwich A	42	11	5	5	35	20	4	7	10	16	29	57
Southampton	42	11	5	5	36	22	4	7	10	18	36	57
Stoke C	42	13	4	4	34	21	3	5	13	19	43	57
Norwich C	42	10	6	5	30	18	4	6	11	22	40	54
Notts Co	42	12	4	5	37	25	3	3	15	18	46	52
Sunderland	42	7	10	4	30	22	5	4	12	18	39	50
Birmingham C	42	9	7	5	29	24	3	7	11	11	31	50
Luton T	42	7	7	7	34	33	5	6	10	31	51	49
Coventry C	42	10	5	6	29	17	3	4	14	19	42	48
Manchester C	42	9	7	5	26	23	4	3	14	21	47	47
Swansea C	42	10	4	7	32	29	0	7	14	19	40	41
Brighton & HA	42	8	7	6	25	22	1	6	14	13	46	40

1983-84
DIVISION 1

	P	W	D	L	F	A	W	D	L	F	A	Pts
Liverpool	42	14	5	2	50	12	8	9	4	23	20	80
Southampton	42	15	4	2	44	17	7	7	7	22	21	77
Nottingham F	42	14	4	3	47	17	8	4	9	29	28	74
Manchester U	42	14	3	4	43	18	6	11	4	28	23	74
QPR	42	14	4	3	37	12	8	3	10	30	25	73
Arsenal	42	10	5	6	41	29	8	4	9	33	31	63
Everton	42	9	9	3	21	12	7	5	9	23	30	62
Tottenham Hotspur	**42**	**11**	**4**	**6**	**31**	**24**	**6**	**6**	**9**	**33**	**41**	**61**
West Ham U	42	10	4	7	39	24	7	5	9	21	31	60
Aston Villa	42	14	3	4	34	22	3	6	12	25	39	60
Watford	42	9	7	5	36	31	7	2	12	32	46	57
Ipswich T	42	11	4	6	34	23	4	4	13	21	34	53
Sunderland	42	8	9	4	26	18	5	4	12	16	35	52
Norwich C	42	9	8	4	34	20	3	7	11	14	29	51
Leicester C	42	9	8	4	40	30	2	7	12	25	38	51
Luton T	42	7	5	9	30	33	4	7	10	23	33	51
West Bromwich A	42	10	4	7	30	25	4	5	12	18	37	51
Stoke C	42	11	4	6	30	23	2	7	12	14	40	50
Coventry C	42	8	5	8	33	33	5	6	10	24	44	50
Birmingham C	42	7	7	7	19	18	5	5	11	20	32	48
Notts Co	42	6	7	8	31	36	4	4	13	19	36	41
Wolves	42	4	8	9	15	28	2	3	16	12	52	29

Ossie Ardíles takes the ball away from Manchester United's Arthur Albiston at White Hart Lane in the 1980s.

1984-85
DIVISION 1

	P	W	D	L	F	A	W	D	L	F	A	Pts
Everton	42	16	3	2	58	17	12	3	6	30	26	90
Liverpool	42	12	4	5	36	19	10	7	4	32	16	77
Tottenham Hotspur	**42**	**11**	**3**	**7**	**46**	**31**	**12**	**5**	**4**	**32**	**20**	**77**
Manchester U	42	13	6	2	47	13	9	4	8	30	34	76
Southampton	42	13	4	4	29	18	6	7	8	27	29	68
Chelsea	42	13	3	5	38	20	5	9	7	25	28	66
Arsenal	42	14	5	2	37	14	5	4	12	24	35	66
Sheffield W	42	12	7	2	39	21	5	7	9	19	24	65
Nottingham F	42	13	4	4	35	18	6	3	12	21	30	64
Aston Villa	42	10	7	4	34	20	5	4	12	26	40	56
Watford	42	10	5	6	48	30	4	8	9	33	41	55
West Bromwich A	42	11	4	6	36	23	5	3	13	22	39	55
Luton T	42	12	5	4	40	22	3	4	14	17	39	54
Newcastle U	42	11	4	6	33	26	2	9	10	22	44	52
Leicester C	42	10	4	7	39	25	5	2	14	26	48	51
West Ham U	42	7	8	6	27	23	6	4	11	24	45	51
Ipswich T	42	8	7	6	27	20	5	4	12	19	37	50
Coventry C	42	11	3	7	29	22	4	2	15	18	42	50
QPR	42	11	6	4	41	30	2	5	14	12	42	50
Norwich C	42	9	6	6	28	24	4	1	13	18	40	49
Sunderland	42	7	6	8	20	26	3	4	14	20	36	40
Stoke C	42	3	3	15	18	41	0	5	16	6	50	17

1985-86
DIVISION 1

	P	W	D	L	F	A	W	D	L	F	A	Pts
Liverpool	42	16	4	1	58	14	10	6	5	31	23	88
Everton	42	16	3	2	54	18	10	5	6	33	23	86
West Ham U	42	17	2	2	48	16	9	4	8	26	24	84
Manchester U	42	12	5	4	35	12	10	5	6	35	24	76
Sheffield W	42	13	6	2	36	23	8	4	9	27	31	73
Chelsea	42	12	4	5	32	27	8	7	6	25	29	71
Arsenal	42	13	5	3	29	15	7	4	10	20	32	69
Nottingham F	42	11	5	5	38	25	8	6	7	31	28	68
Luton T	42	12	6	3	37	15	6	6	9	24	29	66
Tottenham Hotspur	**42**	**12**	**2**	**7**	**47**	**25**	**7**	**6**	**8**	**27**	**27**	**65**
Newcastle U	42	12	5	4	46	31	5	7	9	21	41	63
Watford	42	11	6	4	40	22	5	5	11	29	40	59
QPR	42	12	3	6	33	20	3	4	14	20	44	52
Southampton	42	10	6	5	32	18	2	4	15	19	44	46
Manchester C	42	7	7	7	25	26	4	5	12	18	31	45
Aston Villa	42	7	6	8	27	28	3	8	10	24	39	44
Coventry C	42	6	5	10	31	35	5	5	11	17	36	43
Oxford U	42	7	7	7	34	27	3	5	13	28	53	42
Leicester C	42	7	8	6	35	35	3	4	14	19	41	42
Ipswich T	42	8	5	8	20	24	3	3	15	12	31	41
Birmingham C	42	5	2	14	13	25	3	3	15	17	48	29
West Bromwich A	42	3	8	10	21	36	1	4	16	14	53	24

1986-87
DIVISION 1

	P	W	D	L	F	A	W	D	L	F	A	Pts
Everton	42	16	4	1	49	11	10	4	7	27	20	86
Liverpool	42	15	3	3	43	16	8	5	8	29	26	77
Tottenham Hotspur	**42**	**14**	**3**	**4**	**40**	**14**	**7**	**5**	**9**	**28**	**29**	**71**
Arsenal	42	12	5	4	31	12	8	5	8	27	23	70
Norwich C	42	9	10	2	27	20	7	6	6	26	31	68
Wimbledon	42	11	5	5	32	22	8	4	9	25	28	66
Luton T	42	14	5	2	29	13	4	7	10	18	32	66
Nottingham F	42	12	8	1	36	14	6	3	12	28	37	65
Watford	42	12	5	4	38	20	6	4	11	29	34	63
Coventry C	42	14	4	3	35	17	3	8	10	15	28	63
Manchester U	42	13	3	5	38	18	1	11	9	14	27	56
Southampton	42	11	5	5	44	24	3	5	13	25	44	52
Sheffield W	42	9	7	5	39	24	4	6	11	19	35	52
Chelsea	42	8	6	7	30	30	5	7	9	23	34	52
West Ham U	42	10	4	7	33	28	4	6	11	19	39	52
QPR	42	9	7	5	31	27	4	4	13	17	37	50
Newcastle U	42	10	4	7	33	29	2	7	12	14	36	47
Oxford U	42	8	8	5	30	25	3	5	13	14	44	46
Charlton Ath	42	7	7	7	26	22	4	4	13	19	33	44
Leicester C	42	9	7	5	39	24	2	2	17	15	52	42
Manchester C	42	8	6	7	28	24	0	9	12	8	33	39
Aston Villa	42	7	7	7	25	25	1	5	15	20	54	36

1987-88
DIVISION 1

	P	W	D	L	F	A	W	D	L	F	A	Pts
Liverpool	40	15	5	0	49	9	11	7	2	38	15	90
Manchester U	40	14	5	1	41	17	9	7	4	30	21	81
Nottingham F	40	11	7	2	40	17	9	6	5	27	22	72
Everton	40	14	4	2	34	11	5	9	6	19	16	70
QPR	40	12	4	4	30	14	7	6	7	18	24	67
Arsenal	40	11	4	5	35	16	7	8	5	23	23	66
Wimbledon	40	8	9	3	32	20	6	6	8	26	27	57
Newcastle U	40	9	6	5	32	23	5	8	7	23	30	56
Luton T	40	11	6	3	40	21	3	5	12	17	37	53
Coventry C	40	6	8	6	23	25	7	6	7	23	28	53
Sheffield W	40	10	2	8	27	30	5	6	9	25	36	53
Southampton	40	6	8	6	27	26	6	6	8	22	27	50
Tottenham Hotspur	**40**	**9**	**5**	**6**	**26**	**23**	**3**	**6**	**11**	**12**	**25**	**47**
Norwich C	40	7	5	8	26	26	5	4	11	14	26	45
Derby Co	40	6	7	7	18	17	4	6	10	17	28	43
West Ham U	40	6	9	5	23	21	3	6	11	17	31	42
Charlton Ath	40	7	7	6	23	21	2	8	10	15	31	42
Chelsea	40	7	11	2	24	17	2	4	14	26	51	42
Portsmouth	40	4	8	8	21	27	3	6	11	15	39	35
Watford	40	4	5	11	15	24	3	6	11	12	27	32
Oxford U	40	5	7	8	24	34	1	6	13	20	46	31

1988-89
DIVISION 1

	P	W	D	L	F	A	W	D	L	F	A	Pts
Arsenal	38	10	6	3	35	19	12	4	3	38	17	76
Liverpool	38	11	5	3	33	11	11	5	3	32	17	76
Nottingham F	38	8	7	4	31	16	9	6	4	33	26	64
Norwich C	38	8	7	4	23	20	9	4	6	25	25	62
Derby Co	38	9	3	7	23	18	8	4	7	17	20	58
Tottenham Hotspur	**38**	**8**	**6**	**5**	**31**	**24**	**7**	**6**	**6**	**29**	**22**	**57**
Coventry C	38	9	4	6	28	23	5	9	5	19	19	55
Everton	38	10	7	2	33	18	4	5	10	17	27	54
QPR	38	9	5	5	23	16	5	6	8	20	21	53
Millwall	38	10	3	6	27	21	4	8	7	20	31	53
Manchester U	38	10	5	4	27	13	3	7	9	18	22	51
Wimbledon	38	10	3	6	30	19	4	6	9	20	27	51
Southampton	38	6	7	6	25	26	4	8	7	27	40	45
Charlton Ath	38	6	7	6	25	24	4	5	10	19	34	42
Sheffield W	38	6	6	7	21	25	4	6	9	13	26	42
Luton T	38	8	6	5	32	21	2	5	12	10	31	41
Aston Villa	38	7	6	6	25	22	2	7	10	20	34	40
Middlesbrough	38	6	7	6	28	30	3	5	11	16	31	39
West Ham U	38	3	6	10	19	30	7	2	10	18	32	38
Newcastle U	38	3	6	10	19	28	4	4	11	13	35	31

1989-90
DIVISION 1

	P	W	D	L	F	A	W	D	L	F	A	Pts
Liverpool	38	13	5	1	38	15	10	5	4	40	22	79
Aston Villa	38	13	3	3	36	20	8	4	7	21	18	70
Tottenham Hotspur	**38**	**12**	**1**	**6**	**35**	**24**	**7**	**5**	**7**	**24**	**23**	**63**
Arsenal	38	14	3	2	38	11	4	5	10	16	27	62
Chelsea	38	8	7	4	31	24	8	5	6	27	26	60
Everton	38	14	3	2	40	16	3	5	11	17	30	59
Southampton	38	10	5	4	40	27	5	5	9	31	36	55
Wimbledon	38	5	8	6	22	23	8	8	3	25	17	55
Nottingham F	38	9	4	6	31	21	6	5	8	24	26	54
Norwich C	38	7	10	2	24	14	6	4	9	20	28	53
QPR	38	9	4	6	27	22	4	7	8	18	22	50
Coventry C	38	11	2	6	24	25	3	5	11	15	34	49
Manchester U	38	8	6	5	26	14	5	3	11	20	33	48
Manchester C	38	9	4	6	26	21	3	8	8	17	31	48
Crystal Palace	38	8	7	4	27	23	5	2	12	15	43	48
Derby Co	38	9	1	9	29	21	4	6	9	14	19	46
Luton T	38	8	8	3	24	18	2	5	12	19	39	43
Sheffield W	38	8	6	5	21	17	3	4	12	14	34	43
Charlton Ath	38	4	6	9	18	25	3	3	13	13	32	30
Millwall	38	4	6	9	23	25	1	5	13	16	40	26

David Howells in action for Spurs against Norwich City in October 1987. Spurs lost this one 2-1 at Carrow Road.

1990-91
DIVISION 1

	P	W	D	L	F	A	W	D	L	F	A	Pts
Arsenal*	38	15	4	0	51	10	9	9	1	23	8	83
Liverpool	38	14	3	2	42	13	9	4	6	35	27	76
Crystal Palace	38	11	6	2	26	17	9	3	7	24	24	69
Leeds U	38	12	2	5	46	23	7	5	7	19	24	64
Manchester C	38	12	3	4	35	25	5	8	6	29	28	62
Manchester U†	38	11	4	4	34	17	5	8	6	24	28	59
Wimbledon	38	8	6	5	28	22	6	8	5	25	24	56
Nottingham F	38	11	4	4	42	21	3	8	8	23	29	54
Everton	38	9	5	5	26	15	4	7	8	24	31	51
Tottenham Hotspur	**38**	**8**	**9**	**2**	**35**	**22**	**3**	**7**	**9**	**16**	**28**	**49**
Chelsea	38	10	6	3	33	25	3	4	12	25	44	49
QPR	38	8	5	6	27	22	4	5	10	17	31	46
Sheffield U	38	9	3	7	23	23	4	4	11	13	32	46
Southampton	38	9	6	4	33	22	3	3	13	25	47	45
Norwich C	38	9	3	7	27	32	4	3	12	14	32	45
Coventry C	38	10	6	3	30	16	1	5	13	12	33	44
Aston Villa	38	7	9	3	29	25	2	5	12	17	33	41
Luton T	38	7	5	7	22	18	3	2	14	20	43	37
Sunderland	38	6	6	7	15	16	2	4	13	23	44	34
Derby Co	38	3	8	8	25	36	2	1	16	12	39	24

*Arsenal had two points deducted for disciplinary reasons.
†Manchester United had one point deducted for disciplinary reasons.

1991-92
DIVISION 1

	P	W	D	L	F	A	W	D	L	F	A	Pts
Leeds U	42	13	8	0	38	13	9	8	4	36	24	82
Manchester U	42	12	7	2	34	13	9	8	4	29	20	78
Sheffield W	42	13	5	3	39	24	8	7	6	23	25	75
Arsenal	42	12	7	2	51	22	7	8	6	30	24	72
Manchester C	42	13	4	4	32	14	7	6	8	29	34	70
Liverpool	42	13	5	3	34	17	3	11	7	13	23	64
Aston Villa	42	13	3	5	31	16	4	6	11	17	28	60
Nottingham F	42	10	7	4	36	27	6	4	11	24	31	59
Sheffield U	42	9	6	6	29	23	7	3	11	36	40	57
Crystal Palace	42	7	8	6	24	25	7	7	7	2	36	57
QPR	42	6	10	5	25	21	6	8	7	23	26	54
Everton	42	8	8	5	28	19	5	6	10	24	32	53
Wimbledon	42	10	5	6	32	20	3	9	9	21	33	53
Chelsea	42	7	8	6	31	30	6	6	9	19	30	53
Tottenham Hotspur	**42**	**7**	**3**	**11**	**33**	**35**	**8**	**4**	**9**	**25**	**28**	**52**
Southampton	42	7	5	9	17	28	7	5	9	22	27	52
Oldham Ath	42	11	5	5	46	36	3	4	14	17	31	51
Norwich C	42	8	6	7	29	28	3	6	12	18	35	45
Coventry C	42	6	7	8	18	15	5	4	12	17	29	44
Luton T	42	10	7	4	25	17	0	5	16	13	54	42
Notts Co	42	7	5	9	24	29	3	5	13	16	33	40
West Ham	42	6	6	9	22	24	3	5	15	15	35	38

1992-93
FA PREMIER LEAGUE

	P	W	D	L	F	A	W	D	L	F	A	Pts
Manchester U	42	14	5	2	39	14	10	7	4	28	17	84
Aston Villa	42	13	5	3	36	16	8	6	7	21	24	74
Norwich C	42	13	6	2	31	19	8	3	10	30	46	72
Blackburn R	42	13	4	4	38	18	7	7	7	30	28	71
QPR	42	11	5	5	41	32	6	7	8	22	23	63
Liverpool	42	13	4	4	41	18	3	7	11	21	37	59
Sheffield W	42	9	8	4	34	26	6	6	9	21	25	59
Tottenham Hotspur	**42**	**11**	**5**	**5**	**40**	**25**	**5**	**6**	**10**	**20**	**41**	**59**
Manchester C	42	7	8	6	30	25	8	4	9	26	26	57
Arsenal	42	8	6	7	25	20	7	5	9	15	18	56
Chelsea	42	9	7	5	29	22	5	7	9	22	32	56
Wimbledon	42	9	4	8	32	23	5	8	8	24	32	54
Everton	42	7	6	8	26	27	8	2	11	27	28	53
Sheffield U	42	10	6	5	33	19	4	4	13	21	34	52
Coventry C	42	7	4	10	29	28	6	9	6	23	29	52
Ipswich T	42	8	9	4	29	22	4	7	10	21	33	52
Leeds U	42	12	8	1	40	17	0	7	14	17	45	51
Southampton	42	10	6	5	30	21	3	5	13	24	40	50
Oldham A	42	10	6	5	43	30	3	4	14	20	44	49
Crystal Palace	42	6	9	6	27	25	5	7	9	21	36	49
Middlesbrough	42	8	5	8	33	27	3	6	12	21	48	44
Nottingham F	42	6	4	11	17	25	4	6	11	24	37	40

1993-94
FA PREMIER LEAGUE

	P	W	D	L	F	A	W	D	L	F	A	Pts
Manchester U	42	14	6	1	39	13	13	5	3	41	25	92
Blackburn R	42	14	5	2	31	11	11	4	6	32	25	84
Newcastle U	42	14	4	3	51	14	9	4	8	31	27	77
Arsenal	42	10	8	3	25	15	8	9	4	28	13	71
Leeds U	42	13	6	2	37	18	5	10	8	28	21	70
Wimbledon	42	12	5	4	35	21	6	6	9	21	32	65
Sheffield W	42	10	7	4	48	24	6	9	6	28	30	64
Liverpool	42	12	4	5	33	23	5	5	11	26	32	60
QPR	42	8	7	6	32	29	8	5	8	30	32	60
Aston Villa	42	8	5	8	23	18	7	7	7	23	32	57
Coventry C	42	9	7	5	23	17	5	7	9	20	28	56
Norwich C	42	4	9	8	26	29	8	8	5	39	32	53
West Ham U	42	6	7	8	26	31	7	6	8	21	27	52
Chelsea	42	11	5	5	31	20	2	7	12	18	33	51
Tottenham Hotspur	**42**	**4**	**8**	**9**	**29**	**33**	**7**	**4**	**10**	**25**	**26**	**45**
Manchester C	42	6	10	5	24	22	3	8	10	14	27	45
Everton	42	8	4	9	26	30	4	4	13	16	33	44
Southampton	42	9	2	10	30	31	3	5	13	19	35	43
Ipswich T	42	5	8	8	21	32	4	8	9	14	26	43
Sheffield U	42	6	10	5	24	23	2	8	11	18	37	42
Oldham A	42	5	8	8	24	33	4	5	12	18	35	40
Swindon T	42	4	7	10	25	45	1	8	12	22	55	30

1994-95
FA PREMIER LEAGUE

	P	W	D	L	F	A	W	D	L	F	A	Pts
Blackburn R	42	17	2	2	54	21	10	6	5	26	18	89
Manchester U	42	16	4	1	42	4	10	6	5	35	24	88
Nottingham F	42	12	6	3	36	18	10	5	6	36	25	77
Liverpool	42	13	5	3	38	13	8	6	7	27	24	74
Leeds U	42	13	5	3	35	15	7	8	6	24	23	73
Newcastle U	42	14	6	1	46	20	6	6	9	21	27	72
Tottenham Hotspur	**42**	**10**	**5**	**6**	**32**	**25**	**6**	**9**	**6**	**34**	**33**	**62**
QPR	42	11	3	7	36	26	6	6	9	25	33	60
Wimbledon	42	9	5	7	26	26	6	6	9	22	39	56
Southampton	42	8	9	4	33	27	4	9	8	28	36	54
Chelsea	42	7	7	7	25	22	6	8	7	25	33	54
Arsenal	42	6	9	6	27	21	7	3	11	25	28	51
Sheffield W	42	7	7	7	26	26	6	5	10	23	31	51
West Ham U	42	9	6	6	28	19	4	5	12	16	29	50
Everton	42	8	9	4	31	23	3	8	10	13	28	50
Coventry C	42	7	7	7	23	25	5	7	9	21	37	50
Manchester C	42	8	7	6	37	28	4	6	11	16	36	49
Aston Villa	42	6	9	6	27	24	5	6	10	24	32	48
Crystal Palace	42	6	6	9	16	23	5	6	10	18	26	45
Norwich C	42	8	8	5	27	21	2	5	14	10	33	43
Leicester C	42	5	6	10	28	37	1	5	15	17	43	29
Ipswich T	42	5	3	13	24	34	2	3	16	12	59	27